Texas Politics

Texas Politics

An Introduction

THIRD EDITION

James E. Anderson

Richard W. Murray

UNIVERSITY OF HOUSTON

Edward L. Farley

Harper & Row, Publishers

New York / Hagerstown / Philadelphia / San Francisco / London

Sponsoring Editor: Dale Tharp
Production Manager: Marion A. Palen
Compositor: Port City Press, Inc.
Printer and Binder: The Maple Press Company
Art Studio: J & R Technical Services, Inc.

TEXAS POLITICS: An Introduction, third edition

Library of Congress Cataloging in Publication Data

Anderson, James E
    Texas politics.

    Includes index.
    1. Texas—Politics and government—1951—
I.   Murray, Richard W., Date—   joint author.
II.   Farley, Edward L., Date—   joint author.
III.   Title.
JK4825 1979.A5 1979   320.4′764   78-25817
ISBN 0-06-040263-6

Contents

Preface

This book is intended to be an introduction to the fascinating world of Texas politics. Our major focus is on the description and analysis of political institutions, processes, and behavior at the state level. However, in addition to including a chapter on local government, we say much that is pertinent to local politics. Although it is perhaps unnecessary to say this, we basically view politics not as some form of nefarious or selfish activity (although it may include some such elements) but as the very essence of democracy, involving conflict and struggle among individuals and groups over issues of public policy and governance. Those seeking an exposé of Texas politics, a lot of "inside skinny," or a defense of the status quo will not find it here. We do believe that we have presented a realistic framework for understanding Texas politics whatever one's particular ideology or interests. We have chosen not to grind our own axes here.

We have sought to keep this volume reasonably short. To this end we have not defined or explained many basic political science terms and concepts. We assume that students using the book, and they constitute the main audience to whom it is directed, either will have had a course involving American national government or will be currently enrolled in one. Such a course should provide the necessary background for our book.

Very little material on political or governmental reform is included, although this has been traditionally part of the content of textbooks on Texas government and politics. We are, however, neither uninterested in reform nor believers in the perfection of the present Texas political system. Rather, it is our belief that an understanding of existing political institutions and practices and their impact on society must precede the consideration of reform if the latter is to be meaningful and realistic. Not having space for everything, we decided it was proper to devote our full attention to the discussion of existing institutions, practices, and behavior—a rather large task in itself.

Another way in which we depart from textbook tradition is in our inclusion of only one chapter specifically devoted to public policy matters. Again a disclaimer and an explanation are in order. We are not uninterested in public policy. However, a lack of adequate materials makes it impossible to treat many policy areas in other than fragmentary or formal descriptive fashion. This we did not want to do. Also, the desire to keep down the size of the book helped us decide not to include the standard policy chapters. On the other hand, we have tried to use policy materials throughout the book as illustrations and examples in order to provide a better understanding of the substance of Texas politics.

This edition of the book, like the two earlier editions, is truly a joint effort on the part of the authors. While each of us was primarily responsible for the preparation of particular chapters, all of the chapters were jointly planned, edited, and revised by all of us. Fortunately, we are an agreeable group. We have benefitted from this collaborative effort; it is hoped that our readers will also.

The third edition includes a number of significant changes including new or expanded material on the style of Texas governors; the sunbelt thesis as it applies to Texas; the role of minority groups in Texas politics; zero-based budgeting; voter rejections of the proposed new constitution; and elections through the fall of 1978. There has also been a general updating of the book to take account of developments since the previous edition was published.

We wish to acknowledge the contributions of several people in the preparation of this book. Brazoria County Judge Neil Caldwell drew some original cartoons for the book, while William D. Wittliff, publisher of the Encino Press, give us permission to use some of Representative Caldwell's cartoons originally included in a book published by the Encino Press. Members of the Political Science Department at the University of Houston acted variously as critics, sounding boards, and contributors of information. Colleagues at other colleges have also provided helpful criticism and suggestions. Finally, we must mention our wives, who once again put up with us while we were revising the book and who share our interest in Texas politics.

James E. Anderson
Richard W. Murray
Edward L. Farley

The Constitutional Context

In the United States written constitutions provide an overarching legal context for the "great game of politics." A constitution is essentially a set of basic rules, regarded as superior to ordinary law, that are intended to regulate the political process in a particular community, such as the United States or the state of Texas. To this end, a constitution typically indicates the manner in which the government shall be organized, assigns powers and responsibilities to the various units or branches of government, and places some specific limitations on governmental action as, for example, by a bill of rights. Constitutions may differ substantially in their style, length, and detail in treating these matters, as a comparison of the U.S. and Texas constitutions will readily indicate. The use of written constitutions to limit governmental power is an American contribution to the practice of government and, as a people, Americans tend to be much enamored with things constitutional.

Although important insights may be gained, an adequate understanding of how a government operates cannot be derived from a study of its constitution. There may, for instance, be a sharp divergence between formal constitutional rules and actual political behavior. Although the Fourteenth Amendment to the U.S. Constitution provides that the states shall not deny equal protection of the laws to anyone within their jurisdiction, in the past (and occasionally still) they have discriminated against racial and religious minorities. Constitutional authorizations for governments to legislate on various matters

1

usually tell us little about the actual policies that result. While it is necessary for a government to have constitutional power to levy taxes, a variety of political and economic factors help determine the types and levels of taxes actually levied, exemptions from particular taxes, how they are collected, and the like.

Nonetheless, governmental action in the United States appears in substantial conformity with the relevant constitutional rules, which are often quite general. Americans are still much concerned with questions of constitutional power and practice, especially when personal rights and liberties are involved. But the regulation of economic activity, while not lacking in controversy, does not stir the intense constitutional debates it did a few decades ago.

It is useful, and traditional, to begin an examination of the Texas political system with a brief description of its constitutional context. To this we now turn.

THE AMERICAN FEDERAL SYSTEM

As a member of the federal union, the government of the state of Texas is affected in what it can do by the U.S. Constitution and federalism as well as by the Texas Constitution.[1] The U.S. Constitution divides governmental power between the national government and the several state governments, places some limitations on them, and sets forth some obligations of each to the other.

Certain powers are delegated to the national government, such as those to regulate interstate and foreign commerce, establish post offices and post roads, raise and support armies and navies, and tax and spend for the general welfare. The national government is also given all power necessary and proper (implied power) to carry out its delegated powers. Powers not delegated to the national government (residual powers) are left to the states or the people. The basic arrangement is succintly stated in the Tenth Amendment: "The powers not delegated to the United States by the Constitution, nor prohibited by it to the States, are reserved to the States respectively, or to the people." Essentially, the U.S. Constitution is a source of power for the national government and a series of limitations on the state governments. The latter are free to do anything not prohibited to them by the U.S. Constitution (unless they limit themselves through their own constitutions) and are thereby in a semiautonomous position.

Some limitations on the states are contained in the main body of the U.S. Constitution. In Article I, Section 10, a variety of state actions are prohibited, such as entering into treaties or alliances, coining money, passing bills of attainder and ex post facto laws, and taxing exports or imports. Other limitations are found in amendments to the constitution. The Fourteenth Amendment broadly prohibits the states from depriving persons of their life, liberty, or property without due process of law; abridging the privileges and immunities of citizens of the United States; or denying persons within their jurisdiction the equal protection of the laws. By judicial interpretation, the liberty protected by the due process clause has been held to protect most of the rights listed in the Bill of Rights against state action, including all of the rights enumerated in the First Amendment. The Fifteenth and Nineteenth amendments provide that the right to vote cannot be denied on grounds of race or color and sex, respectively.

Some limitations on the states are implicit in the U.S. Constitution. By judicial construction, the states are forbidden to unduly burden interstate commerce or interfere with the exercise of national power. As a general rule, the delegations of power to the national government act as limitations on the states, the inference being that power granted to the national government is denied the states. The two levels of government do have concurrent power to tax, including taxation of the same objects, such as personal incomes and tobacco products. Neither, however, can use its power to tax to interfere with the basic governmental functions of the other, as in the operation of their court systems.

Article VI provides for national supremacy. According to the "supreme law of the land clause," the Constitution, laws made in pursuance thereof, and treaties made under the authority of the United States take precedence over conflicting provisions in state constitutions and laws. In short, when national and state actions come into conflict and the national government is acting within its area of constitutional power, the conflicting state action must give way. Thus, a provision of the Texas Constitution authorizing separate schools for "the white and colored children" became null and void because it conflicted with the equal protection clause of the Fourteenth Amendment as interpreted by the Supreme Court in *Brown* v. *Board of Education* (1954). Congress, however, may choose to yield to state action in some matters. A notable example is Section 14(B) of the Taft-Hartley Act, which permits the states to enact laws outlawing the union-shop arrangement, although it is permitted by national law. In the absence of this provision, the Texas "right-to-work" law, which bans the union shop in the state, would be unconstitutional as it would then conflict with national policy.

Some limitations may also arise out of the obligations the states owe one another. For example, Article IV of the U.S. Constitution ordains that the states shall give "full faith and credit . . . to the public acts, records, and judicial proceedings of every other State" and that fugitives from justice shall be returned, upon request, to the state from whence they fled. The return of fugitives has been held to be a moral rather than a mandatory obligation, there being no effective way to compel a state to meet this obligation against its wishes. Customarily, though, requests for the return of fugitives do receive compliance.

Within the framework of these various limitations, the states can legally take whatever actions they see fit on economic, social, and political matters subject to whatever limitations they may impose upon themselves. Indeed, the states are probably more restricted in many matters, such as taxation and economic regulation, by their own constitutions than they are by the U.S. Constitution. Although much comment is made relating to the decline in power of the states, the "march of power to Washington," and the like, the states have greatly expanded the range of their activities in the twentieth century. They have frequently been encouraged to do this by national grant-in-aid programs, which in 1975 funneled $49.7 billion to state and local governments.

At this point it should be helpful to indicate the general scope of governmental powers available to the states. They are grouped conventionally into four categories.

Police power. This can be defined broadly as the power of the states to protect and promote the public health, safety, welfare, and morals. This can entail such actions as the enactment and enforcement of criminal laws, licensing of occupations, regulation of local businesses and utilities, regulation of wages and working conditions, control of fire hazards, operation of welfare programs, promotion of economic activity, and control of diseases and pests (e.g., fire ants). Exact definition of the police power is not possible.[2]

Taxing power. The states possess full power to tax, subject to self-imposed limitations and the requirement of noninterference with national governmental activities. Although the basic purpose of taxation is to raise revenue to finance the government, it can be used for other purposes. The various states have shown substantial ingenuity in the types of taxes they levy. High tax rates may be used to discourage the consumption of some products, and favorable tax provisions may be used to encourage or promote desired activities.

Proprietary power. This designates the power of the states, or their subdivisions, to own and operate economic enterprises. As far as the U.S. Constitution is concerned, the states are free to engage in as much government ownership of enterprises (which some might call "socialism") as their inhabitants desire. Although there is no single standard definition of *public enterprise* (as is the case with most political phenomena), the term can usefully be held to designate activities of a commercial or businesslike nature that could be handled by private enterprise. Collectively, a variety of government enterprises can be found in the several states—power production facilities, public forests and parks, recreational facilities, liquor stores, airports, subways, bus companies, cement plants, and insurance companies to name a few. Texas is among the less innovative and active states in the enterprise field.

Eminent domain. The states possess power to take private property for public use, upon payment of just compensation for the property so taken. This power can be used, for example, to acquire rights-of-way for highways, sites for public buildings, and land for public parks. This power can also be granted to public utility companies to secure easements and the like for utility lines. In cases of the sort mentioned, the theory runs that private rights should give way to the general welfare. Public officials, of course, make these determinations; this may stir considerable controversy, as when a utility company seeks land for a nuclear power plant.

These four categories comprise the "pool of power" available to the states under the U.S. Constitution. The extent and purposes for which a state exercises the power available depends first of all on two general factors: (1) limitations imposed by the state constitution and (2) internal political processes. To illustrate the first factor, the Texas Constitution (as of 1978) prohibits the state government from spending more than $80 million annually on public assistance programs for the needy. (Texas is the only state to have such a limitation.) Although the state is constitutionally free to levy personal or corporate income taxes, it has not done so—despite revenue needs—because of the strong political opposition to such taxes, especially from conservative citizens and businessmen; here, then, the limitation is political rather than constitutional.

THE POSITION OF THE STATES

Two comments need to be made here concerning the division of power between the national and state governments in the American federal system. First, the division of power is not a clear-cut, never changing allocation. The actual division of power has fluctuated as changing social, economic, and political conditions have given rise to new or different interpretations of the broad general language of the U.S. Constitution or to action to shift the balance of power. The Nixon administration's "New Federalism" represented an effort to shift power from the national to the state and local governments by general revenue-sharing and other means. What the administration accomplished still remains to be determined. Second, the two levels of government do not operate in separate and distinct spheres but, rather, act jointly in many areas (e.g., highway construction, welfare, and pollution control), with both cooperation and conflict characterizing their relationship. To use a metaphor, the American federal system is best thought of as a marble cake rather than a layer cake because of the extensive intermingling of national, state, and local activities, as in the several hundred federal grant-in-aid programs.

The twentieth century has seen a vast expansion of national governmental power and activity, whether measured by such indexes as civilian personnel employed (208,000 in 1900, 2.9 million in 1975), size of the national budget ($521 million in 1900, $324 billion in 1975), or number and range of programs undertaken. Among the causes often mentioned for the expansion of national action are the following: (1) Many problems, such as inflation, unemployment, monopoly, energy shortages, and poverty, are national in scope and can be dealt with only by a government having nationwide jurisdiction. (2) National defense, of course, is solely the prerogative of the national government. (3) The states have been unable or unwilling to act, or act effectively, on many matters because of constitutional limitations, deficient legislatures, poor administrative systems, and internal political factors. (4) The national government has better financial resources and greater ability to act than have the states. But whatever the causes, and whether or not one considers the expansion of national power desirable, the national government is clearly a much more powerful and active entity today than it was at the turn of the century.

The growth of national power has produced much hand-wringing and many dismal proclamations concerning both the present and the future position of the states. However, reality does not seem to lend much support to the view that the states are in the process of decline or destruction. The states, as well as the national government, have greatly expanded their activities in recent decades and appear considerably more powerful than in the past, at least in an absolute sense. Item: Total expenditures of state and local governments increased from $10.9 billion in 1942 to $226.0 billion in 1974.[3] In Texas, the state's budget grew from $165 million in 1940 to $5.1 billion in 1975. Item: Total government expenditures in the United States for *domestic* purposes was $393.1 billion in 1975. The state and local spending of $226.0 billion was all for domestic purposes and made up 57 percent of the total. Item: In 1975, of the total of 15.0 million government employees, 12.1 million, or 80.7 percent, were employed by state and local governments. Item: Public education, highway construction and maintenance, law enforcement, local business regulation and occupational licensing, land-use control, regulation of consumer utilities, and parks, recreation, and wildlife are policy areas still largely under the control and financing of the states.

In short the states, and their local governments, are still quite important in the United States and have a large impact on the day-to-day lives of most citizens. To neglect them in the study of American politics is to neglect much of the subject.

THE TEXAS CONSTITUTION

The present constitution of the state of Texas, adopted in 1876, is the seventh constitution under which the state has been governed. Previous constitutions were adopted in 1827, for Texas and Coahuila (under the Republic of Mexico); in 1836, for the Republic of Texas after it became independent from Mexico; in 1845, when Texas entered the Union; in 1861, when Texas left the Union to join the Confederacy; in 1866, when Texas reentered the Union; and in 1869, to meet the requirements for Reconstruction laid down by the Radical Republicans in Congress. The Constitution of 1876 has thus lasted substantially longer than all of its predecessors combined, notwithstanding long-continued criticism and a variety of efforts toward revision.

FRAMING THE CONSTITUTION

After the Constitution of 1869 was adopted, a Radical Republican regime led by Gov. E. J. Davis (1870–1874) came to power. Both the constitution and the Republicans apparently caused a great amount of dissatisfaction within the state, especially on the part of the Democrats. A standard interpretation of the era asserts, "The Radical Republican regime in Texas was one of oppression, corruption, graft, and blackmail. It sought to centralize the government and brought about a large growth in government expenditures, an increase in taxation, and a rapid accumulation of a comparatively heavy debt."[4] Whether fully accurate or not, and some recent historical research indicates it is not, this was apparently the view of things that influenced the majority of the framers of the Constitution of 1876. It is, after all, what people *believe* to be real or true that influences their behavior.

In 1872 the Democratic party had regained control of the legislature and in the following year elected the governor and other state officials. Two years later, after the Democrats had taken complete control of the state government, they turned their attention to the state constitution, which to them was a symbol of Republicanism and carpetbag domination. After an abortive attempt to use a joint legislative commission to write a new constitution, in 1875 the legislature adopted a resolution calling for a constitutional convention, subject to the approval of the voters. The voters agreed, and three delegates from each of the state's 30 senatorial districts were elected to a constitutional convention that met in Austin in the fall of 1875.

The constitutional convention was composed of 76 Democrats and 14 Republicans (of whom five were blacks).[5] Forty-one of the delegates were farmers, 29 were lawyers, and the others had occupations such as merchant, editor, and physician. Many were either members of the legislature or had other governmental experience. Thirty-eight were members of the Grange, a major nineteenth-century farm organization, which had a strong following in the state. More than 20 had served as officers in the Confederate Army. Generally, the delegates were "old-line Texans" and were of a conservative mood. Accounts of the constitutional convention agree that the Grange, with its program of "Retrenchment and Reform" in government, was the most important single influence on the convention. The economy-mindedness of the delegates was manifested in such actions as their refusal to employ a stenographer or have the proceedings of the convention published because of the financial costs involved.

The constitution written by the delegates provided for a governmental system intended to be characterized by more popular control, greater economy in operation, and less power to act than that under the Constitution of 1869. Most state officials, including judges, were to be elected; they were generally bestowed with low salaries, short terms of office, and limited power. Many limitations were imposed on the legislature, and the state debt was limited to $200,000. Adequate provision was made for regulation of railroads and corporations, matters of especial concern to the Grangers. Concerning the handiwork of the convention, Prof. Rupert N. Richardson comments:

> All in all, the constitution complied with public opinion quite faithfully. Biennial sessions of the legislature, low salaries, no registration for voters, precinct voting [the previous constitution had required voting at the county seat], abolition of the road tax and a return to the road-working system, a homestead exemption clause, guarantees of a low tax rate, a more economical [and segregated] school system under local control, a less expensive court system, popular election of officials—all these were popular measures with Texans in 1876. The constitution was the logical product of its era. It was to be expected that men who were disgusted with the vagaries of a radical regime would design a government that was extremely conservative. Furthermore, the low prices and low wages of hard times had created a demand for the severest economy in government.[6]

Although there was considerable criticism of the new constitution (especially in more urban counties) because of its restrictive nature, it received popular ratification in February 1876 by a vote of 136,606 to 56,652. Generally, rural areas voted strongly in favor of it while most larger cities, including Dallas, Galveston, Houston, and San Antonio, were opposed.

CONSTITUTIONAL DEVELOPMENT

The meaning of a constitution can be altered and expanded or restricted in a number of ways to meet new needs and conditions. Methods of change include custom and usage, judicial interpretation, statutory elaboration, formal amendment, and general revision. All of these except the last one have been important in the development of the U.S. Constitution, while formal amendment has been the primary means of constitutional change in Texas since 1876. The state courts have generally taken a restrictive view in their interpretation of the Texas Constitution which has had the effect of further stimulating, and necessitating, formal amendment. Between 1879 and 1977, some 361 amendments to the Texas Constitution were proposed, of which 223 were adopted. Partly a consequence of the length, detail, and rigidity of the constitution, this plethora of amendments has further added to its length, detail, and rigidity. In a very real sense, detail begets detail.

The procedure for amending the constitution was itself changed by a constitutional amendment adopted in 1972. Amendments are proposed by resolutions approved by two-thirds of the members elected to each house of the legislature. This can be done either during a regular biennial session or (since 1972) a special session opened to such action by the governor. Although the governor can recommend amendments or give this approval to proposed amendments, he has no constitutional power to veto proposed amendments.

The ratification of amendments is a task for the voters, at either regular general elections or elections called specifically for the purpose, as determined by the legislature. A brief explanatory statement of the amendment, including the way the proposition will be worded on the election ballot, is prepared by the secretary of state with the approval of the attorney general. The approval procedure was provided because it was thought too dangerous to permit one person alone to prepare explanations of proposed amendments; his viewpoint might bias the explanation. An absence of trust is noticeable here, as is often the case in Texas politics.

The secretary of state's statement is published twice in most newspapers in the state several weeks prior to the election, and a complete copy of each proposed amendment is posted in each county courthouse at least 30 days prior to the election. (Under the old procedure the actual amendments, without any explanation, were printed four times prior to the election in a newspaper in each county in which one or more newspapers was published.) The thought behind the new publicity procedure is that it will better inform voters of the meaning of proposed amendments. Given their legalese, the comprehensibility of constitutional amendments is probably only slightly better than that of insurance policies. Under the old procedure, most of those voting on amendments probably had little knowledge of what they were voting on. Whether the new procedure has improved the situation is conjectural.

Approval of an amendment requires favorable action by a majority of those actually voting on it. As evidenced by voter turnout, there is considerable public disinterest in the amending process. When amendments are voted on at special elections, only a very small proportion of the voters participate. In November 1973, nine amendments submitted to voters drew a turnout of approximately 600,000, about 15 percent of the eligible voters. When amendments are voted on at regular elections, a phenomenon called "voter fatigue" occurs, and only about half of those who vote for major elective offices vote on amendments. Voters tend not to vote on matters on which they have little or no information, and constitutional amendments clearly fall into this category for many voters.

The range of constitutional amendments has been quite broad in recent years. Consequently, voters may have had great difficulty in separating the vital from the trivial, the necessary from the merely desirable for some group—assuming they had the information and inclination to attempt the task. Note the topics of amendments voted on in 1973: expand the size of the Court of Criminal Appeals; permit limitation of bail for accused felons; expand the membership and change the name of the Judicial Qualifications Committee; authorize the sale of an additional $200 million in Veterans' Land Fund bonds; provide property tax relief for historical properties; authorize legislation on electronic funds transfers by banks; and allow agricultural associations to assess members to raise funds for research and marketing programs. The first five were approved. Most did not involve anything really fundamental or basic. Certainly the typical voter would be pressed to exercise an informed judgment on such a diverse range of issues.

The long-range trend has been one of an increasing frequency of amendment of the constitution, as Table 1.1 indicates. (The table does not include the first amendment, which was adopted in 1879.) As the constitution has become more detailed through amendment, and as government has become more active—especially since the New Deal era—amendments have proliferated. The need for frequent amendment of the constitution can be taken as one indication of its inadequacy. On

TABLE 1.1 • CONSTITUTIONAL AMENDING ACTIVITY, 1881-1978

Decade	Number of amendments submitted to voters	Number of amendments approved
1881–1890	15	7
1891–1900	15	9
1901–1910	20	11
1911–1920	34	10
1921–1930	25	15
1931–1940	45	32
1941–1950	35	22
1951–1960	43	37
1961–1970	84	56
1971–1978	53	33

the other hand, given the rigidity of the constitution, frequent amendment has helped keep it somewhat viable and responsive to pressing needs.

In a study of the amending process for the 1951–1972 period, Prof. Janice C. May indicates some of the reasons for amending the constitution.[7] These include: (1) avoidance of financial restrictions, such as those on government debt and taxation; (2) elimination of limitations on the activities of local governments; (3) responses to national policies and court decisions, as in welfare and suffrage; and (4) accommodation to decisions of the Texas courts and opinions of the state attorney general, as in workmen's compensation and dissolution of hospital districts. Many amendments are proposed to amend previous amendments because the initial amendments were either narrowly drawn or poorly drafted. Also, amendments defeated by the voters are frequently resubmitted by the legislature. Legislative pay proposals are the leader here, nine having been submitted and only one having been adopted.

THE CONSTITUTION TODAY

As it exists today the Texas Constitution is a long, detailed, cumbersome document. As a consequence of its original length, plus over 200 amendments, it is approximately 65,000 words in length. Only three state constitutions are longer, with the range extending from less than 8,000 words for Vermont to approximately 500,000 for Georgia. The Texas Constitution is not very readable because of its length and complex, legalistic language.[8] A brief description of its content follows.

Bill of Rights. The Texas Bill of Rights is contained in the first article of the constitution and includes 29 sections. All of the provisions of the U.S. Bill of Rights, plus many of the personal guarantees in its main body (e.g., the prohibitions of ex post facto laws and bills of attainder), are repeated in the Texas document. Also included are a variety of guarantees and declarations not found in the U.S. Constitution, such as the provisions that there be no imprisonment for debt and no religious tests for public office—with the stipulation that one "acknowledge the existence of a Supreme Being"; some profess to see an inconsistency in the latter guarantee.

The provisions of the Texas Bill of Rights fall generally into three categories.[9] First, there are statements of general political values and philosophy, as in the declaration that "the maintenance of our free institutions and the perpetuity of the Union depend upon the right of local self-government unimpaired to all the states." Second, there are declarations of substantive rights to liberty and property. Illustrative are the guarantees of liberty of speech and press, prohibition of the "outlawry" of citizens (an action which would make them legally "fair game" for all shooters), and protection of the right to keep and bear arms. Third, several provisions deal with procedural rights, especially in criminal proceedings, such as the guarantees of trial by jury, due course of law, and no double jeopardy.

Governmental organization. The three branches of government—legislative, executive, and judicial—are established by Articles III, IV, and V, respectively. Provision is made for the qualifications, selection, and tenure of members of each branch; their powers and duties are set forth; and limitations on them (particularly on legislators) are imposed, all in substantial detail. Not only does the constitution deal with the substantive power of the legislature, but it also includes many provisions pertaining to the internal organization, behavior, and procedure of that body. In contrast, the U.S. Constitution leaves most of those matters to Congress itself to determine. Many of the state's important executive offices and the structure of the court system are also provided for by the constitution.

Article II explicitly ordains that the state government shall be organized according to the principle of separation of powers:

> The powers of the government of the State of Texas shall be divided into three distinct departments, each of which shall be confided to a separate body of magistracy, to wit: Those which are legislative to one, those which are executive to another, and those which are judicial to another; and no person, or collection of persons, being of one of these departments, shall exercise any power properly attached to either of the other,

except in the instances herein [elsewhere in the constitution] expressly provided.

Other sections of the constitution create a system of checks and balances whereby each branch is given some power to interfere with, or check, the exercise of power by the other branches. Thus, the governor is given legislative veto power, the Texas Senate is authorized to approve most gubernatorial appointments, the courts can hold legislative acts unconstitutional, and so on. The courts, however, have tended to construe the separation of powers quite strictly, with a slight encroachment by one branch on the powers of another being held unconstitutional. Such construction has added to the rigidity of the constitution and hindered the effective operation of government.

Local government. Various articles and sections cover the establishment, organization, legal authority, and selection of officials of local governmental bodies, including counties, municipalities, school districts, and various forms of special districts. In legal theory, local governments are dependent on the state government for their formal powers and, under the Texas Constitution, the state legislature is empowered to enact a variety of legislation involving local governments. Such legislation is supposed to take the form of general laws pertaining to all local governments, a point emphasized by the detailed constitutional prohibition against most local or special legislation; however, this prohibition has often been breached in practice.[10] The constitution also contains provisions permitting cities to adopt home-rule charters (see Chapter 9).

Citizen political participation. The constitution prescribes the qualifications for voting in state and local elections; provides for the disfranchisement of particular persons, such as "idiots and lunatics" and convicted felons; and authorizes the annual registration of voters. By requiring the election of many state and local officials, referenda on many tax levies and bond issues, and popular approval of amendments, the constitution insures a long ballot at elections.

Substantive material. Many sections of the constitution are concerned, often in minute detail, with matters of substantive public policy. Among the topics dealt with at some length are public education, taxation, welfare programs, the veterans' land program, retirement programs for teachers and public officials, conservation and resource development, public lands, and liquor control. For example, there are provisions in Article VII for the creation of a permanent university fund for support of the University of Texas and Texas A. & M. University, regulation of the way this fund can be invested, and control of the use of the income derived therefrom. As a consequence of the large volume of material of this sort, the Texas Constitution takes on the appearance of a legal code. Few would argue that it contains items only of a "fundamental" nature.

AN EVALUATION OF THE CONSTITUTION

Scholars, public officials, and interested citizens have expressed several major criticisms of the Texas Constitution. First, it is too long and detailed, poorly written, badly organized, and often unclear in meaning. Stylistically, the constitution leaves a lot to be desired. Second, it is not confined to fundamental matters and contains a lot of essentially statutory material. Third, the constitution's excessive detail and *restrictive* orientation hamper the operation of the government and help prevent it from adequately meeting the needs of a modern urban society. Fourth, it contains a lot of deadwood, that is, provisions that are no longer necessary or applicable. The "deadwood argument" was substantially countered by a 1969 amendment that deleted 52 outdated or superfluous sections. Some of the provisions eliminated were those that denied the right to vote or hold office to persons who engaged in dueling, authorized pensions for those who fought in the Texas War for Independence (1835–1837), permitted the appropriation of funds for a state centennial celebration in 1936, and dealt with Spanish and Mexican land titles. Some deadwood remains, as in the case of an authorization for the governor to use the militia to "protect the frontier from hostile incursions by Indians and other predatory bands" (Article IV, Section 7).

Although the length and detail of the Texas Constitution, as such, are not especially important, what is really important are the *consequences* of the length, detail, and complexity and their impact on the operation of government and its ability to respond to public problems. Much of the detail is statutory in nature (e.g., the sections on hospital districts, the veterans' land fund, and taxation of agricultural land) in that it seeks to solve problems rather than simply authorize someone to solve them. But, whether the detail is conceived as statutory or fundamental, much of it has the effect of helping some groups and hindering others in getting what they want from government. As one authority remarks: "Many constitutional provisions protect a variety of interests. People like to be remembered in the Texas Constitution; but, unfortunately, not all people are remembered equally, and the sum of those special interests protected does not necessarily add up to the general or public interest."[11]

Getting Around the Constitution

A much noted characteristic of the Texas Constitution is its many restrictions on state government. However, constitutional restrictions can be circumvented in a number of ways. One is simply to ignore them, as several dozen counties do in not electing the four justices of the peace required for each county. A second is to use interpretations and practices which permit the avoidance of limitations. Two prominent examples can be noted.

State debt is limited to $200,000 (Article III, Section 49) unless authorized by constitutional amendment, as in the case of bonds for the veterans' land program. However, there also exist "gimmick" bonds, such as those issued by state colleges and universities for building construction. These are backed by the "building use" fees levied on students. Estimates are that "gimmick" bonds total over $1 billion. Since, technically, they do not pledge the credit of the state, they do not fall within the prohibition on state debt.

In an effort to prevent legislative meddling in local government affairs, the constitution prohibits the enactment of local legislation (applying to name local governments) on a wide range of matters. The legislature gets around this limitation by the use of "bracket" legislation, that is, legislation which looks general but which contains such precise population limits as to apply to only one or a very few local governments. Many laws of this sort have been enacted, usually at the request of local officials needing authority to deal with local problems.

Can such action simply be accepted as necessary to adapt an old constitution to new conditions? If not, how would one act to bring governmental practice into close conformity with the constitution?

Much of the detail is designed to prevent the enactment of legislation or otherwise restrict governmental power. Thus, more than half of the 64 sections in the article dealing with the legislature involve restrictions on it.[12] In all, the state government is undoubtedly more limited by its own constitution than by the U.S. Constitution when it comes to the enactment of social and economic legislation. Much of the criticism of the Texas Constitution has come, unsurprisingly enough, from those who want a more active and positive government.

Because the states possess residual powers under the U.S. Constitution, it is not necessary for state constitutions to authorize the enactment of particular laws in the fashion of the Texas Constitution. However, once started, the process of adding detail and specific authorizations leads to further detail as needs and circumstances change. Prof. Duane Lockard comments:

If the wealth of details grows sufficiently complex, it may become necessary to authorize a particular kind of legislation for the simple reason that so many kinds of legislation are authorized that doubt may be cast on the constitutionality of a law unless it is possible to point to some authorizing constitutional provision.[13]

This appears to be the case in Texas, as indicated by the flood of proposed amendments since 1960 (see Table 1.1), many of which were designed to authorize particular changes in state programs or specific actions by designated local governments. The amending process, because of constitutional restrictions and details, tends to displace the regular legislative process on many policy matters. An illustration of this involves Sections 59, 60, and 61 of Article III. Section 59, adopted in 1936, authorized workmen's compensation for state employees; Section 60, adopted in 1948, extended coverage to county employees; Section 61, adopted in 1952, covered municipal employees. Section 60 was itself amended in 1962 to permit coverage of employees of special districts. It would seem that one general amendment when the problem first arose would have been a sound constitutional approach.[14]

A constitution containing much detail and many restrictions on the actions of public officials will not guarantee good government or responsible officials. Although apparently such was a consideration motivating the framers of the Texas Constitution, a variety of provisions directed to requiring honesty in government have not prevented Texas from having its share of dishonest officials and political scandals. Neither, however, will a constitution confined to fundamental matters and general statements phrased in clear language automatically yield good government and honest, responsible officials. Nonetheless, given Americans' veneration of constitutions and their tendency to follow most of the constitutional rules most of the time, a restrictive and inflexible constitution can hinder a government in responding to public needs and demands.

Everyone does not agree, however, that the state's government has been unduly hampered by its constitution. It has been contended, for instance, that the "nature of the constitution of the state of Texas is only incidental to whether Texas has an honest, efficient, principled government. The caliber of the men who guide the state's affairs determine the type of government Texas has."[15] This viewpoint, while not without some validity, neglects two important considerations: (1) The constitution, directly through such matters as salary limitations and indirectly through its impact on governmental organization and practice, may affect the "caliber" of the men who hold public office. (2) Even "high caliber" public officials can be hindered or frustrated by restrictive constitutional procedures and limitations that place many matters beyond change or current control or that fragment authority and diffuse responsibility. Particular allocations of tax funds and limitations on the governor's administrative authority are cases in point.

CONSTITUTIONAL REVISION

Critics have long advocated that the Texas Constitution should be either revised or replaced with a new constitution more in accord with the requirements of government in a modern urban society. Newspaper editorial writers, educators, the League of Women Voters, various political officials (including some recent governors), and others have spoken in support of revision.[16] Public opinion polls also indicate general public support for constitutional reform.

One impediment to revision has been the fact that until recently the constitution did not provide explicit authorization for calling a constitutional convention, although the power to call such a convention is widely considered to be inherent in legislative bodies. The situation was made murky in Texas by an attorney general's ruling in 1911 that an amendment authorizing a convention was necessary; some legislators have cited this as the basis for not calling a convention. Another question over which there has been controversy is whether a call for a constitutional convention would require approval by the voters. In 1919 the legislature, by simple majority vote, did pass a resolution calling for a convention. Referred to the voters for approval, it was rejected by a vote of 71,376 to 23,549 (representing about 10 percent of the eligible electorate).

Another means for constitutional revision is the use of a specially created constitutional revision commission (appointed by legislative or executive officials) to propose changes subject to legislative approval and the regular amending process; this could take the form of either article-by-article revision or a single comprehensive amendment. Final approval by the voters would be required to put the changes into effect. Popular approval of a constitution (or changes therein) provides legitimation and distinguishes it from ordinary legislative enactment. Popular approval also symbolizes its status as fundamental law, an expression of "the will of the people" as some are wont to say.

A number of factors have contributed to the failure of efforts at constitutional revision.

First, there has been a lack of really strong public support for reform. The League of Women Voters is the only organized group that shows active and continued interest in revision. While many people have indicated they are in favor of reform, they apparently do not feel intensely about it and it is not a salient issue. The result is a kind of "permissive opinion" environment, which permits but does not compel action. Consequently, in the absence of strong political leadership (as by a popular governor) that could direct and lead it, public opinion seems unlikely to produce significant action.

Second, opposition arises because the Texas Constitution is a political document that affects the distribution of power in the political system. It does this by distributing power among participants in the processes of policy formation and administration and by incorporating policies that confer advantages to some while withholding them from others. Those who benefit from provisions in the existing constitution thus have a stake in its retention; revision might not remove or alter their advantages, but it does hold that risk. Respecting those who oppose revision on this ground, Prof. J. William Davis suggests some illustrations:

> This category might include special business and financial interests that prefer the present somewhat irresponsible administration controls . . . teachers who have constitutionally protected pension provisions; construction firms and highway enthusiasts who can boast of the best roads in the country; agrarian interests that find themselves protected by special constitutional provisions [e.g., the homestead exemption]; recipients of, or participants in, special earmarked funds of taxes, who fear losing a favored position in the state financial scheme; policemen and firemen who have received some constitutional protection from their municipal employers. . . .[17]

Third, the legislature has not shown much enthusiasm for constitutional change.[18] It tends to be the dominant branch of the state government, and legislative leaders are reluctant to permit changes that would reduce legislative power or increase gubernatorial power significantly. Although they are not apparently opposed to revision in principle, they have been concerned with retaining control over the revision process. Governors have been more strongly in favor of revision because the position of the executive, from their viewpoint, needs to be strengthened (see Chapter 6).

Fourth, many persons apparently do not find the present constitution seriously lacking in any major way and do not consider revision necessary. If they do perceive a need for some changes, they contend this can be accomplished satisfactorily through the regular amending process. Thus, a few years ago the director of the Texas Legislative Council (see p. 122) argued that the Texas Constitution was "basically good" and any needed changes could be made by amendments. He went on to say that "our Constitution is too precious to be tinkered with just for the sake of change alone or to 'modernize' it in the interests of theoretical perfection. Neither do I subscribe to the idea that we should have a short 'model constitution'."[19]

Partly as a consequence of the reform mood generated by the Sharpstown bank scandal (see Chapter 4), a major effort to revise the constitution got under way in 1971, when the legislature initiated an amendment containing the following provisions:

1. The members of the Sixty-third Legislature, elected in 1972, would meet as a constitutional convention in January 1974.
2. The legislature in January 1973 would create a Constitutional Revision Commission to make recommendations to the members of the legislature.
3. "The convention by vote of at least two-thirds of its members could submit for a vote of the qualified electors of this state a new constitution which could contain alternative articles or sections, or it could submit revisions of the existing constitution which could contain alternative articles or sections."
4. No changes were to be made in the Bill of Rights of the constitution. (Many regarded this as "sacred" and something the people would not permit to be altered.)

Opposition to the amendment came from conservatives, who opposed major revision of the constitution, and others, including many liberals, who questioned the wisdom of permitting the legislature rather than a specially selected constitutional convention to rewrite the constitution. However, only by having the constitutional convention composed of the members of the legislature could the two-thirds vote to propose the amendment be secured. The amendment easily won approval at the polls in November 1972 by a margin of 1,549,982 to 985,282. Apparently the voters were motivated by a desire for reform because they also approved amendments changing the procedure for amending the constitution and increasing the terms of office to four years for statewide elected officials.

In January 1973, the legislature acted to establish a 37-member Constitutional Revision Commission, the members being appointed by a committee composed of the governor, lieutenant governor, attorney general, speaker of the house, chief justice of the supreme court, and presiding judge of the court of criminal appeals. Working through a series of committees and aided by a large staff, the commission made a thorough study of the existing constitution and proposed changes. Public hearings were held throughout the state. When it began its final deliberations, the commission decided to draft a new constitution rather than merely streamline the present one. On November 1, 1973, it presented its recommendations to the legislature.[20]

The proposed constitution drafted by the revision commission was much shorter and written in terms more general than those of the present constitution. Major changes included annual legislative sessions and election of all legislators from single-member districts; greater administrative powers for the governor; streamlining of the judicial system, including merger of the Supreme Court and the Court of Criminal Appeals into a single court of last resort; appointment of appellate judges by the governor from among those recommended by a special nominating committee and nonpartisan election of district and county judges; authorization for the legislature to determine whether the state treasurer and land commissioner should be elected or appointed; provision for county home rule; and elimination of much of the statutory material found in the present constitution. The commission members were motivated both by a desire to write a "good" constitution and by "practical" political considerations. Thus some earmarked taxes, special funds, and tax exemptions in the existing constitution were included in their proposal because of the strong opposition their elimination would have engendered. In all, however, the commission proposed rather extensive alterations in the governmental system.

In January 1974, the 181 members of the legislature met in the remodeled House chamber as the state constitutional convention to begin consideration of the revision commission's recommendations. Speaker of the House Price Daniel, Jr., was elected president of the convention. Eight substantive and five procedural committees were authorized and appointed to perform much of the work of the convention. Under the rules governing the convention, individual articles required majority votes for approval while a two-thirds vote was required to submit a new constitution to the voters. The convention was initially scheduled to end on May 31, but its life was subsequently extended through July 30, 1974. (The convention was in recess for a month during the spring so that members could campaign for renomination or for nomination to other offices.) As one might guess, in operation the constitutional convention looked and acted much like the legislature.

Early in July, following committee action and floor debate, the convention completed work on a proposed 11-article constitution which did not make as many or as extensive changes in the governmental structure as the revision commission had proposed. The convention, for example, decided to continue the election of all judges and currently elected state administrative officials. Several items, which were productive of substantial controversy, were proposed for separate submission to the voters. These included proposals to write the state's "right-to-work" law (which prohibits union-shop agree-

"And it only cost $5 million, folks."

ments) into the constitution, prohibit parimutuel gambling, increase
the terms of state representatives to four years, authorize
limited county home rule, and increase legislator's salaries to $8,750
per year. It then became the task of the convention's committee on
submission and transition to put together a package of constitutional
articles and separate submission items which could win the two-thirds
vote necessary to send it to the voters of the state. This the committee was unable to accomplish although it presented 30 different
proposals to the convention, and at midnight on July 30 the constitutional convention came to an end. Minutes earlier the last proposal
before the delegates had received 118 votes, three short of the total
needed for approval. Constitutional revision in Texas had again failed.

Several factors contributed to the failure of the convention to
submit a new constitution to the voters. One, because the delegates

were also legislators, they were subject to pressure from interest groups because of the impact their votes might have on their political futures. Antagonism existed among some delegates because of past legislative conflicts. Moreover, the campaigning for speaker of the house, which went on during the convention, was a distracting and somewhat divisive influence. Two, some of the delegates were opposed to constitutional revision of any sort. Three, the rule requiring a two-thirds majority vote to submit the proposed constitution to the voters proved to be an insurmountable obstacle. Only simple majorities had been required to approve articles and separate submission items as the convention proceeded in its work. Four, the governor, who is in the best position to exercise leadership on constitutional revision, chose to leave the convention to itself except when it proposed to reduce the gubernatorial veto power. He then readily got what he wanted. Five, some emotional issues, especially that of right-to-work, served to polarize the delegates and exacerbate conflict.

The issue on which the convention ultimately foundered was that of right-to-work. Conservative delegates refused to vote for a constitutional package which did not include the right-to-work submission item while many liberal or pro-labor delegates refused to vote for one which did. The right-to-work issue was really symbolic because the guarantee has no more impact in the constitution than in statute law, and, in either case, its existence depends upon continued authorization in national labor legislation. Nonetheless, it became *the* labor issue in the convention, and no compromise proved possible. The final constitutional package, which included a right-to-work proposal, failed by a vote of 118 to 62. The 62 negative votes came mostly from liberal-labor delegates plus a few conservatives opposed to any constitutional revision.

When the legislature met in January 1975, however, the drive for constitutional revision was revived. Apparently stung by public criticism of the convention's failure and under the leadership of the speaker and lieutenant governor, the legislature went briskly to work considering a multitude of proposals for constitutional revision. The approach settled upon was article-by-article revision. In April the legislature approved a series of eight propositions (which collectively contained ten articles) to be submitted to the voters in November. Each proposition took the form of an amendment to the existing constitution and, in total, provided a new constitution except for the Bill of Rights. There was little difference between the content of the ten articles and the proposed constitution which had been rejected by the convention the previous July. One authority stated that if adopted, the new constitution would be "among the best, perhaps the best, drafted state constitutions in the nation."

In November 1975, following a somewhat desultory and unexciting campaign for and against the proposed constitution, the voters went to the polls and overwhelmingly rejected all eight propositions by margins of three to one. Only in Webb and Duval Counties were all eight propositions approved; in El Paso County seven were approved; and in Kenedy County two were approved. Everything was rejected in the other 250 counties. Approximately 25 percent of the eligible voters went to the polls. Whatever the reasons for their decision—opposition to revision by the governor, lack of understanding of the new constitution, opposition to revision by the legislature rather than a people's convention, or whatever—it appears to have spelled the end of the movement for comprehensive constitutional revision.

In its regular session in 1977, the legislature returned to its old habit of tinkering with the Constitution of 1876. A total of fifteen proposed amendments were passed, seven of which were submitted to the voters in 1977 (five were approved) and eight (six were approved) in 1978. Detail continues to beget detail.[23]

NOTES

[1]For discussions of federalism, see W. Brooke Graves, *American Intergovernmental Relations: Their Origins, Historical Development and Current Status* (New York: Scribner, 1964); and Daniel J. Elazar, *American Federalism: A View from the States* (New York: T. Y. Crowell, 1966).

[2]Cf. Minor B. Crager, *Legal Aspects of Fire Prevention and Control in Texas* (Austin: University of Texas, Institute of Public Affairs, 1969), pp. 16–18.

[3]Most of the data in this paragraph are derived from *Statistical Abstract of the United States, 1976* (Washington, D.C.: GPO, 1976), sections 8 and 9.

[4]Citizens Advisory Committee on Constitutional Revision, *Interim Report to the 56th Legislature and the People of Texas,* March 1, 1959, as reprinted in Fred Gantt, Jr., Irving O. Dawson and Luther G. Hagard, Jr., eds., *Governing Texas: Documents and Readings* (New York: T. Y. Crowell, 1966), p. 39.

[5]Joe E. Ericson, "The Delegates to the Convention of 1875: A Reappraisal," *Southwestern Historical Quarterly* 62 (July 1963): 22–27.

[6]Rupert N. Richardson, *Texas: The Lone Star State,* 2nd ed. (Englewood Cliffs, N.J.: Prentice-Hall, 1958), p. 226.

[7]Janice C. May, *Amending the Texas Constitution 1951–1972* (Austin: Texas Advisory Commission on Intergovernmental Relations, 1972).

[8]For those desiring to read the Constitution, a convenient place to find it reprinted is in *The Texas Almanac.*

[9]T. C. Sinclair and Werner F. Grunbaum, "Personal Rights and Liberties," vol. 5, *Arnold Foundation Monographs* (Dallas: Southern Methodist University Press, 1960).

[10]Texas Legislative Council, *Laws Based on Population* (a report to the 58th Legislature, Austin, December 1962).

[11]Janice C. May, "Constitutional Revision in Texas," in *The Texas Constitution: Problem and Prospects for Revision* (Arlington: University of Texas at Arlington, Institute of Urban Studies, 1971), p. 84.

[12]Limitations in the Texas constitution are well covered in George D. Braden, *Citizen's Guide to the Texas Constitution* (Austin: Texas Advisory Commission on Intergovernmental Relations, 1972), esp. pp. 61–72.

[13]Duane Lockard, *The Politics of State and Local Government* (New York: Macmillan, 1963), p. 89.

[14]Op. cit., p. 9. There are, incidentally, two Section 61s in Article III because one was misnumbered when adopted.

[15]A. J. Thomas, Jr., and Ann Van Wynen Thomas, "The Texas Constitution of 1876," *Texas Law Review* 35 (October 1957): 917, This entire issue of the law review examines the Texas Constitution.

[16]See Dick Smith, "Constitutional Revision, 1876–1961," *Public Affairs Comment* 7 (September 1961).

[17]J. William Davis, "The Abortive Movement for Constitutional Revision, 1957–1961," in Gantt, Dawson, and Hagard, op. cit., p. 63.

[18]May, *Constitutional Revision in Texas,* p. 88.

[19]Quoted in Stuart A. McCarkle and Dick Smith, *Texas Government,* 6th ed. (New York: McGraw-Hill, 1968), p. 29.

[20]These recommendations are contained in three documents: (1) *A New Constitution for Texas;* (2) *A New Constitution for Texas: Text, Explanation, Commentary;* and (3) *A New Constitution for Texas: Separate Statements of Commission Members.* The second item contains biographical data on members of the commission. Also see Jay G. Stanford, "Constitutional Revision in Texas: A New Chapter," *Public Affairs Comment,* 20 (February 1974), pp. 1–6.

[21]For a thorough account of constitutional revision activity in Texas, see Janice C. May, *The Texas Constitutional Revision Experience in the 70's* (Austin: Sterling Swift Publishing Co., 1975).

[22]Janice C. May, "The Proposed 1976 Revision of the Texas Constitution," *Public Affairs Comment* 21 (August 1975), p. 1.

[23]An amendment providing for tax reduction and expenditure limitation was proposed by special session of the legislature in the summer of 1978 and approved by the voters in the fall. This was Texas' response to California's Proposition 13.

Political Participation and the Electoral System

Political systems define and attempt to implement policies deemed to be in the best interest of the society at large. The forms and means of definition and implementation have varied, but little effort was made in the past to significantly involve ordinary individuals in the processes through which political rules and decisions were made. That, of course, is no longer the case. As two leading scholars of modern politics note, "If there is a political revolution going on throughout the world, it is what might be called the participation explosion."[1] The belief that the ordinary man is politically relevant and ought to be an involved participant in the political system has taken firm hold throughout the world. People who have been outside of politics are demanding entrance into the political system; people who have been without influence or power are demanding a share of political control.

One might question the relevance of these general comments to Texas politics. Have not the United States and the state of Texas been committed to citizen participation since their beginnings? And do not most Americans, including Texans, support the values of democracy and citizen involvement? In the abstract, the answer is yes. The Declaration of Independence and the U.S. and Texas constitutions all emphasize that government is an instrument to be wielded in the interests of the people. Similarly, evidence exists that the American public strongly prefers "democratic" as opposed to "nondemocratic" political systems. Nonetheless, a tension has existed through much of our history between our abstract commitment to democracy and popular participation and the practical implementation of these ideals.[2]

This discrepancy between democratic ideals and political realities is evident in the operation of the electoral system. Theoretically, it is the fundamental means by which citizens can control and direct their government. Parties and their candidates, officeholders and challengers, can present themselves for popular scrutiny, and the citizenry—via the ballot—can pass judgment on them. In this way individuals, since they help to select their political leaders, are presumably obligated to accept and obey the government, pending another opportunity to vote their approval or disapproval. And political leaders, selected by the votes of the citizenry, are presumed to be legitimately entitled to their official positions.

Turning from the ideal to the historical record, one notes that large segments of the adult population in the United States, including Texas, were legally excluded from meaningful political participation until well into the twentieth century. Open legal exclusion has by now been virtually eliminated, but substantial numbers of the populace are still not involved in the electoral politics of their state or the nation. This is especially true in Texas, where—despite a record turnout in the 1976 presidential election—half the adults in the state failed to cast ballots in that contest. State and local contests, as we shall see, usually draw even smaller turnouts. There are, of course, forms of citizen involvement and expression other than voting, but voting is one of the most economical means of political action in that it requires only a slight investment of a person's time and energy. As such, it provides a useful standard to measure political performance against accepted democratic ideals.

Questions concerning the nature and extent of public participation in Texas politics thus remain relevant despite widespread abstract support for democracy and the present relative absence of legal barriers to individual involvement. This relevance is enhanced by the fact that electoral participation is selective; that is, those who regularly participate are not representative of the general Texas population. Some groups have been very active in Texas politics while others have been only slightly involved. Because of the selective participatory patterns, state and local governments have often been especially responsive to certain group interests and demands and relatively insensitive to others. This remains substantially true today, despite the increasing efforts of new groups representing new interests to influence the political process.

The patterns of participation in Texas electoral politics are examined in the following sections. In discussing this topic, three groups are distinguished: (1) the adult population residing in the state, (2) those legally qualified to take part in the electoral process, and (3) those who actually involve themselves in electoral politics. The variations between the first group and the last two are of particular import to Texas political patterns. (The three groups are discussed under the headings of "Characteristics of the Texas Population," "The Texas Electorate," and "Voter Participation.")

CHARACTERISTICS OF THE TEXAS POPULATION

Virtually all studies of politics have acknowledged a close connection between the demographic characteristics of large groups of people and their political behaviors. The racial, religious, occupational, educational, geographic, and class patterns characteristic of the Texas population are therefore worthy of our attention. In general, Texans are a diverse people. The land is, of course, vast and varied, ranging from western plains and mountains to central hills and eastern forests and the semitropical coastal plains of the south. And the diversity of the 13 million inhabitants is at least equal to that of the terrain.

RACE, ETHNICITY, AND RELIGION

The population of Texas is more racially and ethnically mixed than most other heavily populated states. Out of a total population of 11,196,730 recorded by the 1970 census, 1,395,853 (12.5 percent) were black. The state's Mexican-American minority was even larger; the 1970 census recorded some 2,059,671 (18.4 percent) Texans as being "persons of Spanish language or Spanish surname."[3] The combined minority populations totaled 30.9 percent. Since there are few Texans of Oriental or American Indian heritage, the remaining percentage of the residents is almost entirely of European origin and is often referred to as the "Anglo" majority.

Historically, the black and Mexican-American groups have been geographically concentrated in different parts of the state. Blacks have resided almost entirely east of a line running through Dallas, Austin, and Corpus Christi, while Mexican-Americans have generally lived south of an imaginary line running from El Paso to San Antonio to Corpus Christi. In recent years some dispersion throughout the state has occurred, especially with respect to Mexican-Americans. In 1970, for example, about 20 percent of the Mexican-Americans lived in the Dallas-Fort Worth and Houston metropolitan areas. The national pattern of blacks migrating to big cities holds in Texas. In 1960, 41.2 percent of the black population lived in the four most populous counties; in 1970, 50.8 percent resided in these counties.

The Mexican-American population has increased considerably in Texas since 1970 because of a relatively high birth rate and continued in-migration from Mexico. The migrant population consists largely of "illegal aliens" or "undocumented workers" who enter the United States without complying with the immigration laws of this country. The increasing number of migrants, coupled with persistent high unemployment in the United States, has made their presence a major political issue in the United States and Texas. Estimates usually place the number of illegal migrants in Texas at between 0.5 and 1 million persons. In 1977 President Carter proposed a complicated program to beef up the border patrol, grant certain rights to illegal migrants already in this country, and make it more difficult for future migrants to get jobs in the United States. Passage of this legislation appears doubtful at this writing, but the continued population growth in Mexico, a country that cannot provide jobs for a large fraction of its adult population, insures that many Mexicans will continue to seek entry into the American and Texas job markets. Consequently, the political problems associated with this immigrant population will become more severe, both in the nation and Texas.

The religious preferences of Texans tend toward fundamental Protestantism and Catholicism. The Texas Council of Churches' count of 1967 recorded somewhat less than 5 million church members in the state, of whom about 36 percent were Baptists and 26 percent were Catholics. The Methodists (17 percent) and Church of Christ members (6 percent) followed, with the remainder divided largely among Presbyterians, Lutherans, Episcopalians, and Disciples of Christ. The Protestants are concentrated in the northern and eastern parts of the state, whereas a large Catholic population is found in southern Texas and along the Gulf Coast. This religious-regional pattern is probably not of great political significance save on issues involving public regulation of community mores, such as public sale of liquor by the drink, legalizing bingo, and pari-mutuel betting on horse racing.

The regional division on such issues as liquor and horse racing led Sen. V. E. "Red" Berry of San Antonio to propose to the 1969 legislature that Texas be divided along a line from El Paso to Orange. The new state of "South Texas" could then have the "fun," according to the senator, and North Texas could keep its "money." Berry's proposed constitutional amendment died in a senate committee.

POPULATION PATTERNS

Since 1940 the state's population has increased from less than 6.5 million to nearly 13 million in the late 1970s. Nationally, this has also been a time of significant population increases; but the percentage change in Texas has consistently exceeded the national average. However, the state's rate of growth has slowed in recent years and now more closely approximates the national average; the Texas population increased by 24.2 percent in the 1950s as compared to 16.9 percent in the 1960s. The primary cause for the drop has been a decline in birthrates, which began in the late 1950s.

Of greater importance than the number of Texans has been their tendency to concentrate in the cities. In 1970, 80 percent of the state's residents lived in urban areas as compared to 75 percent in 1960 and 64 percent in 1950.[4] Nearly three-fourths of the people lived in one of the state's 24 standard metropolitan statistical areas. Overall, the metropolitan areas almost doubled in population between 1950 and 1970, while the rural areas lost a fourth of their inhabitants. Since 1960 most of the state's growth has occurred in the very large cities. For example, 84 percent of the population increase in the 1960–1970 decade was accounted for by the Houston-Galveston, Dallas-Fort Worth, and San Antonio-Austin areas. A number of medium-sized cities that grew very rapidly in the previous decade, such as Abilene, Midland, Odessa, and Amarillo lost population during the 1960s.

A distinct residential pattern is emerging. Two sprawling megalopolises are developing around Dallas-Fort Worth and Houston-Galveston. They contained 40 percent of the state's population in 1970 and, if present trends continue, this will approach 50 percent by 1980. A third such giant urban area may soon link San Antonio and Austin. While the big cities grow and spread, the countryside in most parts of the state is being progressively depopulated. More than half of Texas's 254 counties lost population in the 1950s, as did 60 percent between 1960 and 1970. The Texas of the future may well feature a few urban islands surrounded by a largely unpeopled hinterland.

The political implications of this concentrated urban growth have to be very great. Writing in 1949, V. O. Key, Jr., one of the most respected analysts of American politics, noted that "the Lone Star State is concerned about money and how to make it, about oil and sulfur and gas, about cattle and dust storms and irrigation, about cotton and banking and Mexicans."[5] These concerns doubtlessly continue, but as Texans crowd into big cities such issues may well play a secondary role. Primary attention is shifting to the difficulties arising from the concentration of many people with radically different backgrounds into very limited, technologically developed, amounts of space. Problems of air and water pollution have assumed great importance because the cities produce more waste, refuse, and pollutants than they can dispose of easily. Problems of transportation, housing, and schools are taking on a different and more serious complexion. Perhaps even more important are the myriad problems associated with the existence, in the heart of the great urban centers, of poor black and Mexican-American minorities surrounded by affluent suburban whites.

EDUCATION, OCCUPATION, AND INCOME

Texas politics, in contrast to that of other former Confederate States, has focused largely on socioeconomic rather than racial issues.[6] Since an individual's socioeconomic status is determined largely by his education, occupation, and income, some discussion of these characteristics is warranted.

If educational levels are measured by median number of school years completed by those 25 years old and over, Texans rank a little below the national median in 1970 (Texas, 11.7 years; United States, 12.1 years).[7] This gap was consistent across the various levels of education completed. In Texas 3.1 percent of the adults had completed no years of school compared to 1.6 percent nationally. Some 30.2 percent in the state had no more than an eighth-grade education versus 29.6 percent in the nation; 22.3 percent of all Texans had attended college compared to 24.3 percent of all Americans.

Educational attainment in the state is distributed most unevenly among the Anglo, black, and Mexican-American groups. Anglos, as expected, have the best rates, followed by blacks, then Mexican-Americans. In 1970, for example, 14.5 percent of the adult Mexican-Americans had completed no years of school, and 60.2 percent had not gone beyond the eighth grade. Among blacks, the comparable figures were 3.3 percent (none) and 43.6 percent (eighth grade or less). But in the adult Anglo population, only 0.8 percent had completed no years in school, and only 21.6 percent had not progressed beyond the eighth grade. Achievement in higher education is similarly distributed. Adult Anglos were about three times as likely to have entered college as were blacks or Mexican-Americans.

Minority-group Texans did improve their levels of quantitative educational attainment between 1960 and 1970, but there is good reason for continued concern about the quality of education minority children are receiving. Most black and Mexican-American students attend schools either in rural districts in southern and eastern Texas or in the big central-city districts in Dallas, Houston, and San Antonio. The rural districts with large minority populations have generally been among the poorest in the state, and their lack of money has doubtlessly been reflected in the quality of education they have provided. And the big urban districts, while perhaps once among the best in Texas, are today faced with great and growing problems (finance, integration, and white flight, to name three) that imperil their ability to deliver good educational services. Given the cost and complexity of altering these patterns, qualitative differences in the schooling received by whites, blacks, and Mexican-Americans are likely to persist in coming years.

Another drawback in altering these patterns is the refusal of the U.S. Supreme Court to involve itself in the policy area. In March 1973 the Court, in *Rodriguez* v. *San Antonio Independent School District,* upheld the constitutionality of the Texas school finance system. This system effectively precludes districts with low property values from spending as much money on education as do districts with higher property values. Prior to this decision, pressures had been building to revamp the financing of public schools so a much greater degree of equality in expenditures per pupil would be achieved. After the landmark Rodriguez decision, these pressures waned and no action along these lines was taken by the 1973 legislature. In 1975 and 1977 the existence of large budget surpluses enabled the legislature to increase substantially state funding for public education. However, only modest steps were taken to reduce the enormous disparities in per pupil expenditures between districts in Texas.

Although Texas does include a number of oil and cattle barons ensconced in Cadillacs, the great majority of the state's residents—in comparison to their fellow Americans—are not especially blessed with material abundance. Reflecting inflation, per capita income has rapidly increased in recent years, reaching $6243 in 1976.[8] Still, this ranked Texas only 25th among the 50 states, and the state mean per capita income was just 96.9 percent of the national average in 1976.

As is the case with educational attainment, income distribution varies sharply between the minority groups and the Anglo majority. The 1970 census showed that only 8.3 percent of the nonminority families had income below the poverty line, compared to 31.4 percent of the Mexican-American and 32.7 percent of the black families.[9] At the other end of the scale, 20.5 percent of the Anglo families' incomes exceeded $15,000 in 1969, but only 6.5 percent of the Mexican-American and 3.9 percent of the black families were above this level.

The occupational patterns of employed Texans have been changing in recent years. Farm employment fell from 639,226 in 1940 to 288,887 in 1960 and 187,024 in 1970. Declines have also been registered in the percentage of workers employed in private households and as nonfarm laborers. Substantial increases have occurred in white-collar jobs, especially in the professional and technical categories. The percentage of male workers employed in blue-collar jobs (craftsmen, foremen, operatives, etc.) edged up from 36.7 percent in 1960 to 39.7 percent in 1970. Among employed females, increases occurred in the sales, clerical, and service categories.

Anglos held a high percentage of the jobs that had high status and incomes, while low-paying positions were often filled by minority-group members. Among males, 30.1 percent of the employed Anglos had professional, technical, nonfarm managerial, official, or propri-etary jobs in 1970.[10] The comparable figure for black employed males was 7.3 percent; for Mexican-American employed males, it was 13.1 percent. Only 4.2 percent of the Anglo male work force were employed as nonfarm or nonmine laborers, while 12.3 percent of the Mexican-American males and 19.3 percent of the black males were so employed. Blue-collar jobs were more evenly distributed among the three groups. In the female work force, which comprises about one-third of the people employed in Texas, the general patterns of employment were roughly similar; however, Anglo females tended to fill the clerking and sales-worker positions while nonwhite females provided the bulk of the private household workers. The problems of minority-group workers are further aggravated by the fact that their unemployment rates are typically about twice as high as the Anglo average.

Summing up, one finds that in terms of education and income, Texans lag somewhat behind the national averages. More important is the fact that this lag is accounted for by the markedly lower socioeco-nomic status of the state's two large minority groups. There are, to be sure, many poorly educated and poorly paid Anglos in Texas (about 43 percent of the families the census defined as being below the poverty line were Anglos). However, due to their considerably larger numbers, the overall socioeconomic status of this majority group compares favorably with national averages. The situation is reversed with respect to minority-group members. Some blacks and Mexican-Americans enjoy relatively high incomes and status, but on the whole they are much more likely to be poorer, less well educated, and underemployed or unemployed than are other Texans.

TEXAS AND THE SUNBELT THESIS

In concluding this section, some comment is in order on a theme of social analysis that has recently been given great currency—the "sunbelt versus frostbelt" idea. According to this thesis, there has been a dramatic shift of social, economic, and political power away from the Northeast and the Midwest (the frostbelt), to a sunbelt tier of states stretching from California to the Carolinas.[11] The growth of regional industries such as aerospace, the exploitation of local oil and gas resources, increased federal spending in the area, and a moderate climate have been credited with attracting migrants, jobs, and general prosperity into the sunbelt. The frostbelt has been the loser in this process. These changes have, it is argued, produced new and deep regional rivalries in the political arena, with Eastern and Northern politicians contesting Southern and Western forces for public resources.

Economic Prosperity in Texas: A Populist View

Jim Hightower is the editor of the *Texas Observer,* a biweekly journal that has presented a progressive, and usually critical, perspective on state politics for a quarter century. In a recent editorial (May 1978), Hightower summed up what he views as the consequences of the alliance of Texas political leaders with corporate economic interests.

The Lone Star State . . . has become the nation's promised land, with nearly 10,000 migrants crossing the borders into Texas every month to bask in the prosperity of Sunbelt-style growth. The state's official hucksters assure us that we are privileged to live in the new economic mecca, and that it exists because a long line of governors—from Coke Stevenson in 1943 through Dolph Briscoe in 1978—have had the prescience to make the businessman king.

During the last 35 years, this beneficient leadership of corporate and state executives has constructed in Texas the "Number One Climate" in the country for nurturing big business. More than a thousand million-dollar companies are headquartered in Dallas now, with another 600 in Houston. Only New York and Chicago have more. In the last five years alone, Texas attracted 1,200 industries, and the rush continues. But . . . corporate expansion can hardly be equated with general prosperity, and the predictable results of this alliance are that economic growth has been decidedly unbalanced in Texas and our business structure is being thrown permanently out of whack. Some symptoms:

*While per capita income in Texas is rising, the big boost has come at the upper end of the scale, where a corporate management class is growing and profiting.

*The chances of getting a job in Texas are good, but the chances of being paid adequately for your work are poor—the reason for the poverty of many inner-city residents in Dallas and Houston is not unemployment, as it is in Eastern cities, but the low wages paid to Texas workers.

*Texas lost 12,000 family farms in the last four years, and at least 2,000 more will be squeezed out of business in 1978.

*Consumers increasingly are met in the marketplace by monopolies (such as utilities) and shared monopolies (such as supermarkets) that set prices at inflated levels and limit choices.

*A handful of bankholding companies in Dallas and Houston have gained control of a majority of the state's banking deposits and are shifting local investment capital away from hometown businesses to the ventures of giant corporations in Texas, out-of-state and abroad.

Since Texas is usually cited as a typical sunbelt state, we would expect abundant evidence of these changes to be visible locally. There is, to be sure, some evidence supporting the argument. Texas's population is growing, in part because of migration from the East and Midwest; there are more Texans in Congress and the Electoral College than was the case a few decades ago; and the state's economy, both in terms of employment and growth in per capita income, has outperformed the national economy over the last five years. Note should be taken, however, that these changes have been incremental and scarcely portend a substantial realignment of economic or political power. Political representation in Congress can be taken as an example. Local population growth has resulted in the addition of one seat to the Texas delegation in the U.S. House of Representatives after each of the last three censuses, thereby increasing the delegation from 21 to 24 members. This has doubtlessly given the state a bit more clout in Washington, D.C., but one doubts this compares with the influence Texas had in the 1950s when Sam Rayburn was Speaker of the House and Lyndon Johnson was Majority Leader in the Senate.

Economically, Texas has done comparatively well in the 1970s, but the state still has the largest number of residents below the poverty line of any state, and per capita income, as mentioned earlier, remains below the national average. Those who foresee the shift of national financial power from the Northeast to Dallas or Houston should keep in mind the sobering fact that the deposits in either Chase Manhattan Bank or Citibank in New York exceed the total deposits of every bank in Texas.

One of the factors that is often cited as a boon to Texas is the energy crisis that became evident after the oil embargo of 1973. Texas has enjoyed a number of comparative advantages since 1973 over other states. Local businesses and industries have had adequate supplies of natural gas and fuel oil, albeit at much higher prices. Higher prices for oil and gas have more than doubled the state's revenues from severance taxes and produced sizeable budget surpluses in recent years. Tens of thousands of Texans who own oil royalties or shares of energy companies have profited from higher prices, and hundreds of thousands of workers have benefitted from the resurgence of the energy industry. But, even within Texas, the impact of expensive oil and gas is mixed. Irrigation farmers in Reeves County who used natural gas to power their water pumps have been virtually wiped out by a tenfold increase in the price of that fuel. Farmers throughout the state endured a severe recession in 1977–1978, in part brought on by higher energy costs. Millions of Texans, including some of the poorest people in America, have watched helplessly as their gas and electric bills have doubled and quadrupled within a single year.

Two summary points should be drawn from this discussion. First, the "sunbelt-frostbelt" theory of national politics lends itself to gross oversimplification. There is, for example, tremendous diversity in the political interests of various Southern states as a comparison of energy-poor Georgia with energy-rich Texas or Louisiana quickly reveals. Second, within Texas the benefits of recent economic change have by no means been uniformly distributed. In general, most of the benefits have accrued to middle- and upper-class Anglos in the cities of the state. They provide the bulk of the professional, managerial, and technical services required by an expanding, energy-based, economy. Meantime, many of the state's poor, its rural residents, blacks, and Mexican-Americans have lost ground in terms of economic well-being.

THE TEXAS ELECTORATE

Political participation via the ballot is a right possessed abstractly by those who live in a democratic political society. In practice, however, no government extends this right uniformly to all persons within its jurisdiction. The necessity for some restriction seems obvious: Few would argue that children, foreign visitors, the mentally ill, or certain types of criminals should have access to the electoral system. Not only is exclusion practiced, but fear of fraud and manipulation has led to the development of an extensive regulatory process to supervise use of the ballot.

The individual states have discretion to regulate electoral participation within the limits defined by the U.S. Constitution and federal statutes. Texas, like other states, has established a process whereby citizens must present themselves in advance of an election, attest that they meet certain legal qualifications, and be enrolled on a list of qualified electors if they wish to vote. The procedure may sound trivial, but typically from one-half to one-third of the adult population never completes this preliminary process and thus is automatically excluded from direct participation in elections. The reasons for their failure are rooted in an interrelated pattern of historical discrimination, cumbersome registration processes, and a culture that does little to discourage political apathy.

THE HISTORICAL CONTEXT

Historically, the state of Texas has acted to limit electoral participation. For 90 years, from 1876 to 1966, the state assessed a poll tax on individual electors. The tax was provided for in the Constitution of 1876 as a revenue measure but was later used as a device to restrict political participation, especially among poor whites, blacks, and

Mexican-Americans. The fee was small—usually $1.75 in later years—but the bother of paying the tax probably exceeded its expense as a barrier to voter participation. Additionally, poll taxes had to be paid far in advance of most electoral activity. In its last years of operation, the tax for a calendar year was payable from October 1 of the preceding year to February 1 of the year in which it applied. The likelihood that individuals would forget or neglect to pay the fee was heightened considerably by requiring payment months before the May primaries and November general elections. Texans approved a constitutional amendment in 1966 abolishing the poll tax only after a federal court had ruled the tax invalid.

Another, and far more blatant, effort to reduce voter participation was the "white primary." This scheme was used by a number of southern states in addition to Texas to circumvent the Fifteenth Amendment to the U.S. Constitution, which prohibits a state's denial of suffrage because of race, color, or previous condition of servitude. The procedure was simple. The Democratic party dominated Texas politics after the post-Civil War Reconstruction period, so all that was required to exclude blacks from effective participation was to bar them from the party's nominating processes. This exclusion was justified on the grounds that a political party, as a private association, possessed the right to extend or deny membership to anyone for any reason it deemed sufficient. Registered blacks were still free to vote in the general election, but since the Democratic nominee always prevailed, this right was of little importance.

Legal challenges to the white primary were initiated in the 1920s. Finally, after 20 years of legal controversy and four major judicial decisions, the U.S. Supreme Court struck down this exclusion of black voters, reasoning, in *Smith* v. *Allwright,* that party primaries are an inseparable part of the total electoral process and thus come under the protection of the Fifteenth Amendment.

REGISTRATION AND VOTING PROCEDURES

For several years after the poll tax was abolished, Texas retained the most cumbersome registration procedures in the United States. The 1966 constitutional amendment that removed the poll tax continued the system of annual registration far in advance of the party primaries and general election. Such a requirement placed a heavy burden on the ordinary adult, who was only marginally interested, informed, and motivated in political matters. The registration system was challenged successfully in federal court, and a more liberal law was passed in 1971. At present, one can register to vote in any election up to 30 days before polling day. Registration is for a period of two years, and voting in an election automatically extends one's registration for another two years.

The potential electorate in Texas is defined by a set of restrictions that limits access to the ballot. The Texas Constitution denies the vote to idiots and lunatics, paupers supported by the county (that is, persons in county homes for the destitute, which does *not* include ordinary welfare recipients), and felons whose rights have not been restored. A constitutional provision denying the vote to persons under 21 years of age was rendered inoperative by the adoption of the Twenty-sixth Amendment to the U.S. Constitution in 1971, which lowered the voting age to 18. Until 1969 only qualified electors who owned property that had been rendered for taxation were eligible to vote in bond-issue elections, but the U.S. Supreme Court voided this practice as a violation of equal protection of the laws.

Voters are required to cast their ballots in the election precinct in which they reside. An exception is made, however, in the case of qualified electors who expect to be absent from their county on the day of the election or who, because of illness or physical disability, cannot appear at the polling place in their precinct on election day. Such individuals may cast an absentee ballot at the county clerk's office from 20 to 4 days before the election or else secure and cast a mail ballot before election day. Provisions also exist for Texas residents outside the state due to military service or outside the country in the employ of the federal government to ballot by mail.

VOTER PARTICIPATION

Voter turnout in Texas has been low over the years. Nationally, the last seven presidential elections (1952-1976) have attracted an average of 59.5 percent of the voting-age population. In the Lone Star State, the average in the same contests has been only 44.8 percent. Turnout in state and local races is even lower. The last 12 general elections for governor drew the votes of an average 33 percent of the state's adults. The Democratic primaries (which usually produce the winner of the general election), over the same period, attracted only 28 percent of the potential electorate. County and local races are usually even less popular with voters.

Voter participation, like income, educational attainment, and employment, varies greatly among different segments of the Texas population. As one might expect, the poor and minority-group members are less involved in politics than are the more prosperous Anglos. Table 2.1 compares registration and voting levels within four demographically different areas within Houston in 1976.

**TABLE 2.1 • VOTER REGISTRATION AND PARTICIPATION IN FOUR HOUSTON
NEIGHBORHOODS IN THE 1976 PRESIDENTIAL ELECTION**

Nature of Area	Percent of Adults Registered to Vote	Percent of Adults Who Voted	Dem. Percent of Presidential Vote in Area
White, Middle-Class	88	60	29
White, Blue-Collar	63	38	60
Black, Blue-Collar	80	43	98
Mexican-American, Blue-Collar	48	21	80

These data make it strikingly clear how much variation in registration and voting there is along socioeconomic lines. In a middle-class, white neighborhood most adults were registered (88 percent in 1976), and a sizeable majority of 60 percent voted in the 1976 presidential election. Registration was much lower in a white working-class area (63 percent), and only 38 percent of the adults balloted in the 1976 contest. A black neighborhood had a high level of registration (80 percent), which reflected a major voter registration drive undertaken there in the summer of 1976. However, only 43 percent of the black adults went to the polls in November. Finally, in a heavily Mexican-American neighborhood, just 48 percent of the adults were registered, and only 21 percent voted. Comparing the extremes, middle-class white adults had three times the weight in the election as did an equal number of Mexican-American adults.

Some indication of the significance of these differences can be gleaned by looking at the right-hand column in Table 2.1, which lists the vote percentage received in each area by the Democratic presidential ticket of Jimmy Carter and Walter Mondale in 1976. Obviously, there are great differences in the voting tendencies from area to area. The Carter-Mondale ticket got 98 percent of the votes of blacks, 80 percent of the Mexican-American vote, but only 29 percent of the white middle-class vote. Thus, variations in voter participation are of great practical significance. Generally, as in this case, differing rates of voter participation work to the advantage of Republican candidates in general elections. In Democratic primaries, the most conservative candidates are usually the beneficiaries of turnout differences.

Examining county vote totals for the state tends to confirm the pattern found in Houston. The vote-per-population ratio is generally lowest in areas of Mexican-American concentration, such as the Rio

Grande Valley, and highest in areas of relative Anglo affluence, such as the Panhandle. Voting participation has risen sharply among the state's blacks, but both they and the poorer Anglo elements still fall far short of matching the turnout of white middle-class voters.

Many observers felt that the elimination of the poll tax, followed by lowering the voting age to 18 and easing registration procedures, would result in a dramatic increase in voter participation. Figure 2.1 reveals that this has not happened. Voter registration did increase from 3 to 4 million after the poll tax was eliminated in 1966, and it rose another 2 million after the voting age was lowered and registration procedures changed. However, actual voting has edged up more slowly. Increases in presidential voting have barely kept up with population increases, and the percentage of Texans voting in the important party primaries has gone down in the last few years. In 1978, for example, less than 25 percent of the state's adults voted in the Democratic or Republican primaries, compared to 31 percent who voted in the 1956 Democratic primary.

One can infer from these figures that while legal factors such as voting age and the existence or nonexistence of a poll tax affect voter registration and voter turnout, they do not alone explain participation patterns. Whether people vote is not simply a function of whether they *can* legally vote, but also of whether they *want* to vote.

Empirical research into the behavior of the American electorate has shed some light on factors that are associated with voting and nonvoting. No such studies have as yet been done of the Texas electorate, but there is no reason to suspect that Texans differ substantially from other Americans in their general political behavior.

In general, we can say that a person votes or becomes politically active as a result of two sets of factors, one psychological, the other environmental.[12] Some people are "self-starters"; that is, they are moved to political action of their own accord. Ordinarily, they are so motivated because they think their activity will affect electoral or policy outcomes (a sense of political efficacy) and/or because they consider it their civic duty to be politically active. Such individuals usually come from homes where political interest and participation were high. A disproportionate number of them complete at least some college work, and they are often of middle or high socioeconomic status.

For others, political activity is much more a matter of immediate environmental factors. They are moved to political action by external stimuli—their friends, the news media, contact by a party worker, and so on. In such cases the social and political setting in which one operates is crucial. Of course, some people shut out or ignore political

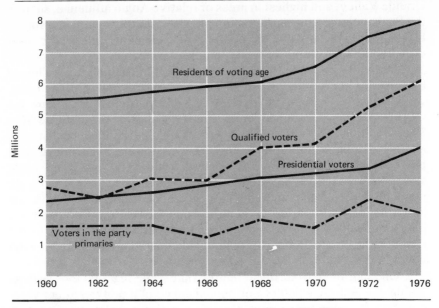

Figure 2.1 • Political participation patterns in Texas: 1960–1976.

SOURCES: Richard Scammon, ed., *America Votes* (Pittsburgh: Univ. of Pittsburgh Press), Vol. 4, pp. 389–404; Vol. 5, pp. 387–403; Vol. 6, pp. 397–414; Vol. 7. pp. 379–392; Vol. 8, pp. 364–377; Vol. 9, pp. 321–332; Vol. 10, pp. 349–365. Also, *Statistical Abstract of the United States* (Washington, D.C.: GPO), *1959*, pp. 25, 27; *1961*, p. 29; *1964*, p. 11; *1967*, pp. 12, 25; *1969*, p. 25; *1971*, p. 25. In addition, recent election and registration data were provided by the Office of the Secretary of State of Texas.

stimuli, but in general the more political information and stimulation people are exposed to, the more likely they are to be politically active.

Applying these general considerations to Texas politics provides some insight into the markedly low participation in the state. Environmentally, little is done to stimulate voter interest. With a single party dominating the political scene for most of the twentieth century, competition over political issues has been muted. Often major public offices are filled without the voters being offered a viable alternative, as in the gubernatorial elections of 1958, 1960, and 1966. Nor is there evidence to suggest that the state's newspapers and radio and television stations do much to encourage political activity. Perhaps most important, however, is the absence of a tradition of widespread political participation. When parents have been inattentive to politics, the likelihood of their children becoming politically apathetic adults is heightened. The patterns of the past are thus extended into the future.

The consequences of a tradition of noninvolvement are most severe among the blacks and Mexican-Americans. For generations they were legally or informally discouraged from political action. Breaking down their long-standing nonparticipation is a painfully slow process, as the political leaders of these groups can attest. Consider the situation of the Mexican-American minority, among whom voting is lowest. Many members of this group came into the state in the last century and found an unfamiliar political culture transacted in a language they did not understand. They were usually exposed to schools of poor quality and had to face a hostile, dominant Anglo establishment. Their cultural background, with its stress on personal action and family ties, hindered political activism and the development of political leaders capable of representing their interests. Their political inactivity—like that of blacks—is ending, but the full transformation requires extensive social and psychological changes as well as the elimination of legal barriers.

THE ELECTORAL SYSTEM

Citizens lack means to directly control public policy in a democratic system, but it is expected that they be given the opportunity to select key policymakers and to set general limits within which these policymakers operate. As we have seen, many adults do not qualify or, even if qualified, do not participate in the process. That aside, the practical implementation of this elective principle can be accomplished in many ways. A cursory survey of the 50 states would reveal that no two have devised electoral systems exactly alike, and a number have very little in common with each other. A basic difference centers on the degree of popular involvement in the selection of state and local officials. In some states only the governor and state legislators, among state officials, are chosen by public balloting. In others nearly all state leaders, including judges and key administrators, must stand for election. Texas—true to the spirit of Jacksonian Democracy, with its stress on popular control—falls in the latter camp.

Changes in the Texas Constitution require majority approval by the state's voters, and voter approval is needed for a number of county and local policies (especially those involving new financial commitments). But more important are the rules and practices that allow qualified citizens to choose public officials. Three types of elections figure in this process: primary, general, and special.

PRIMARY ELECTIONS

State statutes specify that most state and county public officials shall be chosen in a general election held every two or four years. But to be placed on the general-election ballot under the name of one of the major parties, a candidate must first qualify in a party primary. Texas political parties are discussed in Chapter 3, but since their primaries are an inseparable part of the election system and are extensively regulated by state law, this aspect of partisan politics is discussed here.

The importance of primary elections cannot be overemphasized. These preliminary contests narrow the choices presented to the electorate from a potential of thousands to a very few. The importance of party nominations is reflected in the fact that Texas and most other states require that such decisions be made in public elections. Of course, the longtime Democratic party dominance of Texas politics makes the primaries even more significant. In fact, until very recently, most of the state's significant electoral activity was confined to that party's primary.

State law requires that the major parties hold their primaries on the first Saturday in May of even-numbered years. If no candidate for an office receives a majority, the two contenders who polled the greatest number of votes are matched in a runoff election held the first Saturday in June. Texas voters are not required to identify themselves as members of a party when they register and thus are free to vote in any party's May primary, but not in more than one. Voters are also prohibited from balloting in one party's May primary and switching over to another's June runoff.

To secure a position on the primary ballot, a candidate for state office must declare his intention of running by filing an application with the state party chairman or, if a district or county office is sought, with the party's county chairman or chairmen. Application must be made 90 days prior to the May primary. Until 1972 the parties bore the costs of holding their primaries, and substantial filing fees were collected from candidates to cover election expenses. This system was ruled invalid by the courts in 1972, and the 1973 legislature passed a new law providing two means of getting on the ballot: (1) A candidate can still qualify by paying a filing fee that ranges from $1000 for statewide office to $100 for certain local positions. (2) One can qualify by presenting a petition signed by a specified number of voters eligible to vote for the office the candidate is seeking. Statewide offices require 5000 signatures; lower offices require from 25 to 500 signatures, depending on the number of votes the party's candidate for governor received in the last general election in the district where the candidate is running.

Since filing fees are no longer sufficient to underwrite primary-election costs, the state has had to assume most of this obligation. A special fund has been established by the legislature, and the secretary of state oversees payments from it to cover the expenses incurred in holding the primaries.

In 1975 the Texas legislature provided that, for the first time, voters in the May 1976 party primaries would elect delegates to the national party conventions that would nominate the major presidential candidates. This presidential primary bill was drafted by backers of U.S. Senator Lloyd Bentsen, a prospective candidate for the Democratic nomination. The "Bentsen bill" required candidates to go through a difficult petition process in order to get delegates on the ballot, in the belief that this would work to the advantage of the Texas Senator. The bill did not secure its intent, however, as Jimmy Carter qualified delegates for the ballot and swept the May Democratic primary, while Ronald Reagan was routing President Gerald Ford on the Republican side.

The presidential primaries did have important consequences for the electoral system. The spirited GOP contest, for example, drew nearly 500,000 voters into the Republican primary or about three times more than had voted in that party's May election before 1976. Many of these new Republican voters were urban middle-class conservatives who normally voted in the Democratic primary. Their absence left the Democratic primary with an electorate composed largely of rural Texans, blue-collar and older whites, blacks, and Mexican-Americans. Whether 1976 portends a lasting trend cannot be determined because the Bentsen bill applied only to 1976, and the 1977 legislature adjourned without reaching agreement on a new law. Consequently, it will be May of 1979 before Texans know what procedures will govern the selection of delegates in the 1980 presidential conventions.

GENERAL ELECTIONS

General elections are held on the first Tuesday after the first Monday in November of even-numbered years. Members of the Texas House of Representatives and the U.S. House must run every two years. The governor, state senators, and elected county officials run every four years, whereas U.S. senators serve six-year terms. Additionally, Texas voters ballot for presidential electors every other general election. In all cases the candidate who receives the most votes for an office wins; there is no runoff provision, as in the party primaries.

Places on the general-election ballot are quite restricted. Most serious candidates qualify via the Democratic or Republican primaries. Minor party candidates may qualify for the general election ballot via a primary or a convention procedure, depending upon the percentage of the vote their last gubernatorial candidate received. A number of candidates get on the ballot in this fashion, but save for a few Raza Unida party candidates in South Texas, minor party nominees have had no electoral success.

Independent candidates can get on the ballot via a petition process. For state office, a candidate must collect signatures equal to at least 1 percent of the total vote cast for governor in the last general election. Lower-level positions require a varying percentage of the gubernatorial vote with the proviso that no more than 500 names are needed. The petition route has proven a difficult road to the general-election ballot. From 25,000 to 40,000 signatures are needed for a state office, but the important thing is that signees must be registered voters who did not participate in a party primary that year. A candidate defeated in a party primary cannot avail himself of the petition alternative to get in the November election. The last resort for an aspiring office seeker who has failed to qualify by party or petition is a write-in campaign. Texas law permits voters, in a general election, the option of writing in their personal choice if they are unhappy with the candidates on the ballot. But like the petition process, this has been of negligible importance in modern times. In 1977 the legislature tightened the write-in process by requiring such candidates to register with election officials prior to polling day for any votes they receive to be counted.

In sum, those with a good chance of victory are almost always the survivors of the major party primaries.

Texas utilizes the *party-column ballot* and permits *straight-ticket voting*. Candidates for various offices—from the presidency to county constable—are arranged in columns by party affiliation opposite the offices they are seeking. Traditionally, the Democratic party was assigned the first (left-hand) column, but in recent years the party polling the largest vote for governor gets this premier position in the general election. Of course, since Democrats won the governorship for a century prior to 1978, this rule was without effect until the upset victory of Republican Bill Clements. Other parties are given columns to the right of the first in order of their respective standing in the last gubernatorial race. If independent candidates qualify, they are placed to the right of the party nominees; their order is determined by lot. Voters are given the option of voting for all the candidates of a party by marking a single box on paper ballots or by pulling a big lever placed at the top of the voting-machine lists. This option generally works to the advantage of the Democratic nominees since they carry the colors of the party tradition-ally favored by Texas voters.

SPECIAL ELECTIONS

In addition to the biennial party primaries and general elections, special elections are occasionally required. The Texas legislature may schedule a vote on proposed constitutional amendments in a special election, and the governor is required to call special elections to fill vacancies in federal and state legislative offices and elective county posts. No party nomination is needed for a ballot position in a vacancy election. Anyone satisfying the office's legal qualifications can get on the ballot by making application 30 days in advance of the election and paying a filing fee, which varies from $10 for a local office to $1000 for a state office. This ease of access has often resulted in a proliferation of candidates. For example, voters could pick from among 71 entries in the 1961 special election to fill the U.S. Senate seat vacated by Lyndon Johnson. The victor in a special election must secure a majority. Failing this in a first balloting necessitates a runoff between the two top vote getters. The statute requiring a majority for election was enacted by the conservative Democratic faction, which feared that, given a large field, it would be easier for a liberal Democrat or Republican to lead on the first ballot than in a runoff. More recently, the Democratic-controlled legislature amended the special election law so that a candidate could list his or her party affiliation, if any, on the ballot. This would, it was supposed, help Democrats best Republicans in these contests.

ELECTION ADMINISTRATION

State law regulates the electoral process in Texas, but actual administration of elections is largely the responsibility of county officials and local party leaders. A good deal of variation has resulted from this local control. Voting, for example, is on paper ballots in most rural areas, by machine in many cities, and on electronically tabulated punch cards in a few places.

The basic electoral unit in Texas, as in most states, is the precinct. These units are geographic districts drawn by the county commissioners courts, which may legally contain from 100 to 3000 voters—although deviations can be found at both extremes. A single polling place is required in each precinct and all qualified residents, save those casting absentee ballots, must vote in the precinct where they live.

In party primaries the party's county executive committee appoints a presiding judge in each precinct, who then selects several clerks to assist him in running the primary election. The precinct committeeman, who has been elected by the precinct voters in the last party primary, is usually appointed to serve as election judge.

Texas counties assume the costs of general and special elections, and the county commissioners court appoints the election-precinct judge in these cases. Traditionally, the Democrat-controlled courts have chosen the Democratic primary-election judge to run the general election. The Texas Election Code does, however, require appointment of at least one election clerk from each of the major parties. Further provision is made for parties and candidates to place poll watchers in such precincts as they desire. Perhaps because of these specifications, most observers feel that Texas elections have been administered honestly in recent years. An exception to this might be in southern Texas, where Republicans charged—in the 1968 presidential election, as in 1960—they were "counted out" by the Democrat-oriented political machines that survive there. In this regard it is interesting to note that after the Republicans gained control of the White House in 1969, the U.S. Justice Department brought suit against a number of southern Texas officials alleging vote fraud.

Apart from the mechanics of running the actual balloting, a number of officials are involved in the electoral process. The county tax assessor acts as registrar of voters. He must, by March 1 of each year, prepare a list of registered voters and provide this list to election judges. The county clerk is responsible for preparing the ballot and conducting absentee voting in general and special elections. A county election board, which includes the county judge, clerk, and sheriff, plus the major party chairmen, handles the technical problems of securing voting places and distributing necessary supplies.

In case of mechanical failure or if a demand for a recount arises, ballot boxes and voting machines are sealed and stored after the election judge determines and reports the vote count in his precinct. The county judge appoints a referee to supervise any recount, and representatives of the involved candidates may observe the process of reopening and tabulating the ballots or machine totals. Although state law guarantees a recount upon request to a candidate who came within 5 percent of winning an election or making the runoff, such requests are rarely made. Recounts have seldom changed election outcomes and, if recounting does not reverse the results, the seeker of the count must pay a small fee for each precinct involved.

While local party and governmental officials remain responsible for conducting elections, the 1967 legislature did provide for the secretary of state to become the chief election officer of the state. His original role was limited to issuing detailed written instructions and directives concerning election laws, registration of electors, and voting. However, in recent years the importance of the position has increased, probably because court decisions have forced the state to take a more active role in administering elections. For example, the 1973 law providing for state financing of primary elections gave the secretary of state an important supervisory role in overseeing this process.

MONEY AND THE ELECTORAL PROCESS

Mention has been made of the fees candidates must pay to get on the ballot in primary and special elections. Of far greater importance for candidates than that cost is the skyrocketing cost of campaigning for office. James C. Wright, veteran Fort Worth congressman and unsuccessful U.S. Senate candidate, outlined some of the problems in Texas in the 1960s, when costs were much lower:

> Why does the pursuit of public office cost so much? Let me itemize out of my own experience in Texas, which is by no means unique. Just one first-class letter to every family in Texas requires—in production and postage—approximately $300,000. A single billboard in one of our big cities rents for $550 a month. Others can be had for only $75 or $100 a month. But multiply this by the thousands it takes to cover a large state. A 30 minute TV broadcast which I did on eighteen of the fifty television stations in Texas cost me a little over $10,000. The same amount of time, on the same stations, if taken in 20 second spots, would have cost $400,000.[13]

Present-day office seekers in Texas have found there is usually no cheap way to win elections. With the electorate growing yearly and with weak party organization being the rule, most candidates have tremendous problems in reaching the voters. Personal "stumping"' is ineffective, save at the local level, because it touches so few voters. A candidate working 10 hours a day, seven days a week, would need about 40 years to talk one minute with each adult Texan. And campaigns usually last only two or three months. The problem is not limited to statewide races. Candidates in the major Texas cities often compete in districts that contain hundreds of thousands of voters.

Of necessity, candidates must advertise themselves in the electronic media and on billboards if they are to reach most voters. And they must take care to present an image tailored to the constituency they are appealing to for votes. Such candidate advertisement is expensive, as is the public relations advice needed to manage the office seeker's image. Most political observers place the *minimum* cost of an effective statewide campaign at $1 million. John Tower reported spending more than $2.6 million in his successful race for reelection to the U.S. Senate in 1972. Hotly contested local races can easily cost a candidate $100,000 or more. The winning candidate in the 1977 mayor's contest in Houston spent about $900,000 in quest of an office with a two-year term. The costs of running are rising rapidly. Postage rates, production costs, staff salaries, media time—all important elements in a modern campaign—are getting more and more expensive year by year. And as some candidates turn to expensive, professionally directed campaigns, others are forced to counterspend, setting off an escalating cycle.

The influence of money on elections is documented in a recent study of Texas candidates by Chandler Davidson, David Fleischer, and Becky Mathre.[14] They examined 34 contested races for statewide office in 1972 and 1974 and found that of the 115 candidates in these

Who is the man with the shovel?

contests, in 26 of 34 cases the one who reported spending the most money won.

The upshot of the tremendous cost of winning elections is that one must either be personally wealthy or command support from resourceful backers. Once in office, an incumbent has a considerable advantage since he gets free media exposure and publicity not available to challengers. The increasing difficulty that men of modest means face in running for office and the increasing advantage enjoyed by those who possess wealth and are willing to invest it in campaigns has produced cries for reform. In the wake of the Watergate scandals, the movement for fundamental electoral reform has gained considerable support around the country. Congress passed legislation limiting the size of contributions to federal office seekers and the amounts that could be expended in federal elections and providing for an income-tax checkoff system to fund presidential campaigns. The Texas legislature followed suit by enacting the Political Funds Reporting and Disclosure Act of 1975. This law tightened existing disclosure requirements to make it much more difficult to hide political contributions. Stiff penalties were provided for violators. Additionally, ceilings were established on the amounts of money that could be spent in given elections. In statewide contests, for example, only 10¢ could be expended for every voting-age adult in the state in primaries and general elections (about $850,000 at this time). In runoff elections, only 4¢ per adult could be expended. The constitutionality of such limits was challenged in the courts, and these ceilings were struck down by the U.S. Supreme Court in the *Buckley* v. *Valeo* decision.

The *Buckley* decision means that the impact of money on elections in Texas is controlled only in the sense that contributions and expenditures must be reported. Individuals, privately owned businesses or partnerships, and corporate political action funds may give any amount they wish (except in federal elections where a limit of $1000 per person and $5000 for committees prevails), and candidates are free to spend as much as they can raise or borrow. The practical effect is that election expenditures are skyrocketing. Over $800,000 was spent by two candidates seeking a congressional seat from the Houston area in 1976. Gov. Dolph Briscoe spent $3.5 million in his unsuccessful bid to be renominated in the 1978 Democratic primary. Meantime in the May 1978 Republican primary, wealthy businessman Bill Clements spent $2.2 million in an election where only 150,000 persons voted. Clements spent another $5 million (mostly borrowed from himself) to defeat Democrat John Hill in the general election contest for governor.

CONCLUSIONS

A better perspective is gained on the nature of Texas politics if one keeps in mind that no existing "democratic system" lives up to the theoretical expectations often held about democracy. As the authors of an early study of American voting behavior conclude:

> The open minded voters who made a sincere attempt to weight the issues and candidates dispassionately for the good of the country as a whole— exist mainly in deferential campaign propaganda, in textbooks on civics, in the movies, and in the minds of some political idealists. In real life, they are few indeed.[15]

In terms of political interest and motivation, knowledge of the issues, adherence to principle, and rational judgment in making political decisions, individual voters generally fail to satisfy requirements for a democratic system of government as outlined by political theorists.

Texas politics, considered in this general context, does not represent some unique island surrounded by a democratic sea. The deviations from democracy found in the Lone Star State are rather typical of those in other states and the nation, only more severe than is usually the case. The low rates of political participation can be attributed to several factors: a registration process that for years discouraged citizens from qualifying for the ballot; an electoral system that places a heavy burden on candidates for public office; the absence of meaningful competition and alternatives in many instances; and a political tradition of nonparticipation among the poor, blacks, and Mexican-Americans. The financial problems Texas office seekers face are little different from those confronting candidates in other states. These factors and the resulting lack of political involvement are changing, but slowly.

In the meantime, Texas politics has been basically an Anglo affair, often slanted in the direction of status-quo elements. White middle-class Texans have possessed a disproportionate share of the politically relevant resources (income, leisure time, educational skills, political motivation), and the state's political system has, as it must, responded to this reality. Most political leaders are drawn from and supported by this active strata of the population, and their decisions as to who shall benefit by government and who shall pay for government inevitably reflect this. Reducing this to terms of liberalism versus conservatism (which is, one should be cautioned, only one of many legitimate ways of viewing politics), the selective participation patterns characteristic of the state have shifted the mainstream of Texas politics to the right of center somewhat more than one might expect given the socioeconomic diversity of the population.

NOTES

[1]Gabriel Almond and Sidney Verba, *The Civic Culture* (Boston: Little, Brown, 1965), p. 2.

[2]For a discussion of the discrepancies between abstract support for "democracy" and support for the practical application of democratic principles, see James W. Prothro and Charles M. Grigg, "Fundamental Principles of Democracy: Bases of Agreement and Disagreement," *Journal of Politics* 22 (Spring 1960): 276–294, and Herbert McClosky, "Consensus and Ideology in American Politics," *American Political Science Review* 58 (June 1964): 361–379.

[3]U.S. Bureau of the Census, *Characteristics of the Population: Texas, PC(1) 45 Tex* (Washington, D.C.: GPO, 1970), p. 435. Because there are very few persons of Spanish language or surname in Texas who are not of Mexican-American ancestry, we can reasonably infer that the characteristics of the Spanish language or surname group apply to the state's Mexican-American minority.

[4]Census Bureau, *Number of Inhabitants: Texas,* op. cit., p. 5.

[5]V. O. Key, Jr., *Southern Politics* (New York: Knopf, 1949), p. 254.

[6]Ibid., pp. 254–261.

[7]U.S. Bureau of the Census, *Detailed Characteristics: Texas, PC(1) D45 Tex* (Washington, D.C.: GPO, 1970), pp. 1363–1364.

[8]See *The Houston Chronicle,* May 11, 1977, pp. 1–19.

[9]Census Bureau, *Detailed Characteristics: Texas,* op. cit., pp. 2290–2293.

[10]Ibid., pp. 1740–1744.

[11]The best known treatment of this subject is Kirkpatrick Sale's *Power Shift: The Rise of the Southern Rim and Its Challenge to the Eastern Establishment* (New York: Random House, 1975).

[12]Lester Milbrath, *Political Participation* (Chicago: Rand McNally, 1965), pp. 39–141; and Bernard Berelson, Paul F. Lazarsfeld, and William N. McPhee, *Voting: A Study of Opinion Formation in a Presidential Campaign* (Chicago: University of Chicago Press, 1964), pp. 277–304.

[13]*Harper's,* April 1967, p. 89.

[14]Chandler Davidson, David Fleischer, and Becky Mathre, "The Influence of Money on Elections: The Texas Case," unpublished paper delivered at Southwestern Sociological Association meeting, Dallas, Texas, 1977.

[15]Paul Lazarsfeld, Bernard Berelson, and Hazel Gaudet, *The People's Choice* (New York: Duell, Sloan & Pierce, 1944), p. 100.

Political Parties
in Texas

Direct citizen control of government is impossible in large societies. Millions of individual citizens cannot inform themselves on the countless matters requiring public action, or assemble to debate and decide policy, or take time to see that public policies are executed. Even if it were technically feasible for citizens to do these things, they usually display little desire to assume such burdens. Public power and authority must therefore be delegated to legislators, executives, judges, administrators, and, occasionally, unofficial leaders. In an effort to relate the great number of individual citizens to the few decision makers, intermediate structures have developed in democratic societies. Most important among these are political parties and interest groups.

Political parties perform three general sets of activities.[1] They select candidates who compete for public office; they propagandize on behalf of a party program or set of beliefs; and they attempt to guide the elected officeholders of government. In doing these things, parties produce a number of unplanned consequences. They acquaint members of the electorate with political values and information. They offer uninformed or underinformed citizens a simplified map of the political world, help them form political judgments, and make it easier for them to be active politically. Competition between parties recruits political leaders and offers voters periodic choices between alternatives. Of course, as we shall see in the case of Texas, the extent to which any particular party or party system performs these activities or produces such consequences can vary greatly.

THE TEXAS PARTY SYSTEM

Save for the few days every four years when a national convention is in session, the major political parties in the United States can be viewed as loose coalitions of variously organized, virtually autonomous, state parties. The Texas Democratic and Republican parties are not, then, mere branches of encompassing national parties; rather, they exist as state entities that make occasional contributions to national party affairs.

Considerable differences exist in interparty competition from state to state, and Texas is usually rated as one of the least competitive states. For example, a recent study placed the Lone Star State forty-fifth in competition between parties.[2] But such was not always the case. Two-party politics held sway in the state until late in the nineteenth century, when bitterness over Republican-sponsored Reconstruction and the black's place in politics and society wrecked the Texas Republican party. The result was a half century, 1900–1950, in which the Democratic party was seldom challenged and almost never defeated in electoral contests.

This Democratic dominance had great significance for Texas politics. Most importantly, *one-party* politics tended to dissolve into *no-party* politics.[3] When most voters and all the candidates consider themselves Democrats, the party label ceases to be of much significance. Instead of fights between clearly defined parties for electoral support, a far more chaotic factional politics took told in the state. Cleavages among voters formed and reformed from campaign to campaign, depending on the issues and personalities involved. Flamboyant political personalities like Miriam "Ma" and James E. "Pa" Ferguson and W. Lee "Pappy, Pass the Biscuits" O'Daniel often became issues in themselves. At the same time issues of deep meaning to the people of Texas, such as the level of public services to be undertaken and the distribution of costs for these services, were seldom the basis for contesting elections. A politics of the status quo predominated. Elected officials, lacking the support of a meaningful party, were loath to raise basic and controversial issues. The absence of party support left them particularly vulnerable to pressures from such established economic interests as the state's oil, gas, and insurance industries.

Without political parties to channel and simplify political action, the unplanned consequences of party activity mentioned earlier were not produced in Texas. Individual voters, denied a choice between a "Democratic" and "Republican" position, were left to their own devices and judgments in making political decisions. Nor could aspiring political leaders be recruited by or seek the support of established political organizations. In such a situation politics becomes a game of every person for him or herself—a game well-suited for those who begin play with ample economic resources and political influence and skills.

This era of fragmented, personalistic politics began to decline in the late 1930s, when the economic issues raised by the New Deal filtered into Texas politics. A realignment along economic lines had progressed sufficiently by 1948 for V. O. Key, Jr., to note that "the terms 'liberal' and 'conservative' have real meaning in the Democratic politics of Texas."[4] However, the Democratic party of recent years has proven increasingly unable to contain within itself this liberal-conservative split. Consequently, a spillover of conservatives has contributed to an emerging Republican resurgence in partisan politics.

The degree of competition presently provided by the Texas Republican party depends on what level of office is considered. In general the higher the office, the more vigorous the partisan contest. In the five presidential elections since 1960, for example, the Republicans have averaged 50.2 percent of the two-party vote. The GOP share of the two-party vote in the eight U.S. Senate elections held between 1960 and 1978 was a very respectable 48.0 percent. But in gubernatorial contests since 1960, the average Republican vote share was only 35.5 percent. The minority party often fails to contest the Democratic nominees for many positions. In 1972, for example, no Republicans ran for either lieutenant governor or attorney general, the second and third most powerful elective positions in state government. Challengers were fielded in 19 of 24 U.S. House of Representatives races in 1976, in 8 of 16 state Senate contests, and in 54 of 150 state House districts. Outside metropolitan counties, very few Republicans sought local offices.

The weakness of the Texas Republican party as one moves down the ballot is obvious when one looks at the votes received by GOP candidates at various levels in the 1976 election (see Figure 3.1). President Ford got almost 2 million votes, but the Republican vote for lesser offices drops steadily to the point where only a few more than 0.75 million votes were received by GOP state representative nominees. Aside from the top two or three positions on the ballot, the center of political action in Texas is still the Democratic party.

An argument could be made that the factions within the still dominant Democratic party resemble and, to some extent, substitute for the competing parties of a two-party system. Evidence points to the contrary, however. Many voters do not apply labels like "liberal" or "conservative" to themselves and have trouble relating such terms to politicians and public issues. The sources of voter confusion are not hard to fathom. Democratic candidates in Texas often decline open

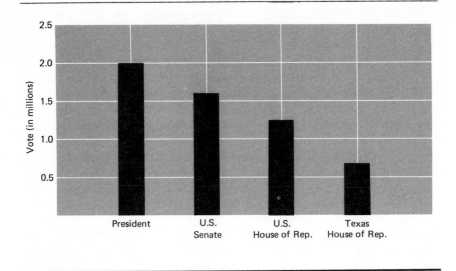

Figure 3.1 • Total vote for Republican candidates for selected Texas offices: 1976.

alignment with either faction, preferring to run as "moderates" or "middle-of-the-roaders." In the 1972 gubernatorial primary, both Frances ("Sissy") Farenthold and Dolph Briscoe stressed their credentials as "reform" candidates rather than stress their liberal (Farenthold) or conservative (Briscoe) leanings.

The conclusion one is driven to is that Texas is still quite a way from having a competitive party system and all that this entails. In presidential and U.S. Senate races, the Republican party candidates run strongly and often successfully; despite Clements' gubernatorial victory in 1978, the GOP lags far behind in most state and local contests. The loosely defined conservative and liberal Democratic factions offer only a pale shadow of partisan competitiveness. Of course, party politics is changing in Texas, and that change may be moving the state toward a competitive party system. The possibilities for such an eventuality are discussed later in this chapter.

PARTY ORGANIZATION IN TEXAS

THE LEGAL STRUCTURE

The organizational form of Texas political parties is prescribed by law. Each party has a *permanent organization* that is legally responsible for managing the partisan process, and provision is made for *temporary organizations* to permit expression of membership views and fill certain party positions.

Figure 3.2 diagrams the relationship of the individual voter to the party apparatus. In Texas individuals do not register as members of a political party; they indicate their partisan affiliation by participating in the primary or convention of the party of their choice. State law requires that political parties whose last gubernatorial candidate received 20 percent of the vote in the general election must nominate their candidates in primary elections. In practical terms this means that Democrats and Republicans have to nominate by primaries and excludes other parties from this requirement.

After voters have balloted in their party's primary (held biennially on the first Saturday in May), they are eligible to attend their party's *precinct convention,* which is held on primary-election day. If their party does not hold a primary election, registered voters who do not vote in any other party primary are eligible to attend their party's precinct convention on election day. The precinct convention offers the individual party member an opportunity for direct expression of his or her views. These meetings entertain, debate, and pass on various questions. More importantly, they select delegates to the next level of temporary organization, which meets a week after the precinct convention. In heavily populated counties containing more than one state

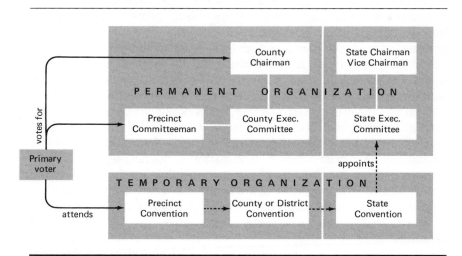

Figure 3.2 • Official party organization in Texas.

senatorial district (Harris, Dallas, Bexar, and Tarrant), delegates convene in a *district convention*. In the other counties they assemble at *county conventions*. Each precinct is allocated a certain number of delegates based on the precinct's vote for the party's gubernatorial nominee in the last general election (the usual quota is one delegate for each 25 votes).

The district and county conventions may consider resolutions if they choose, but their major task is to select delegates to the *state convention* held in September after the primaries. State delegates are also apportioned on the basis of each area's gubernatorial vote—the usual rate is one delegate per 300 votes. The September gathering certifies the party's nominees for the upcoming general election, produces a party platform, and chooses members of the state executive committee. In presidential election years prior to 1976, the state delegates also assembled in June to designate members for the national party committees and choose delegates to the national conventions. The presidential primary law passed in 1975 required that at least three-fourths of the Democratic and Republican national delegates be directly elected in the May 1976 primaries with the remainder being chosen by the June conventions. This had the effect, of course, of reducing greatly the importance of the convention process in 1976. However, as mentioned earlier, the primary law applied only to 1976, and the manner of delegate selection to future national conventions has not been determined.

Like the temporary organs, the permanent organization of the parties breaks down into three levels. First, there is the *precinct committeeman,* elected by the primary voters in each precinct or appointed by the precinct convention if no primary is held. The committeeman (or precinct chairman as he is sometimes called) occupies a pivotal position in the party, for it is at the precinct level that the party apparatus directly interacts with the individual voter. Besides running the primary election, the committeeman is expected to stimulate and coordinate party activities in his area. All precinct committeemen are automatically members of the *county executive committee*. This committee is responsible for arranging the county primary election and the county convention. Much of the actual work is performed by the chairman of the county executive committee, who is either elected in the party primary, if such an election is held, or appointed by the county executive committee. The *state executive committee* heads up the party. This committee consists of 64 members: a chairman and vice chairman and a man and woman from each of the 31 senatorial districts. The principal duties of the state committee include certifying statewide candidates for the primaries and setting up the state conventions.

PATTERNS OF ORGANIZATIONAL ACTIVITY

There are three reasons why one cannot assume that the legal structure mirrors the actual manner in which party politics is organized. First, the parties have often been unable to fill many of the legally defined posts. In recent years the Republicans have had precinct committeemen in only about half the precincts in the state. Minor parties usually staff only a tiny fraction of the party positions created by law. Only the dominant Democratic party approaches filling all the party slots, but even here vacancies are common.

Second, much of the actual political work is done outside the official party structure. This is especially true in the fragmented Democratic party. Unofficial party groups representing various factional positions raise money, recruit and endorse candidates, organize house-to-house canvassing, pass out slate cards, and provide transportation to the polls. The reason for their existence is simple. The legal organization cannot endorse candidates in primary elections, but oftentimes the Democratic primary is *the* crucial election. Those interested in influencing the outcome of the primary must work outside of, or around, the legal party structure.

Even in the Republican party, a great deal of partisan and electoral activity is channeled through extralegal organizations. Candidates often build their own organizations and avoid close identification with the regular party organs. In the 1972 general election Hank Grover, the GOP gubernatorial nominee, was forced to do this when John Tower, the party's nominee for reelection to the U.S. Senate, refused to tie his campaign to Grover's in any form or fashion. Dolph Briscoe, out of choice, carefully distinguished his successful campaign from that of the 1972 Democratic presidential nominee, George McGovern.

A third factor that has diminished the importance of the official party apparatus, especially at upper levels, is that party officials have typically been dominated by elected public officials in the state. The governor, for example, has usually been able to control the state Democratic conventions and delegations to the national conventions. Elected Republicans like U.S. Sen. John Tower and State Rep. Fred Agnich have exercised considerable control over the Texas GOP apparatus.

There is evidence, however, that this traditional dominance of the party organizations by elected officials is eroding. The adoption of reform rules by the national Democratic party in the early 1970s weakened the control of that party's elected officials over the national delegate selection process. The requirement that backers of any candidate able to muster 15 percent support from those attending the party meetings must be given a proportionate share of delegates resulted in a 1972 national Democratic delegation that was split about evenly between supporters of George McGovern, George Wallace, and uncommitted independents. Gubernatorial nominee Briscoe was an ineffectual leader of that delegation in Miami Beach. Briscoe got along better with the Carter-dominated delegation to New York in 1976, but he had no control over the makeup of the group. On the Republican side in 1976, Senator Tower committed early to President Ford and was selected to be a floor leader for Ford at the convention in Kansas City. That selection became meaningless, however, when the Senator and 95 other Ford delegates were beaten by backers of Ronald Reagan in the May primary. Reagan supporters, despite the opposition of Tower, assumed control of the state party structure in 1977.

These triumphs of outsider forces against elected officials do not mean that the latter have lost all their considerable influence over party affairs. But, such officials will have to bargain and compromise more than was their custom in the past.

Despite the limited relevance of the formal party structure, it has often served as a battleground. Factional elements have sought to strengthen their intraparty position by acquiring control of official party posts. Such local party leaders as precinct committeemen and county chairmen are not mere figureheads, but often wield real power and influence. A second thing is at stake here. The conventions offer an opportunity for symbolic victories in that they provide for the expression of "party" views on various issues and questions. Many of the bitter fights at Democratic precinct, county, and senatorial conventions in 1972 can be understood in this light. These gatherings offered proponents and opponents of legalized abortion and marijuana, war or peace in Southeast Asia, and numerous other issues an opportunity to press their views in a public forum. In 1976 thousands of conservatives turned out at Republican meetings to pass resolutions opposing the Equal Rights Amendment, "giving away" the Panama Canal, and legalized abortion.

Finally, the convention process has offered the individual voter a means of influencing the outcome of the most important decision made by American political parties: the nomination of candidates for the presidency of the United States. The influence of Texans has been crucial on occasion, as in 1952 and 1972. In 1952 thousands of Eisenhower supporters descended on Republican precinct conventions around the state; swept aside the Taft forces, which had the backing of the Texas GOP establishment; and sent an Eisenhower delegation to the Republican National Convention in Chicago. That Texas delegation played a pivotal role in the general's capture of the Republican presidential nomination. The turnout of McGovern supporters in 1972 gave the South Dakota senator a large bloc of delegates from a state noted for sending solid establishment delegations to the Democratic national convention. McGovern's Texas support was crucial in the early convention fights over delegate seatings, where he insured his eventual nomination.

THE IMPACT OF PARTY ORGANIZATION

The organizational dimension of political parties accounts for much sound and fury, but of what significance is it? The organizational structure provides a stage on which individuals can act out their political feelings, but what matters the play itself?

Realistically, one must conclude that party organization is not very important in Texas politics. Organizations, if they are to succeed, require the investment of money, energy, and skills. But to attract such investments, organizations must offer something in return. Therein lies the weakness of party organization in Texas. According to a common conceptualization, partisan organizations can recruit resources by offering three kinds of incentives to individuals—material, solidaristic, and purposive. Material incentives refer to tangible goods and services such as money, property, jobs, and so on. Solidaristic incentives include the enjoyment of social interaction, of being "where the action is," or of associating with important people. Purposive incentives come into play when an organization is viewed as a means of achieving some desired goal, such as repealing the income tax, legalizing abortion, or electing honest men to office.

Most of the strong party organizations in the United States, including the fabled big-city machines, were built primarily on material incentives such as patronage jobs, contract preferments, and direct aid to the needy. And most of the strong party organizations that have survived (such as the Daley organization in Chicago or the Democratic and Republican parties in Indiana) retain control of jobs and favors they can dispense to the faithful and deny the infidels. But in Texas, precious few jobs and contracts can be used freely for organizational purposes. There is a little federal patronage available when a party controls the White House, and public officials have some discretion in awarding things like architectural contracts for public projects, but, in general, the parties' cupboards are bare. About the only widespread source of patronage available is provided by the tradition of appointing precinct committeemen as public election judges for their precincts. Of course, the Democratic-controlled county commissioners courts usually reserve these positions for members of their own party. Even here the amount of money involved is miniscule. Election judges work from 7:00 A.M. to late at night for about $50. They can appoint a few clerks to assist in operating the polls, but they receive less than $40 for a long day's work. Such pay, offered two or three days a year, is not likely to attract many party laborers.

In many other states, the cities nurture party organizations, but cities in Texas usually elect their leadership via nonpartisan ballots and place most of the municipal jobs under civil service. Few rewards are available for distribution under this setup, and urban party organization has been weak. More material incentives exist in rural areas, where "courthouse" jobs and favors can be dispensed more freely and with greater impact. It should come as no surprise that the most notable instances of machine politics in the state occur in rural southern Texas. Courthouse-based establishments in counties like Duval and Starr use material incentives to control the votes of the impoverished, unacculturated Mexican-American residents and thus dominate local politics in these areas.

This relative absence of material incentives means that party activists in Texas are recruited into party work primarily by solidaristic or purposive incentives. That is, they work because they enjoy the social life associated with political activity or because they see party work as a means of realizing goals or values they prize. A study of 216 Democratic and Republican committeemen in Houston found that only nine were interested in partisan activity because of material rewards. The remainder were attracted for social or goal-oriented reasons.[5] Such motives are usually acclaimed in civics texts and materialistic ones are condemned, but organizations that must rely almost exclusively on such incentives are seriously hampered. Two problems arise: turnover and ideological rigidity.

People who donate their labor and treasure to parties because they derive social gratification from the excitement of a campaign or working for a particular candidate tend to tire of the sport relatively quickly. The campaign and its attendant social life ends, the candidate is defeated and fades from view or is elected and goes on to Austin or Washington. For most of those who work in party organizations, the press of personal, nonpolitical matters eventually reasserts priority in their lives. Thousands of Texans were caught up in the presidential efforts for Barry Goldwater in 1964, Eugene McCarthy in 1968, George McGovern in 1972, or Ronald Reagan in 1976. But few continued to work for the Republican or Democratic party after the bell tolled for their favorite. Texas parties, and those elsewhere in most cases, are thus rather like balloons periodically blown up in the course of a campaign, only to be released on election night. For the months and years between campaigns, the party organization is little more than a shriveled, inert facsimile of its former self.

Ideological rigidity is often associated with those who are drawn into a party because they have a deep desire to influence public policy in some direction. They are willing, nay eager, to invest their time, energy, and part of their fortune in partisan battles. But they exact a price. The price is that they expect their party to remain true to the principles or causes they associate with it. By demanding that their party stick to the straight and narrow path of righteousness, these committed supporters often cripple its ability to make the sort of broad appeal essential to electoral success. Simply put, they would rather be right than win, a luxury that few parties which remain competitive can afford. All factions in Texas politics have their share of such individuals, but the Republicans and liberal Democrats have probably experienced the most difficulty in this respect.

Part of the responsibility for the weak status of party organization in Texas rests with the statutory provisions designed to insure democracy in the partisan process. For example, the requirement that major parties nominate candidates by primary takes away the most crucial power a party organization can command: the power to give or withhold the party label from those contending for public office. Ironically, the attempt to insure open, vigorous parties by statute has, besides weakening the party organization, not contributed much to democracy within the parties. The party primaries draw poorly in contrast to the general elections, and only about 5 percent of the electorate avail themselves of the opportunity to participate in the precinct conventions held on primary-election day.

There is, in all of this, a circularity. Parties are organizationally weak in Texas, and because they are weak, they cannot recruit the kind and quantity of resources needed to exert much influence in Texas politics. In their stead individual officeholders, candidates, and interest groups assume a more important role—a role they, of course, are not likely to vacate willingly. There is nothing inevitable about the cycle, but clearly the establishment of strong, effective, state party organizations capable of counteracting this cycle will be a most difficult task, if accomplishable at all.

THE RISE AND FALL OF FACTIONALISM WITHIN THE DEMOCRATIC PARTY

THE EMERGENCE OF PARTY FACTIONS

Ever since the Democratic hegemony was established at the turn of the century, divisions and fissures have plagued the party. Sometimes the divisions centered around issues, sometimes personalities, sometimes a combination of the two. In the last decade of the nineteenth century, Gov. James Hogg fought for progressive reforms opposed by such powerful commercial interests as the banks and railroads. The flamboyant Fergusons divided Texans from the 1910s to the 1930s, for reasons of both personality and politics. James "Pa" Ferguson, a vigorous opponent of prohibition, was impeached and removed from the governor's office in 1917. Barred by state law from public office, he ran his wife, Miriam "Ma" Ferguson, for governor five times. She won twice. Despite occasional challenges, Texas Democratic politics remained conservative in tone and responsive to established economic interests in the state throughout the first third of the twentieth century.

More permanent and pervasive divisions began to take shape in the 1930s. The severe hardships associated with the depression and the controversy surrounding President Franklin Roosevelt's New Deal policies resulted in a realignment of the national parties along economic policy lines. A somewhat similar shift occurred within the Texas Democratic party. By the late 1930s, a clear gap had opened between those who supported Roosevelt and the national party and those who opposed both. The latter group, stressing their continuity with the state's political heritage, had evolved into an identifiable conservative faction by the end of World War II. Support for the conservative faction came primarily from business, professional, and agricultural segments of the society; the rapidly growing white middle class; and most public officials in the state. Aligned opposite them were those political leaders whose first loyalty was to the national Democratic party and its leadership; the state's nascent organized-labor movement; some survivors from earlier Populist movements still dissatisfied with the power of special interests in the state; and segments of the black and Mexican-American groups just beginning to enter, or reenter as the case might be, Texas politics.

The governor's election of 1946 was fought along liberal versus conservative lines. The liberal standard-bearer, Homer Rainey, who had just been fired as president of the University of Texas, challenged conservative Beauford Jester in the Democratic primary. Rainey lost, and a pattern was established. The half dozen hotly contested gubernatorial primaries from the late 1940s to the early 1970s all featured liberal Democratic candidates taking on conservative Democratic opponents. The liberals continued to lose.

THE CONSERVATIVE FACTION

The impression should be avoided that the conservative Democratic faction was a well-oiled political machine that periodically ground up liberal and Republican challengers at the polls. The faction really was a loosely defined coalition, drawing support from a multiplicity of interests, citizens of a conservative ideological bent, and people eager to associate themselves with a winning team. There was no clearly defined power elite within the conservative Democratic group, and no single leader commanded the faction. There was an exceptional period in the mid-1960s when Gov. John Connally, a man of forceful personality and the possessor of substantial political assets, dominated Democratic conservatism in a fashion rarely seen in Texas politics. But even Connally could not perpetuate his influence beyond his gubernatorial tenure. Preston Smith, a longtime conservative rival, succeeded him as governor in 1969; Connally's protégé and heir apparent, Ben Barnes, was smitten in the 1972 Democratic primary.

The most striking thing about the conservative Democrats in Texas has been their political success. From the 1930s to the 1970s every governor elected was supported by this faction. Most U.S. congressmen were elected with conservative support, as were a majority of state legislators. Liberals achieved parity at times in one house of the legislature, but conservatives retained firm control of either the Texas Senate or House in all sessions.

Several interrelated factors have contributed to the conservatives' success at the polls. Some have been alluded to before, but a summary list at this point is useful.

Low level of political participation. As mentioned in the previous chapter, participation is considerably higher in the more conservative segments of the Texas population than in the liberal-leaning elements.

Superior access to resources. Electoral success usually requires money, the investment of certain skills, and publicity. The conservative faction was fortunate in this regard because it has enjoyed the support of those best able to supply these things—the well-to-do, major economic concerns, and the owners of major mass media organs in the state.

Absence of party competition. As long as the Democratic party dominates Texas politics, political control can be maintained by winning the party primaries. This is somewhat easier to do than winning general-election contests because voter participation is much lower in the primaries and incumbent officials or those they back have a great advantage over challengers.

Ability to define the rules of the game. Over the years conservative representatives manipulated the electoral rules to maximize their faction's advantage. Incumbent interests were protected by filing dates set far in advance of primary elections and by primaries held in May rather than late in the summer, as is the case in most states. Voters are not required to register by party so that "presidential Republicans" can vote in the Democratic primaries without difficulty. In the last few years the federal courts have reversed a number of the more blatant rule manipulations of the conservative faction. Annual registration, high filing fees, and several redistricting plans have been overturned, with a resulting increase in Republican and liberal and moderate Democratic representation.

As in all things, success breeds success. Because conservative Democrats won and controlled public offices, they could recruit the candidates and backing necessary to continue winning. Business and governmental support materialized behind conservative candidates since they were expected to win. Individuals donated their time and money, confident that even if their cause was not entirely righteous, it would at least prevail. To cite an example: Governor Briscoe's fund-raising dinner in the fall of 1973 reportedly raised $800,000. It may be assumed that many of those who paid $100 each for boxes of chicken did so not because of a taste for cold fowl or the governor's politics, but because it was simply good business to chip into the war chest of the likely leader of state government through 1978.

The self-perpetuating effect of winning is nowhere more evident than in the case of the southern Texas political machines. Most of the machine-controlled votes come from impoverished Mexican-Americans, whose political interests would seem more aligned with liberal issue positions (support for minimum-wage legislation, more social welfare benefits, etc.). Nevertheless, the machines usually aligned themselves with conservative Democrats in party primary fights. The machines needed the rewards that came from supporting winners, and thus they hunted where the ducks were without much regard for ideological considerations.

Geographically, conservative strength in the primaries was greatest in central and western Texas. Liberals usually ran best along the Gulf Coast and in eastern Texas. Since the late 1950s conservative Democrats have fared much better in rural areas and small towns than in big urban centers. Two factors largely account for the poor showing of conservative Democrats in heavily populated counties. First, Mexican-American and black voting has increased in the big cities, and conservatives have had little success in attracting support from these new voters. Second, the Republican primary draws most of its voters in the metropolitan areas, and this reduces the vote potential for conservatives in the Democratic primary. Within cities, conservatives got most of their votes from middle- and upper-income whites and received a decent share of the blue-collar vote and a very small percentage of the ethnic minority vote. Combined with their rural-small town support, this was usually enough to win.

THE LIBERAL FACTION

If conservatives represent the better-off and status quo elements within Texas, who are the liberals? The liberal faction has typically been a loosely defined collection of officeholders, party activists, and voters. Lacking a state organization and denied control of the regular party structure in the state, Texas Democratic liberalism has been as much a state of mind as anything else. And the extent of that state of mind is often in doubt.

Nonetheless, several general areas of agreement within the liberal faction can be discerned.

Support for the national party and its presidential nominees. Historically, liberals have been loyalists and have roundly condemned those Democrats who periodically supported Republican national candidates. Allan Shivers, Governor from 1949 to 1957 who supported Eisenhower in 1952 and 1956, was the favorite object of liberal derision in the 1950s and 1960s. Another former governor, John Connally, seems likely to be the new bête noire of liberals because he headed up the national "Democrats for Nixon" movement in the 1972 campaign and switched to the Republican party in 1973. Ironically, many liberals' loyalties to the national ticket were strained in 1968 and 1972 for quite different reasons. Antiwar liberals were unhappy in 1968 with Hubert Humphrey's general support for the Vietnam War and threatened to bolt the party. In 1972 the shoe was on the other foot, and many traditional liberal elements (e.g., organized labor) had trouble warming up to the "peace" candidacy of George McGovern. In retrospect it appears that most liberals, after months of fretting, ended up supporting the party nominees in both cases.

Expanding the role of state government, especially in the areas of welfare, education, health, and employment. Examples of this orientation can be found in recent legislative sessions, where liberals led efforts to eliminate the constitutional limitation on state appropriations for public welfare and to improve workmen's compensation and unemployment insurance.

Shifting the tax system so it depends less on consumer taxation and more on taxes of business profits and high incomes. The liberal position on these matters was evident in the 1969 special legislative session, where senate liberals provided most of the votes to defeat extending the sales tax to food and drugs. In addition to fighting the extension of sales taxes, legislative liberals have provided the few votes cast for corporate and personal income taxes.

Reducing the role played by "special interests." Liberals have long protested the influence of such groups as the oil, gas, and insurance industries and utilities, arguing that they are virtually exempt from effective state regulation and/or can determine public policy in areas of direct concern to themselves. The control of industrial pollution, one of the most pressing problems of modern society, often divides liberals and conservatives into opposing camps. Everyone opposes pollution in the abstract, but liberals are more willing to insist that industries bear the costs of eliminating whatever air and water contamination they cause than are conservatives, who are concerned lest an unreasonable economic burden be placed on the manufacturing sector of the state's economy.

In contrast to other southern states, racial issues in Texas have not emerged as major points of contention between the Democratic factions. Evidence of this can be seen in the fact that Texas liberal candidates sometimes run well in central-city black precincts *and* in the deep east, an area where George Wallace polled a plurality in the 1968 presidential election. This absence of factional polarization along racial lines results from several factors. The black population is relatively small, constituting an eighth of the residents, and poses little threat to the white majority in most parts of the state. Also, since the black and Mexican-American minorities are concentrated in different regions of Texas, there is no possibility of a minority coalition endangering local Anglo political control.

Probably more important is the fact that the issues that divide Texans along racial lines, such as school integration, fair housing, and equal opportunity in employment, have been contested primarily at the *federal or local* level. Most of the controversial legislation and judicial decisions have come from the national government, and enforcement or implementation has fallen to local school boards, municipal councils, and county governments.

One might wonder why conservative Democrats, who rarely get much black support in the party primaries, do not play up racial issues to strengthen their position with white Texans. The answer is that they simply cannot afford to do so. Conservative Democrats get few black votes in the primaries, but they depend on substantial black support in the general elections. Because liberals are usually defeated in the primaries and therefore do not appear on the general ballot, blacks vote for conservative Democrats rather than for conservative Republicans. Dolph Briscoe's vote percentage in Houston's black precincts rose from less than 5 percent in the 1972 primary runoff to an average of 95 percent in the November 1972 general election.

Liberal voting support is drawn from the state's minorities, the rural poor (especially in eastern Texas), unionized workers, and a small but often vocal segment of the white middle class. Black support for liberal candidates in the primaries has been most firm in recent years. The Mexican-American minority has been less predictable—especially in rural southern Texas, where local machines often deliver their votes to the conservative Democrats. Organized workers account for a good share of the votes and an even greater share of the campaign volunteers and funds that go to liberal candidates. The labor movement's influence, however, is limited by the fact that it represents less than an eighth of the state's workers. Union strength and status are low in most parts of Texas, a major exception being the highly industrialized upper Gulf Coast area.

The liberal faction usually has great difficulty in getting out its vote. Since liberal supporters tend to be poorer, less well educated, and less politically aware, they are less likely to register and go to the polls than are other citizens. Low turnout is an especial problem in the party primaries because they typically arouse little voter interest or enthusiasm.

The liberal voter coalition—blacks, Mexican-Americans, union members, the rural poor, some middle-class whites—is so diverse that, while together all these elements might constitute a majority in the Democratic primary, holding them all together is extremely difficult. But there were occasional successes. Ralph Yarborough, an unabashed liberal, won three U.S. Senate elections and served from 1957 to 1971. Five or six Texas congressmen are usually of liberal persuasion, and about a third of the legislature can typically be claimed by the faction. The liberals' best innings have come in presidential politics. Texas electoral votes were won by Republican Dwight Eisenhower in 1952 and 1956, but liberal Democrats helped hold off strong GOP challenges to John Kennedy in 1960 and Hubert Humphrey in 1968. In 1972 Texas liberals provided critical support to George McGovern at the national Democratic convention, and in 1976 they worked to hold the state in the Democratic column for Jimmy Carter.

A Liberal Reminisces
About Democratic Party Politics in Texas

Billie Carr is a Democratic National Committeewoman from Texas, a frequent guest at the Carter White House, and a power broker within the state party—a political insider by almost any standard. Her prominence, and that of the liberal wing of the Democratic party in Texas, contrast markedly with the longtime status of that group in the state's majority party.

Billie Carr, could you begin by telling us a little about how things used to be for the liberals in party politics?

The first thing you have to realize is that we started out every year knowing that no matter how well we did in the local precinct and county meetings, the conservative faction, with the help of whoever happened to be governor, was going to steal the state convention and dominate the Democratic State Executive Committee. The only question was would they steal it openly, by throwing our delegates out in a credentials fight on the floor, or in secret, by dreaming up some kind of crazy rule that nobody had ever heard of until the convention began.

Can you think of specific examples?

My most vivid memories are of one of the first state conventions I attended in the early 1950s at Mineral Wells, Texas, To begin with liberal delegates were not assigned any hotel rooms. We were not allowed to hold a caucus in Mineral Wells. When we tried to gather in the park, the Palo Pinto Mounted Posse came with billy clubs and threatened to arrest us for meeting without a permit. Inside the convention we were seated in the back of the auditorium and given half as many chairs as we had delegates—and, of course, no one was allowed to stand so this meant that we had to rotate and take turns sitting on the steps in the hot sun every hour. I don't know why we stayed because our mikes were cut off and we were not allowed to make motions or speak from the floor. We were referred to by the keynote speaker as the "communists" in the party. No cafe would serve food to those of us wearing liberal badges, so we were very happy when a church women's society offered to make us sandwiches and lemonade. Our happiness at this Christian charity suffered a bit when we found out that the sandwiches cost $2.00 each and the lemonade was 50¢ a glass. Finally, at the end of the convention we found that many of our cars had been towed away and we had to pay $13.00 to get them out of the city pound.

What about the situation of liberals in the Democratic party today?

Well, of course, with the help of the McGovern-Fraser national party rules, we get a much fairer shake today. The state party is reasonable, open, accessible. Liberals are now, to some degree, part of the party establishment. And, in some ways that makes things more difficult. Now we just can't criticize, we have responsibilities. Another problem is that we don't have the old clear-cut issues. In the 1950s and 1960s we had issues like civil and political rights for blacks and ending the war in Vietnam. There are still good issues around like women's rights, but it is harder to mobilize people, to get them interested and active about these problems. Texas liberals, like liberals all over the country, need a new agenda.

Still, the liberal faction within the state has generally endured failure and frustration. Able to command no more than a firm third of the state's primary voters, liberal success has come only when they have backed a strong candidate running under favorable conditions. Particularly galling to most liberals has been their inability to support a successful candidate for governor since victory there might have enabled them to consolidate a significant power base within the state.

THE DECLINE OF FACTIONALISM IN THE 1970s

Partisan politics are constantly changing in this country and the 50 states. Public figures come and go; new issues appear and old ones fade; some voters move away or die; others move in or come of political age. Texas is no exception in this regard as an analysis of recent trends within the Democratic party makes clear. Such an analysis reveals that a deterioration of the conservative versus liberal factionalism has occurred in the 1970s.

The decline of factionalism is illustrated by the political career of former Gov. Dolph Briscoe. Briscoe won the Democratic nomination in a runoff with Frances "Sissy" Farenthold in June 1972. That contest, like all the modern primary battles for the governorship, was fought along relatively clear conservative-liberal lines, with Briscoe cast as the conservative. Briscoe's tenure as governor, however, is less easily understood in a traditional conservative versus liberal sense. To be sure, Dolph Briscoe was a conservative governor in a number of respects. His passive gubernatorial style, his reluctance to use political power to deal with social problems, his appointment of conservative Anglos to most available positions, his opposition to any new taxes—all can be taken as evidence he kept the conservative faith. But one should also note that Briscoe vigorously supported the national Democratic ticket in 1976. During his tenure as governor, the Texas budget increased at a more rapid rate than under any previous chief executive. Briscoe actively sought, with some success, to broaden his political base with appeals to black and labor leaders. Such actions do not fit the traditional Texas conservative mold.

The 1978 gubernatorial contest between Governor Briscoe and Texas Attorney General Hill is difficult to interpret in factional terms not only because of the incumbent but also because the challenger did not clearly fall in either the liberal or conservative camp. The press tended to depict Hill as the more liberal of the two, but note should be taken that the Attorney General came to prominence as a supporter of conservative Democrat John Connally in the 1960s and that he took many conservative positions during the 1978 campaign. Poll data from the 1978 primary indicated that while liberals were a little more likely to support Hill than Briscoe, self-described "conservatives" were about evenly divided between the two candidates. Hill's victory over Briscoe in the May 6th election mostly hinged on the respective personalities of the candidates, their styles of political leadership, and short-term issues such as whether anyone should serve ten years as governor.

Further evidence of the decline of factionalism within the Democratic party can be found by looking at the second tier of elected Democrats in Texas from whose ranks future governors and senators will likely emerge. Public figures like Lt. Gov. William Hobby, Comptroller of Public Accounts Bob Bullock, and Land Commissioner Bob Armstrong are very different in their approach to politics, but all have avoided identification as party liberals or conservatives. Consequently, there is a dearth of committed leaders around whom either party faction can rally.

As the preceding discussion suggests, the blurring of the liberal-conservative split within the Democratic party is partly related to the personalities of major public figures in the state. In the 1950s and 1960s the schism within the party was exacerbated by the personal bitterness between conservative leaders like Allan Shivers and John Connally and liberals like Ralph Yarborough. The Dolph Briscoes, Lloyd Bentsens, and John Hills of the 1970s do not stir the same factional animosities.

Something fundamental has also been occurring within the Democratic electorate and among party activists in Texas. In the first place, the participating electorate in the Democratic primary has gotten *proportionately smaller* in recent years. In the 1970s from 20 to 25 percent of the adults in the state vote in the Democratic primaries, compared to 30 to 40 percent in the 1950s. Even in nonpresidential years, many more Texans now vote in general elections than do in the Democratic primary. Participation has dropped off most sharply among persons who identify themselves as Republicans and among conservative independents in the cities and suburbs of the state. Conservative activists as well as voters have left the Democratic party, further eroding the hardcore conservative element.

On the other hand, along with registration increases, blacks and Mexican-Americans have become a larger part of the Democratic primary electorate. This would, it might be supposed, be a boon to the liberal faction given traditional voting patterns. Things have not turned out so simply. As ethnic voter groups have grown in size and political sophistication, they have developed an acute sense of their special political interests. Black and Mexican-American alignments within the Democratic party often reflect how particular candidates relate to these groups' special interests rather than some general liberal or conservative criteria. Something akin to this has occurred within organized labor where support for broad liberal programs has been increasingly replaced by a concern for special issues and appointments that relate directly to unions and their memberships.

We thus see that while the conservative base in the primary has shrunk, the liberal coalition has fragmented. The obvious result is a decline of bifactionalism and the emergence of a more pluralistic, pragmatic politics within the party. Democratic aspirants for elective office find it much easier to operate in this environment by avoiding factional labels and assuming flexible positions on most public issues.

This flexibility is also helpful in dealing with Republican challengers in general elections, a topic discussed in the following section.

THE REPUBLICAN PARTY

THE REPUBLICAN REEMERGENCE

After a half century of near dormancy as little more than a patronage-distributing club, the Texas Republican party has reemerged as a political force to be reckoned with. Republican presidential candidates have contested Democrats on at least an equal footing since 1952. GOP gubernatorial nominees ran strong races in 1962, 1968, 1970, and 1972, before winning in 1978, and Republican John Tower has held a U.S. Senate seat since 1961. The party now fields candidates in most of the congressional districts and in about half of the state legislative races. Victories are no longer rare, as indicated by the fact that in 1979 the GOP held four of 31 state Senate seats, 22 of 150 state House seats, and county executive positions in a dozen counties, including Harris.

The improved Republican performance is related to several political and social changes that have occurred in recent years. First among

Party distinctions in Texas are often illusory.

these has been the rather steady movement of the national Democratic party toward a more liberal or leftist position. This national shift, dramatized by the nomination of George McGovern in 1972, has strained the loyalties of many Texas Democrats of conservative and moderate persuasion. A number have forsaken the ancestral party. Most prominent among these is John Connally, a man who led the state Democratic party in the 1960s but campaigned for Republican Richard Nixon in 1972 and declared himself a Republican in 1973. Most dissatisfied Democrats have adopted an ambivalent stance. They support Democratic nominees when their conservative credentials are in order and Republicans when those credentials are not. Former governor Allan Shivers, a delegate to the 1968 Democratic National Convention who came home and endorsed Richard Nixon, epitomizes this type of behavior.

Second, changing socioeconomic conditions in Texas have worked to the Republicans' advantage. The party draws much of its support from the white, urban middle class, a group that has grown very rapidly since World War II. Some of these people may have become Republicans because their income, status, or outlook changed; others are transplanted Republicans who moved to Texas from other parts of the country.

A third factor benefiting the Texas GOP is the decline in straight-party voting. This trend has been evident in national politics for some time and seems well established in Texas. This aids the state's Republicans because most Texans who identify with a political party consider themselves Democrats and, if voting decisions were made on this basis alone, GOP candidates would be doomed from the outset. Obviously, many Texas voters are now looking beyond party labels in casting their ballots. The personalities of the candidates and the issues involved in particular races have assumed greater importance than was previously the case. Of course, this assures the Republicans nothing save a fighting chance in any specific election.

Fourth, court-ordered reapportionment of legislative seats has helped Republican candidates. Much of the Republican voting strength is concentrated in the large metropolitan areas, but these were—until recently—seriously underrepresented in the U.S. Congress and the Texas legislature. Federal courts have forced a more equitable distribution on these legislative seats. And, in the case of the legislature, they have forced the adoption of single-member districts, both of which have helped the GOP elect more people in recent elections.

The operation of these factors has resulted in a somewhat improved Republican performance, but the party's success has not yet been substantial. As was true of the liberal Democrats, Republicans can win statewide races only under most favorable circumstances.

Specifically, there must be a sizable defection of normally Democratic voters if the party's candidates are to stand a chance.

A basic Republican difficulty stems from the moderate to conservative image many Democratic nominees have been able to present in general elections. That image has kept many conservative and moderate Texans in the Democratic fold who might otherwise have gravitated to the Republican party. The Texas Republicans' claim that they are the truly conservative party elicits a strong response in presidential voting, but does not work nearly as well in state and local contests.

The effort of Republicans to attract conservatives out of the Democratic party is not without costs. In trying to outbid the Democrats, the GOP necessarily restricts its appeal to the great mass of voters, who are neither consistent liberals or conservatives. Furthermore, this attempt to base the Republican party on solid conservatism has attracted many far-right supporters to its banner, many of whom are active in the party organization. Their presence has led to a good deal of bickering within the party because they vehemently oppose efforts to broaden the GOP's electoral base by diluting its ideological base. Moderate Republican candidates like George Bush of Houston and Alan Steelman of Dallas often have considerable campaign problems with their own right flank. Ironically, though, Republican success has usually been achieved only when Republican candidates could appeal to disgruntled Democrats of moderate or liberal persuasion.

PATTERNS OF REPUBLICAN ELECTORAL SUPPORT

As discussed earlier, Republican electoral support in Texas varies greatly from one governmental level to another. In presidential and U.S. Senate contests, the party competes with the Democrats on an equal footing. But in congressional, gubernatorial, and state legislative races, Republicans do considerably less well. GOP candidates rarely file for county offices.

Geographically, as Figure 3.3 shows, Republicans run especially well in the Panhandle, the Permian Basin, and in the German counties of the hill country. Patches of Republican strength are also found in the Tyler-Longview area of East Texas, and in the Dallas-Fort Worth and Houston metropolitan areas. Statewide Republican candidates tend to do especially poorly in a broad belt that stretches from west central Texas down to the Rio Grande and South Texas. Other strongly Democratic counties are found in central East Texas and in the northeast corner of the state.

A county-by-county geographic presentation of electoral data like that in Figure 3.3 does not, of course, reflect the enormous vote differential between counties. In the 1976 general election there were

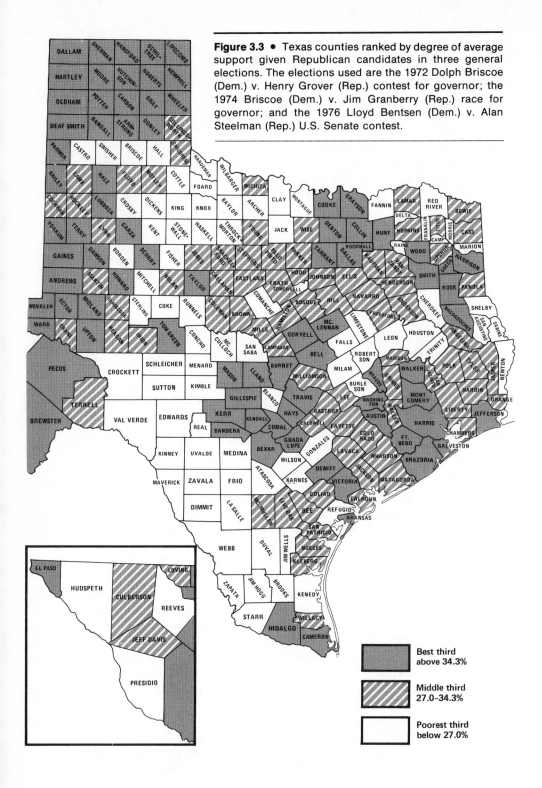

Figure 3.3 • Texas counties ranked by degree of average support given Republican candidates in three general elections. The elections used are the 1972 Dolph Briscoe (Dem.) v. Henry Grover (Rep.) contest for governor; the 1974 Briscoe (Dem.) v. Jim Granberry (Rep.) race for governor; and the 1976 Lloyd Bentsen (Dem.) v. Alan Steelman (Rep.) U.S. Senate contest.

Best third
above 34.3%

Middle third
27.0–34.3%

Poorest third
below 27.0%

686,000 voters in Harris County, while Loving County has 86. In most elections the two most populous counties in Texas (Harris and Dallas) have more voters than the 200 or so counties with fewer than 30,000 residents. To convey some sense of how partisan voting varies along urban-rural lines, we have grouped Texas counties into four categories and examined the vote patterns in three recent statewide contests. Table 3.1 presents these data.

In the eight most populous counties of Texas, Republicans do reasonably well, garnering an average vote of 46.5 percent. Since about half the state's electorate is in these counties, Republican success here is of great import. GOP candidates did less well in the 15 counties with betwee 75,000 and 200,000 inhabitants, averaging just 42.2 percent of the two-party vote.

Republican candidates run poorly in less well-populated counties. The GOP average falls to 38.2 percent in the 43 counties with between 25,000 and 75,000 people, and it plummets to 30.5 percent in the 188 counties with less than 25,000 population. It is obvious that the traditional Democratic loyalties of voters in the small towns and rural areas are still very much intact.

As one might expect, Republican support within the urban centers is greatest in white, middle-class precincts. The party does fairly well in blue-collar boxes (precincts), although it usually does not win majorities. Republican candidates have had little success in appealing to the big-city ethnic minorities. The Texas GOP candidates rarely get

TABLE 3.1 • VOTE PERCENTAGE IN GENERAL ELECTIONS FOR REPUBLICAN CANDIDATES GROUPED BY COUNTY POPULATION*

County Population	Grover (R) v. Briscoe (D) 1972	Granberry (R) v. Briscoe (D) 1974	Steelman (R) v. Bentsen (D) 1976	Average Republican % in All 3 Elections
Above 200,000 (8)	53.4	39.4	46.8	46.5
75,000 to 200,000 (15)	48.6	35.6	42.3	42.2
25,000 to 75,000 (43)	45.0	28.7	40.8	38.2
Below 25,000 (188)	36.4	22.5	32.5	30.5
State Totals	48.4	33.6	42.6	41.5

*The Republican candidates' percentages are of the two-party vote. This is especially significant for the 1972 election because about 6.5 percent of the total vote went to neither the Democratic nor the Republican candidate for governor.

even a tenth of the black vote and usually lose Mexican-American areas by margins of more than two to one. In elections where Republican candidates have gotten a respectable minority vote, as did John Tower from Mexican-Americans in 1966 and George Bush from blacks in 1970, indications are that this resulted less from minority support for the GOP nominees themselves than from a considerable disaffection with their Democratic opponents.

A summary of support patterns for Republican candidates points up problems for the party. About a fifth of the Texas electorate are blacks or Mexican-Americans, but the GOP gets few votes from these minorities. A fifth of the electorate (including, of course, some blacks and Mexican-Americans) reside in rural Texas, and Republicans usually get only 30 percent or so of this vote. Democratic candidates usually carry low-income, urban white areas. When one combines the Democratic strength in these sectors of the population with the quarter or so of the middle-class, urban white vote the majority party gets, the Democrats have a clear majority.

The Texas Republican party's white middle-class electoral base is simply too narrow to produce statewide electoral victories. Data on voter attitudes toward political parties confirm the pattern we find in election results. Surveys consistently show that only about 16 percent of the adults in Texas identify with the Republican party. There is a very large number of self-described independents in the state (about 40 percent), but the percentage of Democratic identifiers remains at about 45 percent, or roughly three times the size of the Republican base. The percentage of Democratic identifiers has gone down a little in recent years, but the offsetting increase has occurred in the ranks of independents, not Republicans.

THIRD PARTIES IN TEXAS

From time to time in Texas new political parties have appeared and sought a role in the political system. The Populist party emerged in the 1880s and was, for a few years, a force to be reckoned with in many parts of the state. More recently, supporters of George Wallace launched a major bid for Texas electoral votes in the 1968 presidential election under the banner of the American Independent party. The Wallace party received 584,269 votes (18.3 percent), led in 22 counties, and finished second in 38 others. The Raza Unida party has been active in Texas in the 1970s, having elected several county officials in South Texas and put up a few statewide candidates. Their most successful candidate, Ramsey Muniz, got 214,118 votes for governor, or 6.3 percent, and helped to make the 1972 contest between Democrat Dolph Briscoe and Republican Hank Grover very close. A number of national minor parties, such as the Socialist Workers, the American party, and the Libertarian party, have also placed candidates on the ballot in Texas. But, whether homegrown or transplanted, old or new, these parties have shared a common fate of failure.

At first glance the Lone Star State would seem a hospitable place for a multiparty system. The state is large and has a most diverse population, and there is little evidence of any enduring consensus on issues within the electorate. But the truth is that third parties have not been able to become stable, significant forces within the political system. The reasons for their failure include the following four factors:

1. *The electoral rules of the game under which parties operate in Texas.* The "winner take all" quality of elections in Texas and the United States, as opposed to the proportional representation systems common in Europe, makes it difficult for third parties to establish a political base. Ten or 20 or even 30 percent of the vote usually elects no one to office in Texas, so minor parties usually achieve significance only as "spoilers" by taking votes from major party candidates. Additionally, the major party candidates are guaranteed the best places on the general election ballot, and they have primaries paid for by the taxpayers of Texas. Minor parties do not share in such largesse. Since elected Democrats, with the assistance of a few Republicans, will continue to write the rules by which state politics is played, this pattern of advantage to major parties will likely continue.

2. *The nature of the major parties in Texas.* As mentioned earlier, American political parties tend to be loose, decentralized entities. They are not highly organized, nor often committed to any firm set of principles. Such characteristics certainly apply to the dominant party in Texas, the Democrats, and are reflected in Democratic candidates who follow rather flexible, pragmatic courses. This flexibility of Democrats, and to a lesser extent Republicans, tends to undercut the potential of third parties because if opinion shifts occur within the electorate, major party candidates can usually adapt to such new realities.

3. *The nature of the minor parties in Texas.* Ironically, it has been the small parties not the big ones in Texas that have often been inflexible in their approach to voters. Many of these parties are composed of individuals strongly committed to political goals or positions that command little support among the state's voters. In most cases such parties have disdained compromises to win votes because such a "sellout" would be, in their

leaders' view, but an imitation of the corrupt politics practiced by the major parties.

4. *The natural advantages major parties enjoy in Texas.* The rule in electoral politics, as elsewhere in life, is: "Them that has, gits." Expressed less crudely, those who enjoy current benefits are usually in the best position to make sure they continue to reap future benefits. The case of political parties competing for candidates, money, media attention, and votes illustrates this point. Most able, serious, and experienced office seekers in Texas (along with, to be sure, many lacking in ability, seriousness, and experience) choose to run as Democrats or Republicans because they think only major party candidates can win. Financial contributors invest their dollars in Democrats or Republicans because they think no one else can win. Television, radio, and newspapers give coverage to Democrats and Republicans because they think no one else can win. Voters narrow their choices to Democrats and Republicans because they think no one else can win. Of course, under these conditions, they are right—no one but Democrats and Republicans *can* win. The expectation produces the reality.

In light of the above factors, the prospects for third parties are bleak indeed in Texas. A popular national figure denied a major party nomination might again mount a serious bid for Texans' presidential votes, as George Wallace did in 1968. Or, local conditions might enable a third party based in a segment of the state's electorate, such as urban blacks or irrigation farmers in the High Plains, to enjoy local electoral success the way the Raza Unida party did among Mexican-Americans in South Texas in the early 1970s. But such special conditions aside, there is virtually no chance for the establishment of stable, influential third parties at the statewide level in Texas. That should hardly be surprising, given the great difficulties the Republicans have encountered in becoming a competitive second party.

If third parties have little future in Texas, what is likely to occur within the state's party system? The following section speculates on that subject.

THE FUTURE OF PARTY POLITICS IN TEXAS

Two central questions arise when one tries to assess the future of party politics in Texas. What will occur within the dominant Democratic party, and will the Republican party become truly competitive with the Democrats? Opinions naturally differ on these matters, but we believe some patterns can be identified.

WHITHER THE DEMOCRATS?

In a lengthy earlier section, we discussed the decline of factionalism within the Democratic party in the 1970s. This decline has been especially notable in the case of office seekers, but in some areas the longstanding split between liberals and conservatives continues. This is most clearly the case within the organizational structure of the party where reasonably distinct factions still contend. There also continue to be important differences on issues within the electorate that can be framed in liberal versus conservative terms, so the potential exists for a revival of the feisty factionalism of the 1950s and 1960s within the Democratic party.

We doubt that this potential will become a reality soon. One major constraint on the renewal of intraparty warfare is the growing Republican threat. Texas Democrats of the late 1970s may agree on little else, but they share the view that the management of the state's political affairs is better off in Democratic rather than Republican hands. Democrats know that once Republicans get a foothold in state government, dislodging them will be very difficult. Consequently, Democrats will be under great pressure to mute their internal differences in order to present a united front against Republicans in general elections.

The decline of stable bifactionalism within the Democratic party probably means that personalities will assume even greater importance in the state's political affairs. Office seekers must build their own ad hoc coalitions to win elections, and the composition of such coalitions will shift quickly depending on short-term factors. Such instability of political alignments will make it more difficult for primary voters to relate competing Democratic candidates to general issue positions. This kind of everyone for themselves politics will also increase the advantage of incumbents and other candidates with superior financial backing.

THE REPUBLICAN FUTURE

For 15 years Republicans have been predicting the imminent emergence of a real two-party system in Texas. Many harbingers of this transformation have been identified. The election of a U.S. senator in 1961; strong races for governor in 1962, 1968, and 1972; the defection of former Governor Connally in 1973. But one thing or another always seems to frustrate the minority party just as it is getting within striking distance of the Democrats. Texas Republicans were primed for an all-out offensive against John Kennedy in 1964, only to see Texan Lyndon Johnson assume national power after the President's assassination in November 1963. Expected gains in the late 1960s from public dissatisfaction with the Democrats about Vietnam and social unrest did not materialize when the 1970 recession focused voters' attention on economic issues. The ultimate opportunity seemed at hand in 1973. Texas voters had massively rejected George McGovern, the 1972 Democratic presidential nominee; the majority party was split into three quarreling groups; and Governor Connally had just come on board the Republican ship. Then, Watergate, and the GOP had to start all over again.

Most analysts have contended that a key condition for establishing a competitive party system in Texas is the election of a Republican governor. That condition was satisfied in the 1978 general election. Bill Clements' surprising victory (his own pollster showed him 10 points behind his opponent a week before the election) raises two important questions: Does the election of a Republican governor indicate that, at long last, Texas is a two-party state? And, just what will be the consequences for party politics of having a Republican chief executive in Austin?

In answer to the first question, while the 1978 election showed Republicans can win the governorship under favorable circumstances, it does not indicate that a two-party system has been established. Republicans have come close to winning the governorship in 1962 and 1972, so Clements' win was not a dramatic turnabout. In fact, Clements got 300,000 fewer votes in 1978 than did Hank Grover, the losing Republican candidate in 1972. Analyzing the 1978 returns shows few shifts in vote patterns—traditional Democratic voters stayed Democratic, traditional Republicans voted for the GOP. What was different from 1972 and other years was that the turnout was exceptionally light among Democratic voter groups such as blacks, Mexican-Americans, blue-collar workers, and the rural poor. Republican voters in the big-city suburbs and areas like the Permian Basin voted in great numbers. Overall, only 28 percent of the state's 8.4 million adults went to the polls in 1978, compared to 51 percent in 1976.

This low turnout of Democratic voters compared to that of Republicans reflects a number of short-term conditions. These would include the absence of a presidential contest; the public concerns in 1978 with "Republican" issues, such as inflation and government spending, rather than with "Democratic" issues like unemployment; and the much better funded campaign efforts that Republicans Clements and John Tower were able to mount against Democrats John Hill and Bob Krueger, who opposed Tower in the U.S. Senate contest.

The election aside, what are the consequences of having a Republican governor? Several partisan effects should result in the near future. For the first time in modern history, Republicans should get many of the political, administrative, and judicial appointments Texas governors make. This should help build a statewide base for the minority party, especially if Clements is reelected in 1982, so he can fill virtually all appointive positions in the state. The GOP should also get better treatment in legislative and congressional redistricting and other electoral matters. Having a Republican governor in office should help the party raise money and recruit candidates for state and local office. In sum, the Republican party should be a more visible and active force in state politics than ever before.

This is especially likely because Bill Clements, an outspoken and aggressive campaigner, is expected to be an activist governor. There is in this, of course, both potential and danger for the Texas Republican party. As the unquestioned leader and symbol of the Texas GOP, Clements' success or nonsuccess as governor will have profound consequences for the party in the state. If Bill Clements is perceived as an effective, competent leader, he will enormously enhance the prospects for the Republican party, just as the election of Linwood Holton boosted the Virginia Republican party in the late 1960s. On the other hand, if things go badly for Clements, his tenure may simply convince Texans there was a good reason why they had elected Democrats for 100 years the way Republican Claude Kirk's (governor from 1967–1971) did in Florida.

In any case, Texas will remain for some time a state where the Democrats have a great advantage in most elections. Over 98 percent of the state's county officials are Democrats, as are 85 percent of the legislature and over 80 percent of the congressional delegation. The election of a Republican governor can help to break down this Democratic dominance, but even under the most favorable circumstances, change will come slowly.

NOTES

[1]Frank Sorauf, *Party Politics in America,* 3rd ed. (Boston: Little, Brown), pp. 12–16.

[2]See Austin Ranney's article, "Parties in State Politics," in Herbert Jacobs and Kenneth Vines, eds., *Politics in the American States,* 2nd ed. (Boston: Little, Brown), pp. 84–89.

[3]V. O. Key, Jr., *Southern Politics* (New York: Knopf, 1949), pp. 298–311.

[4]Ibid., p. 255.

[5]See Frank Forbes, "Party Activists in Houston" (Master's thesis, University of Houston, 1969), p. 39.

4

Interest Groups in Texas Politics

In every democracy, interest groups emerge to press political demands. The reasons are simple enough. In any political system the institutional structure, composition of political leadership, and public policies generate conflict, dissatisfaction, and frustration among people. These produce demands for certain political actions. Some, but not nearly all, of these demands can be aggregated and processed through political parties. Parties, by their nature, are limited in their ability to transmit a multiplicity of citizen demands. They must make broad appeals, shy from specific commitments to groups, and subordinate virtually all else to their first priority—winning elections. So, many people turn to more specific associations, interest or pressure groups, to seek or promote certain governmental actions or policies.

The limits of political parties are especially apparent in Texas because, save for a few brief intervals, there has been no real competition between parties.

Paradoxically, scholars have paid little attention to interest groups' contribution to Texas politics save for certain groups that lobby in the legislative, executive, and administrative branches of state government to secure favorable policy decisions. Lobbying represents an important aspect of group activity, but other activities are also of great significance. A Dallas business group pours funds into a favored candidate's race; farmers in Lubbock block distribution of a newspaper opposed to a farm strike; thousands of ladies in pink converge on Austin to urge rescision of the Equal Rights Amendment; and Texas oil companies purchase full-page ads in big-city newspapers extolling the virtues of the commission that regulates their industry. All such activities contribute to the sum of group involvement in the Texas political process.

Any discussion of Texas interest groups is handicapped by the relative inattention they have received and by the fact that much group political activity is purposefully hidden from public view. These factors limit the following discussion of the bases of group organization, the tactics used by such organizations, and interest groups' general impact on Texas politics.

THE BASES OF GROUP ORGANIZATION

Interest groups are organized aggregates, or, more simply, groups of people who have joined together for some common purpose. This purpose might be protection or advancement of the group's economic interest, as is the case with trade associations, professional groups, and labor unions. Or it might be more general in nature, as with groups that oppose environmental pollution or wish to eliminate corruption from government. Generalization is difficult. Some groups pursue long-term objectives (e.g., bettering employee working conditions or arresting a perceived Communist influence in American politics), while others seek short-term goals (e.g., preventing a specific tax increase or purging sex education courses from the public school curriculum).

Granted the complexity of purposes that distinguish groups, a more basic issue must be dealt with: Why do some groups that share interests organize and engage in political action while others do not? Why are doctors, lawyers, and steelworkers in Texas well organized for protection of their economic interests while secretaries, janitors, and farm laborers are hardly organized at all? Why do residents of one area in the path of a proposed freeway organize a vigorous protest against losing their property while citizens in another place accept relocation without complaint? There is virtually an infinite number of common purposes that could serve as organizational bases, but only a limited number of organized groups do in fact exist.

Several general factors promote or retard the degree of collective political action engaged in by a group with common interests.

Size of the group. Contrary to what one might think, the *smaller* the group, the more easily it can be organized. Large groups are cumbersome and hard to coordinate. Each individual's contribution to the collective enterprise is small, and "letting George do it" is a persistent problem.[1] With small groups, each person's contribution is important to group success, and one's share of the group benefits is larger, thus, organizational participation is more rational from the individual's viewpoint. A practical illustration of the size principle can be seen in the fact that it is far easier for the few oil-exporting nations to organize than it is for the many oil-importing nations to do so.

Group concentration. The more concentrated the potential group, the more easily it can be organized. The organizational costs of communication and coordination increase sharply when a group's membership is scattered. Four thousand young people concentrated on a college campus can be combined for political action with a great deal less effort than it would take if the same number were scattered in 100 different places.

Membership resources. Organization entails costs, especially if the group is too large for face-to-face interaction. Means for communicating with members are usually necessary in all but the simplest organizations, and employment of a permanent staff is often necessary. Since organizational costs are usually borne by group members, the more resources they possess the more easily they can afford organization. Resources include not only money but also such things as leisure time and skills useful for organizational activities.

Organizational resources. People join organizations because they perceive membership to be in their best interest. Organizations must thus provide inducements or incentives to prospective members.[2] Sometimes the incentive is simply that the individual agrees with the goals or purposes of the organization; but this is often insufficient, especially when the group is large. Mass organizations usually develop selective incentives that help them attract individuals into their folds. To work, one may have to join a union; to enjoy good social relations, one may have to become a member in a neighborhood civic club; to achieve career status or prestige, one may have to join a professional association.

Climate for organization. The constitutional guarantees of speech, assembly, press, and petition should equally protect all groups' right of organization, but circumstances make it easier for some groups to associate formally than others. A group that reflects general community values, like a veterans' organization, will likely encounter no opposition; but a group that supports legalizing marijuana might face harassment. An association that challenges a local power structure may find a series of legal and illegal barriers in its path that do not obstruct those who go along with the powers that be.

Applying these considerations to Texas helps one understand

variations in group organization. The 20,000 or so doctors can organize far more easily than can the hundreds of thousands of clerks in the state. Urban blacks can build up an organizational infrastructure that surpasses that found among dispersed rural blacks. Trial lawyers can afford group organizaton; janitors cannot. Unions that control selective incentives for members, like admission to apprentice programs for the skilled trades, have little difficulty in recruiting members. Unions representing workers not qualified through apprentice programs (e.g., auto mechanics) are not so fortunate. Organizers of a Committee to Restore Prayer in the Public Schools would face few problems in a conservative city like Amarillo; the same could probably not be said for a Gay Liberation or Young Socialists League chapter.

BUSINESS GROUPS

Business groups enjoy considerable advantages in American and Texas politics. To begin with, very large corporations such as Exxon and Bell Telephone possess enormous resources. The managers of these firms have access to numerous lawyers, accountants, public relations experts, full-time political lobbyists, and millions of dollars in advertising or public affairs budgets. Few other interested parties enter the political arena with such assets. These economic goliaths can usually take care of their own political needs without relying on collective action.

Most business firms, however, do not have the resources or the interest to operate independently in political matters. Joining with other businesses is not only economical, it also tends to increase the impact these firms can have on political decision makers. Some of these associations represent general business interests, like the Texas Association of Business or local chambers of commerce, but most represent particular segments of the business world. Beer makers have the Texas Brewers Association; oil operators have the Texas Independent Producers and Royalty Owners Association; highway contractors have the Good Roads Association; and so on into the hundreds. The reasons for such collective activity in Texas are easily understood. State government collects over $4 billion a year in taxes; business firms want to pay as little of this as possible. State government has regulatory power over virtually every type of economic activity in Texas; businesses want regulation that, at a minimum, does not interfere with their ability to operate profitably and, at a maximum, enhances their profitability. Finally, state government spends billions of dollars for goods and services; many businesses, such as highway contractors, could not survive wtihout selling their services to the state.

In general, one can say that the business sector in Texas is well organized to protect its political interests. The major exception would be the small independent businessmen and women in fields like retailing. In such cases their large number, diversity of interests, wide geographic distribution, and relative lack of resources preclude effective organization.

OCCUPATIONAL GROUPS

In contrast to the situation in most industrialized states and at the national level, business groups in Texas do not have to contend with a strong organized labor movement. About 400,000 workers are members of unions in Texas, but this represents less than 10 percent of the work force as compared to 21 percent of the country as a whole. Despite vigorous organizing efforts by a number of unions, the percentage of unionized workers in the state has been declining in the 1970s.

The weak status of organized labor in Texas reflects several factors. Public attitudes in the South generally stress individualism rather than collective action, and there is a considerable amount of antiunion feeling, even among blue-collar workers. Many employers in the state, such as Brown and Root, the huge construction firm, are ideologically opposed to unions and fight efforts to organize their workers with great determination. Organized labor also operates under severe legal handicaps. Texas is one of 20 states with a "right-to-work" law which prohibits union-shop arrangements. Under this law no worker can be required by a majority approved company-union agreement to join a union to get or keep a job. The principle sounds admirable, but unions argue that it creates a "free-loader" problem in that many workers will enjoy the fruits of having a union represent them but will refuse to pay their share of the cost of such representation. Other restrictions on unions include an anticheckoff law that prohibits an employer from deducting union dues without prior written permission from the employee concerned, a prohibition of mass picketing and secondary boycotts, inclusion of unions under the state antitrust laws, and a provision that labor unions are liable for damages resulting from strikes in breach of contract.

About a third of the 150,000 farmers in Texas belong to one of several farm groups. The traditional lack of consensus among farmers is reflected in the fact that prominent organizations like the Texas Farmers Union and the state branch of the American Farm Bureau disagree on virtually every public issue affecting agriculture. Periodic efforts have been made to organize farmworkers in Texas, particularly in the lower Rio Grande Valley. However, these efforts have met with no success, and this segment of the Texas work force remains unorganized.

Most high-status professional workers in Texas, such as medical doctors and lawyers, have long had effective associations protecting their public-policy interests. In the 1960s and 1970s other white-collar workers like teachers, nurses, and public employees have turned to group organization to promote their interests.

Nevertheless, no more than 1 of the 5 million employed persons in Texas are represented by any sort of occupational association. Since organization is common only among white-collar professionals and skilled blue-collar employees, this means that virtually all lower paid workers are not represented by groups in the political arena. This has, as we shall see, significant implications for public policy in Texas.

ETHNIC AND RACIAL POLITICAL GROUPS

One of our popular literary traditions maintains that the United States is a "melting pot" in which persons of diverse ethnic origins are assimilated into the mainstream of American life and culture. Certainly, there is some evidence to support this view. For example, Irish and German Americans have become highly assimilated in the last half century, and Polish and Slavic Americans seem to be in the process of doing so at the present time. Nevertheless, there is considerable evidence that for many racial or ethnic groups assimilation has progressed at a much slower pace. This has especially been the case with Americans of African or Hispanic origin. The reasons for their continuing distinctiveness reflect not only high degrees of ethnic consciousness within these populations, but also the effects of centuries of political, social, and economic discrimination that Americans of darker skins have endured in this society.

In Chapter 2 we emphasized that Texas has both a large black and Mexican-American population that accounts for about a third of the state's residents. Stress was also placed on the fact that in terms of almost every objective measure—income, educational levels, occupational patterns—blacks and Mexican-Americans rank far behind the Anglo majority in Texas. Given that distinct socioeconomic status of black and brown Texas, plus the political discrimination that each population has been subjected to, it is hardly surprising that a number of politically active groups are rooted in these communities.

These groups tend to be of two general types. The first are organizations concerned with the general social and political problems facing the minority populations; the second focus on more specific problems or political tasks. A number of groups in the first category are affiliated with national associations. There are, for example, chapters of the National Association for the Advancement of Colored People (NAACP) active in every large metropolitan area in Texas. Similarly, the League of United Latin American Citizens (LULAC) and the American GI Forum represent Mexican-American interests around the state. Such organizations are active on a range of problems: school desegregation, employment and promotion practices, securing more political appointments, etc. The specialized groups include the Mexican-American Legal Defense and Education Fund (MALDEF), the Harris County Council of Organizations (HCCO), the Black Organization for Leadership Development (BOLD), and the Progressive Voters League (PVL). MALDEF is principally concerned with research and litigation relevant to the needs of the Mexican-American community. The other three groups are black voter groups (the first two in Houston, the last in Dallas) that screen candidates for public office, issue endorsements, and work to deliver the minority vote to the endorsed office seekers.

Despite the fact that there are several hundred black or brown organizations in Texas that do get involved in politics, only a tiny fraction of the black and Mexican-American populations are members of these groups. This does not mean that most minority citizens do not support the goals of these groups; available evidence suggests they generally do. Rather, low membership reflects the situation of most adults in these populations. They are poor, lack leisure time, have little access to political information, and have more than enough to do in facing the everyday problems of survival. It is difficult for blacks and Mexican-Americans to invest their time, energy, and money in political efforts that usually have no immediate payoff.

The impact of ethnic political groups in Texas is difficult to assess. Politically, blacks and Mexican-Americans have made obvious headway over the last 30 years. Discriminatory legislation has been erased from the statutes; both groups are reasonably well represented within the Democratic party structure; more minority legislators are getting elected; and a few more political appointments are coming to minorities. Still, there has been only modest progress in closing the socioeconomic gap that separates blacks and browns from Anglos in Texas. One problem these disadvantaged minorities face is the great difficulty they encounter in uniting around a common political program. A current example concerns how the government should deal with nonlegal immigrants from Mexico. LULAC and other Mexican-American groups have stressed that the problem should be approached from the perspective of the human rights of the individuals involved. Accordingly, they have criticized proposals such as those advanced by President Carter that would offer only a limited amnesty to immigrants and tighten access to the country because these policies would be cruel and inhumane when applied to several million people. Blacks, on the other hand, have generally supported proposals to expel illegal immigrants and tighten admissions because they see Mexican immigrants as competitors for a limited number of jobs.

There are, of course, other identifiable ethnic populations in Texas. Most notable among these are the approximately 100,000 Jews in the state. Though relatively small in number, Jews tend to be active in many social and political groups, and they can bring considerable political pressure to bear on issues of great interest to the Jewish population. The Texas Legislature found this out in 1977 when it was pressed to pass legislation making it illegal for any Texas firm to cooperate with the Arab economic boycott of Israel.

Finally, we should note that while many Texans retain a sense of their German, Polish, Czech, or other European heritage, there is virtually no meaningful political organization along these lines in the state.

POLITICAL INTEREST GROUPS

Interest groups rooted in political agreement per se, rather than some kind of economic or ethnic interest, tend to be of two kinds. The first kind are narrow-range groups that concentrate on particular issues; the second kind represent members on a wide range of political matters. Single-issue groups are now active in Texas to reform marijuana laws, to support the Equal Rights Amendment, to defeat the Equal Rights Amendment, to make abortions more accessible, to prohibit abortions, and so forth. The proliferation of these groups reflects the fact that they can organize rather easily because they usually require only a short-term investment (writing legislators, going on a bus trip to Austin, etc.) as opposed to a continuing commitment over a long period of time. General political interest groups active in the state are usually spin-offs from national associations. Typical of this genre are Common Cause of Texas, the Texas Conservative Union, and the Texas Women's Political Caucus.

Common Cause is the largest "public interest" group operating at the national level with about 225,000 dues-paying members. The national organization has helped state-oriented groups emerge to focus on special local issues. The Texas group got a boost by strongly supporting reform measures in the wake of the Sharpstown banking scandal of 1971. By 1973 Common Cause of Texas had some 7000 members and was very active in the legislative session that year. The Texas Conservative Union grew out of the American Conservative Union, a prominent national political group. The Texas Conservative

Union was started early in 1977 and had, within one year, a membership of 4000 and an operating budget of $75,000 per year. The Texas Women's Political Caucus has only a few hundred members, but they employed a lobbyist at the 1977 legislative session and have become a prominent representative of the feminist point of view.

The combined impact of these new political groups is probably not great, but they have added diversity to the Texas interest-group picture.

TACTICS AND STRATEGY OF GROUP POLITICS

Interest groups usually rely on three methods of securing favorable public action: lobbying, mass propagandizing, and electioneering. Additionally, unorthodox and sometimes illegal tactics have occasionally been used by groups in pursuit of their objectives.

LOBBYING

Lobbying refers to the process wherein group representatives interact with public decision makers in the hope of influencing policy. Most of the publicized lobbying in Texas occurs in the state legislature, but lobbying is by no means restricted to the legislative process. Wherever decisions are made that affect group interests—be it city hall, the governor's staff, the courts, or administrative agencies—one finds lobbying activity.

Lobbying, at least successful lobbying, involves a transfer of benefits between groups and decision makers. A lobbyist may dispense material benefits, but often he or she offers political support or information to the public official who in turn takes the lobbyist's position into account in making policy decisions. Outright bribery, public suspicions to the contrary, is rare.

At every session of the Texas legislature one can find hundreds of lobbyists in attendance or around the capitol at various times, serving as spokesmen for various groups. Many lobbyists are longtime political actors, often having served as legislators themselves, and many are quite knowledgeable concerning legislative issues and the operation of the legislative process. They may draft bills, mastermind legislative campaigns, help line up support for or against given bills, and otherwise work to secure their goals.

Lobbyists typically do a goodly amount of wining, dining, and entertaining. Legislators may be taken to luncheon or dinner, invited on hunting and fishing trips and other junkets, and provided with liquor or entertainment.[3] Some lobbyists representing special interest groups are famous in Austin for their breakfasts, buffets, or specialty dinners

"Jim, suppose the people get a lobbyist!"

(e.g., catfish) for elected officials. What the lobbyist seeks to secure by these activities is not so much votes (at least not directly) as "access" and "goodwill." A lobbyist must be able to talk with a legislator when the need arises, and he is much more likely to be able to communicate effectively if that legislator is favorably inclined toward him. No one knows whether the Texas Trial Lawyers Association's maintenance of a buffet throughout the 1973 legislative session was responsible for killing comprehensive no-fault insurance legislation, but the free food certainly did no harm to the lawyers' cause.

Many legislators who are lawyers are employed by corporations and groups and are paid retainer's fees for their efforts. Nonlawyers are sometimes employed in "public relations" positions by banks and other businesses. Such arrangements are quite legal, although some question their propriety. When a bill affecting a corporation or interest group comes before the legislature, does a legislator employed by that group act as the representative of his client or of his constituents? Although the answer is a matter of conjecture, apparently groups believe that employing legislators holds some benefit.

Lobbyists and interest-group representatives often appear at committee hearings and present oral or written statements on the need for, the merits of, and possible effects of given bills. In so doing, they provide legislators with much useful, if self-serving, information on legislation—some of which would not otherwise be available. Also, lobbyists occasionally encourage the attendance at hearings by persons favorable to their position in an effort to create the impression that they have wide public support.

The service role that lobbyists fill is of great importance in the legislature because that body lacks the staff and expertise needed to gather information independently. Charges are sometimes made that the legislature is unduly reliant on outside, biased sources of information. A case in point occurred in 1973–1974. In 1973 Governor Briscoe resisted legislative demands for a thorough overhaul of the statewide property-tax system that largely supports the public schools. The governor's position was that more reliable data on the property tax was needed before he could support substantial reform. The governor asked the Legislative Property Tax Committee to gather this information after the 1973 session ended. This committee, lacking sufficient staff itself, turned to the Texas Research League, a private organization funded by some of the largest business interests in the state, to actually gather the needed data and present recommendations. To no one's surprise, the plan the league eventually recommended did not conflict with the economic interests of its supporters.

Because of the many forces that play on legislators and the legislative process, it is not possible to determine with precision the impact of lobbying efforts. The success of a particular group will depend on such factors as its size, status, resources, cohesion, and position on issues and the attitudes of legislators, public opinion, and so on. Groups are likely to claim substantial power and success for themselves. This, among other things, helps create the impression that they are a force to be reckoned with and at the same time impresses their members and supporters.

Whatever their actual impact, lobbying groups do perform a number of useful functions: (1) They are a major source of demands for the legislative process in that they pressure public officials to act in response to their interests. (2) They provide a great deal of useful, if sometimes biased, information to public officals, much of which is of a specialized or technical nature. (3) They help keep their members and the public informed as to what the legislature is doing and how they may be affected by proposed legislation. (4) In a broad sense, group pressures provide a sort of functional representation that supplements the regular system of geographic representation.

A "New Breed" Lobbyist Comments on Working the Texas Legislature

---

Marion "Sandy" Sanford is a partner in the largest law firm in Texas and one of the biggest in the country. Although a specialist in administrative law, much of Sanford's time is taken up with politics—lobbying for his firm's numerous clients when the legislature is in session. Urbane, low-key, intelligent, he has been cited as one of the new breed of lobbyists that are coming to prominence in Austin.

Sandy, what changes have you observed in lobbying?
    Well, I started in 1969, and just since then there have been many changes. For one thing the issues are getting more complex. The old days when it was liberal versus conservative are gone. Now, it is more often urban versus rural, or one business interest against another. This complexity means that lobbying is getting to be a full-time job. The members have changed, too. They're generally smarter, more capable. You have to be better prepared, know what you're talking about.

Just how does an effective lobbyist work the Texas legislature?
    Basically, you explain things. The key is you've got to figure out just what proposed legislation will do and then explain this in terms that are relevant to legislators. You not only need to know the special interest aspects of legislation, but you've got to talk about the public policy reasons why bills should be killed or passed. One thing you do not do is lie to people. If you give a member bad information, he might go out with it and get his ass blown off. You must have a reputation for integrity.

Do you know and work with most of the members?
    I know all 31 senators and most of the House members that have been around for a term or so. A good lobbyist has to pay attention to the electoral process. You've got to keep up with who is running, help good people out as much as possible with fund raising, other things.

Just whom do you help?
    I represent all kinds of clients, so I can't just work with people on one side of the political fence. On different issues I need different folks, so I basically try to help the competent people, those you can explain your case to.

What are the advantages of having a professional lobbyist in Austin?
    The one thing a lobbyist can do that citizens cannot is to get in to see people. Most of the members are my friends; I know them, they know me. When we talk we are on common ground; we understand what is going on. Now, maybe that is not fair, but just getting in does not sell your deal. You still have to make a good, believable case.
    One thing to keep in mind: Most legislators are pretty sophisticated; they can take care of themselves when it comes to dealing with lobbyists. I think it was Jesse Unruh [former Speaker of the California Assembly] who said: "Hell, if legislators can't eat lobbyists' steaks, drink their whiskey, screw their women, and still do what's right, they don't belong in the legislature."

    The discussion thus far should not be taken to mean that there has been no criticism of lobbying. On the contrary, there has been much criticism of interest groups as being selfish, greedy, corrupt, and undemocratic, especially if their views or interests are in conflict with the person doing the criticizing. Although demands have often been made for the regulation of lobbying on behalf of special interest groups to prevent abuses and corruption, lobbyists have been unregulated for most of the state's history. A 1907 statute did prohibit efforts to influence legislation "by means other than appeal to reason" and provided that persons guilty of lobbying were subject to fines and imprisonment. This rather stringent statute was never enforced.

In 1957 mounting criticism of some lobbying activities and some legislative scandals, such as the taking of a $5000 bribe by a legislator, culminated in the adoption of the Lobby Control Act. Unlike the earlier statute, the 1957 law made publicity rather than prohibition of lobbying activities its purpose. Lobbyists were required to register and provide certain information about themselves, the legislation in which they had an interest, and their expenditures incurred while engaged in "direct communication" with legislators. In general, the law did little to control or modify lobbying activities. Numerous loopholes in the act restricted its effect, and its provisions were not vigorously enforced. A tougher law was enacted in 1973 which seems to have, if nothing else, made lobbyists more circumspect. Traditional practices such as showering selected legislators with expensive gifts on "governor for a day" have disappeared. It would now be surprising to find lobbyists paying for legislators' apartments in Austin, a common practice a few years ago.

Fear of adverse publicity is probably as responsible as new laws are for limiting lobby abuses. The good old days when gentlemen of the press did not write critically about gentlemen of the legislature have passed. For example, *The Texas Monthly,* a magazine with more than 100,000 subscribers, rates legislators after each session. A good way to make the "10 worst" or "furniture" list (this includes members who are neither good or bad, just around) is to be overly responsive to lobby pressures.

MASS PROPAGANDIZING

Groups use mass propagandizing to influence public opinion favorably in the hope that this will eventually produce desired political action. A classic, though unsuccessful, example of the technique was the American Medical Association's radio and television campaign of the early 1960s against Medicare legislation.

Mass propagandizing requires extensive use of the mass media, which entails substantial costs. As a result, this tactic is pretty well restricted to those groups blessed with substantial material resources. Here again, business groups, given their financial resources, operate at an advantage. Business groups have propagandized on behalf of the

"Mr. Speaker, change my vote for 'aye' to 'nay'."
(Some legislators get cues from lobbyists in the gallery.)

state's right-to-work law and to have it included in any revised constitution; unions cannot afford an equal counterattack. Shell dredgers in Galveston Bay launched an intensive "save our jobs" radio and television campaign on behalf of their employees prior to the 1969 legislative session. Conservationist groups opposed to continued dredging bought no rebuttal time. The dredgers won. Publicity campaigns are frequently organized to promote large bond issues for cities, counties, port facilities, and so on. Contributions to these efforts usually come from industries and concerns, like the construction companies, that expect a share of the bond-financed work. In 1977 and 1978 oil companies in Texas conducted a vigorous campaign, using both paid and free media, against the national energy plan proposed by President Carter.

ELECTIONEERING

Interest groups often involve themselves in the electoral process. Organized groups have found they get more favorable responses from public officials they have helped elect to office. Organized labor in Texas has relied heavily on electioneering as a group tactic. Unions, with their large memberships and staffs, can offer candidates campaign workers as well as financial contributions. However, labor union influence is restricted largely to a minority of legislative districts that have substantial numbers of unionized workers. Business groups cannot match labor's manpower, but they can provide financial assistance and technical expertise in selected candidates' campaigns.

The electioneering rule is simple: Elect one's friends and defeat one's enemies. Of course, there are risks involved. Backing a loser does little to ingratiate a group with the winning candidate. Large economic interests sometimes avoid this problem by giving aid to competing candidates. Both John Tower and Robert Krueger, opponents in the 1978 U.S. Senate race, received financial support from the oil industry, though not in equal amounts.

There are legal restrictions on group involvement in Texas elections. Corporations and labor unions are both prohibited from contributing to political races, but this law has had limited practical effect. Business officers simply contribute as individuals to campaigns, and their companies find means of making up the deficit. Unions establish nonpartisan "political education" arms that collect money for "educational" purposes and use it to back candidates friendly to organized labor.

In the aftermath of Watergate, when there were several prosecutions and a great many more "voluntary" disclosures of illegal business contributions to candidates, many corporations have followed labor unions in setting up political action committees (PACs) to collect and distribute funds. A firm or professional association forms a PAC which then solicits contributions from stockholders (or members) and executives. The PAC then parcels out the money to favorite candidates. An October 1977 listing found 76 PACs in Texas with some $2 million collected for future political investment. The Texas Medical Association alone had a war chest of almost $200,000.[4]

Other groups besides business and labor engage in electioneering. Ethnic organizations, such as the Harris County Council of Organizations, a black group in Houston, often take sides in elections. Religious groups, veterans' organizations, and professional associations occasionally get involved in elections when they feel their group interests are specifically affected. There are a number of explicitly political organizations that endorse or condemn candidates according to their ideological coloration. Local chapters of the John Birch Society have led the fight against the fluoridation of drinking water in referenda held in several communities. And there are officially nonpartisan groups, like the League of Women Voters, that publicize the issues and candidates' positions in various elections.

LITIGATION

Americans have become a very litigious people. We have thousands of judges, hundreds of thousands of lawyers, and millions of pending lawsuits clogging a massive judicial system. Almost every important political dispute eventually ends up in the courts. The NAACP pioneered the national use of litigation to secure interest-group objectives by bringing a long series of challenges against segregation laws and practices in the various states. Following the national trend, Texas groups have increasingly turned to the courts to resolve political issues. Sometimes they win, as was the case with black-supported challenges to many aspects of the Texas election laws and with the feminist assault on the state statute restricting abortion rights of women. Sometimes they lose, as was the case with the Mexican-American challenge to the state's system of financing the public schools. Some issues remain in doubt, as illustrated by the numerous pending suits by taxpayers attacking state and local procedures for assessing property.

Seeking a solution to a political dispute via litigation has disadvantages. It usually takes time, some financial backing, legal expertise, and a reasonably good test case. But, there are notable advantages, particularly to groups that have standing in many constitutional areas (i.e., blacks), to groups that are unpopular (homosexuals, for example), or to groups that have already been rejected by nonjudicial decision makers in the political system.

UNORTHODOX TACTICS

Interest groups use tactics that are available to them. And what is available depends on the nature of the group and the context in which it is operating. Groups, such as the Texas Brewers Association, that possess ample material resources and enjoy access to elected political leaders are well suited for lobbying. Those that have high community standing and sufficient resources, as does the Texas Medical Association, many well rely on a media campaign to generate favorable public opinion. The Texas AFL-CIO invests its manpower in electioneering.

However, there are groups very much interested in policy outcomes and political decisions that do not enjoy abundant material

"The Beer Lobby is working overtime this Session."

resources, access to political leaders, high community standing, or considerable manpower. Their situation dictates the use of unconventional tactics. Some of these tactics strain the bounds of legality; others are clearly illegal.

Historically, extralegal or illegal tactics are not new in Texas politics. Populist farmers of the late nineteenth century sometimes resorted to violence against their visible enemies, the railroads and the banks. The various Ku Klux Klan organizations that appeared in Texas after the 1870s had few compunctions about breaking laws when it suited their purposes. Labor unions in Texas, as elsewhere, have relied on picketing, boycotts, and occasional violence in securing their position in the state.

In the 1960s reliance on unconventional political tactics increased in Texas, as in the rest of the country. Organizations or groups of college students, poor people, blacks, Mexican-Americans, and others often felt they could have no influence on state or local political decisions if they relied only on socially acceptable methods. So unorthodox means were utilized. Mothers of dependent children receiving welfare disrupted operations in county welfare offices around the state to protest a cutback in their monthly allocations. College students in Austin had to be forcibly removed from trees that were to be cut so a football stadium could be enlarged. Mexican-American high-school students in Crystal City staged a school walkout to dramatize opposition to school policies that favored the Anglo minority in the community. The Black Panther party in Houston announced it had "liberated" an area in the Third Ward ghetto and warned city police not to enter the section. This led to a confrontation with the police in which one Panther leader was killed and others were wounded.

As the above examples indicate, most of the groups using unorthodox tactics in the 1960s were on the liberal or left side of the political spectrum. In the 1970s the issues that galvanized these groups—the war in Vietnam, racial injustice, police repression—have faded or lost appeal, but the tactics remain with us. Their use, however, has spread across the political spectrum. Conservative Texas farmers, who in 1968 thought a "demonstrator" was a long-haired hippie on LSD, see nothing wrong with massing their tractors around the state capitol and hinting that violence may come unless their demands are met. Middle-class housewives who probably thought it disgraceful for President Nixon to be heckled by protesters carrying placards showing napalmed Vietnamese children, disrupted Jimmy Carter's 1976 campaign appearances in Texas while waving placards depicting aborted fetuses. Antipornography groups have, on occasion, shown scant respect for the "sacred property rights" of X-rated bookstore and moviehouse owners.

More groups are turning to political action in pursuit of their objectives, and they seem increasingly willing to use different methods to secure their goals.

STRATEGIC CONSIDERATIONS

Up to this point we have been concerned with the tactics or specific means groups rely on to accomplish their objectives. Some attention should be given to general considerations that underlie interest-group activity. Of particular importance is the question as to just where in the governmental system tactical effort is directed. The American political system is complex, with power being divided among overlapping local governments, a state government, and the federal government. Where a group concentrates its political effort depends in part on where it expects a favorable hearing. Texas business groups generally feel they enjoy maximum influence at the state and local levels and seek policy decisions at those points. Labor unions concentrate their resources on national, state, and local politics in that order. In the school integration battles of the last 20 years, black Texans have looked to the federal courts for relief; but their white antagonists have looked to local school boards for desegregation decisions. In the Rio Grande Valley labor dispute of the late 1960s, farm laborers hoped for involvement of the U.S. Congress; the growers were content to rest their case with state and local officials.

Abstract arguments about states' rights as opposed to centralized government must be weighed with these facts in mind. Those groups who expect favorable treatment at the state or local level proclaim loudly the benefits of decentralized government. But those who have received letter results from the federal government have no fear of centralized decision making.

THE IMPACT OF GROUP POLITICS IN TEXAS

The preceding sections should have convinced the reader that there are many political groups active in Texas and that they rely on a variety of methods to influence the political system. The important question remains: What difference do interest groups make in Texas politics? Would things be substantially different if such associations did not exist, did not enter the political arena? An answer can be sought in two ways. First, by looking at the specific impact groups have on particular decisions. Second, by assessing the overall effect of group activity on public policy in Texas.

In the first instance, one usually proceeds by examining the track record of lobbying groups because their activities are fairly visible. A problem here, as mentioned earlier, is that most groups are prone to exaggerate their own significance. For example, after the 1973 legislative session, Common Cause of Texas claimed credit for the enactment of a number of "reform" measures, including lobby-control legislation, campaign financial disclosure, an ethics bill, an open meetings law, and legislation providing for public access to governmental records. Given the mood of the legislature that year and the commitments of the speaker of the house, it is likely most of this legislation would have passed without the assistance of Common Cause. At the other end of the spectrum, the Texas Association of Business releases a list after each session of the bills it killed that were inimical to its members' interests. Again, most of these measures would have likely failed irrespective of specific lobby pressures.

Perhaps the best way to get a reading on the relative clout of specific groups in the legislative process is to see what transpires when there is a head-on collision between lobbies on an issue on which most legislators have not formed a prior opinion. An example of such a clash in the 1977 session was the slurry pipeline fight between the railroads and private utilities. The issue was whether the railroads would be forced to give the right-of-way to a pipeline from Colorado that would bring crushed coal, mixed with water, to power plants in Texas. Railroads currently haul this coal, and they would not voluntarily allow competing pipelines to cross their property. After one of the most spirited lobby efforts in recent years, the utilities prevailed over the railroad association. Other disputes in the session matched doctors against trial lawyers on the issue of limited damages from malpractice suits (the lawyers came out on top here) and the pro- and anti-ERA forces (the pros won).

Examining such cases can be instructive, but too close attention to detail can obscure the general role of interest groups in the state. The basic point to keep in mind is that *the generally conservative, status quo forces in Texas enjoy an overwhelming advantage in group politics*. These forces are rooted in the business and high-status associations of the state. They are highly organized, employ skilled political operatives, possess unrivaled financial resources, and have access to virtually all policymakers in state government.

These privileged groups do not have to contend with effective counterforces, given the weakness of organized labor and public interest associations. They are further advantaged because they are usually cast in the role of defending existing policy or practice. The American and Texas political systems, with their great complexity, favor those who want to block, rather than initiate, new policies. Established groups in Texas basically want to preserve the low tax-low service state, to keep economic regulation at a minimum, and to make sure that such regulation that is required continues to be in the best interests of those being regulated.

The success of these groups is reflected in the broad outlines of public policy in Texas. The cost of living for middle- and upper-income Texans is among the lowest in the country, primarily because of the favorable tax treatment such individuals receive. Comparative assessments usually rate Texas as one of the most hospitable states in the country for business and industry. This is reflected in facts such as more insurance companies are chartered in Texas than in any other state. Texas was also the last of the 50 states to establish a commission to regulate private utilities. That delay may have been no great loss since most of the already existing 200 boards or commissions in Texas have been "captured" by the industry they are supposed to regulate. An example of such is provided by the Railroad Commission, which has regulated the oil and gas industry since the 1930s. The Commission has always sought to maintain a close and friendly relationship with the industry. This is hardly surprising since it started its regulatory activities at the behest of oil and gas companies that wanted production controlled to prevent price fluctuations rather than in response to some general public need.

On the other side of the coin, Texas provides minimal public services for its poor, its unemployed, its injured, its mentally ill or retarded. For example, Texas ranked 25th in median income in 1976, but was 38th in per capita expenditures for public education and 45th in payments to families under the aid to dependent children program.[5] It is not accidental that the recipients of these services are not effectively organized to influence public policies.

CONCLUSIONS

Twenty years ago E. E. Schattschneider, a respected analyst of American politics, took issue with the pluralist view that all segments of the population in the United States are represented through interest group politics.

> The vice of the groupist theory is that it conceals the most significant aspects of the system. The flaw in the pluralist heaven is that the heavenly chorus sings with a strong upper-class accent. Probably about 90 percent of the people cannot get into the pressure system.[6]

The general tendencies Schattschneider pointed to are unusually manifest in Texas. Electoral participation is low in the state, and it, too, is biased toward upper-class and conservative interests. Political parties, organizations that Schattschneider thought were essential counters to the class bias of group politics, are weak in Texas. Nor is effective political power vested in the hands of elected public officials in the state.

What this adds up to is a situation that gives organized interests unusual influence. Political leaders must have support for themselves and their policies, and such support is most readily available in Texas from established economic interest groups. Public policy with regard to taxing and spending and apportioning the benefits of government have long reflected that reality and likely will continue to do so for the foreseeable future.

NOTES

[1]This thesis is fully developed in Mancur Olson, *The Logic of Collective Action* (Boston: Harvard University Press, 1965).

[2]A good discussion of this point can be found in Robert Salisbury's "An Exchange Theory of Interest Groups," *Midwest Journal of Political Science* 13 (February 1969): 1–32.

³For two journalistic surveys of the Austin lobby scene, see Lee Clark's "May the Lobby Hold You in the Palm of its Hand," *Texas Observer,* May 24, 1968, pp. 1–3; and the series of articles in the July 1973 edition of the *Texas Monthly* magazine.

⁴See Preston F. Kirk, "The '78 PAC Attack Shapes Up," *The Texas Observer,* December 2, 1977, pp. 10–14.

⁵The data on educational and welfare payments are from *The Book of the States* (Lexington, Kentucky: Council of State Governments, 1976), pp. 321, 386.

⁶E. E. Schattschneider, *The Semi-Sovereign People: A Realist's View of Democracy in America* (Hinsdale, Illinois: Dryden, 1975), pp. 34–35.

The State Legislature

Viewed from a traditional, legal perspective, the primary task of the legislature is to "legislate," to enact statutory laws governing the people and territory over which it has jurisdiction. It is more useful, however, to describe the primary task of the legislature as participation in the formation of public policy. This is so because the form and content of public policies depend not only on statutes passed by the legislature but also on actions by the governor, administrative agencies, and the courts. All help shape public policies, which are the actual courses of action followed by government on topics of concern, such as the regulation of petroleum production, the licensing of barbers, or the rights of the criminally accused. Moreover, there are also many unofficial participants in the policy-formation process, including political parties, pressure groups, the communications media, and private citizens.

In addition to policy formation, the Texas legislature may variously engage in a number of other activities. These include supervising the administrative agencies, approving gubernatorial appointments, conducting legislative investigations, impeaching or otherwise removing executive officials from office, proposing amendments to the state constitution and approving or disapproving amendments to the U.S. Constitution, and handling congressional districting within the state. When it is in session, most of the legislature's time and attention is devoted to policymaking activities, however.

Much has been written in recent years concerning the decline in importance of state legislatures and, concomitantly, the shift of initiative and power in legislative activity to the chief executive. It is indeed probably fair and accurate to depict the state governor, like the president, as playing the role of "chief legislator" in the legislative process. However, whatever the actual relationship between the governor and legislature in a given state, and whatever one might think the relationship should be, it is only the legislature that, in the final analysis, can enact laws or legislation. The governor and others can recommend and urge the enactment of new laws, taxes, or expenditures, but only the legislature can enact them into law, into legitimate and binding public policy. These generalizations are especially apt in Texas, where the legislature is widely regarded as being the dominant branch of state government.

The power to enact legislation is significant, especially when one recalls the discussion in Chapter 1 of the wide range of matters dealt with by the state. In 1975, for example, the Texas legislature enacted over 700 bills into law. Their subject matter ranged from the highly important (e.g., voter registration, strip-mining regulation, and the creation of a public utility commission) to minor changes in local government authority and modification of the quail hunting season in Refugio County.[1] What the legislature does (or does not do) is of much significance for the people of Texas.

LEGISLATIVE PERSONNEL

REPRESENTATION

The Constitution of 1876 set the maximum size of the Texas House of Representatives at 150 and the Texas Senate at 31, with the members to serve two-year and four-year terms, respectively. In comparison with other states, the Texas legislature appears about average in size. Membership of state senates ranges from 17 in Nevada to 67 in Minnesota, while the range for lower houses is from 35 in Delaware to 400 in New Hampshire.

Little is known conclusively concerning the significance of the size factor, but there is no shortage of theory regarding it: For example, a larger legislature will provide better representation of the people, a smaller legislature will be more efficient, and so on. A long-standing generalization in social science literature holds that the larger an organization or group, the more likely it is to be controlled or dominated by a few of its members. This seems borne out by the Texas legislature; most observers would agree that the House has been more tightly controlled than the Senate by a leadership group. In larger groups, relationships tend to become more formal and hierarchical.

The geographical district (an electoral unit based on the number of people living in a defined geographical area, such as a county or portion thereof) has been the standard device for selection of members of the Texas legislature. As in the rest of the nation, the belief (but not always the practice) has been that these districts should be roughly equal in population.[2] Such alternative schemes of representation as functional representation (whereby representatives are selected by specified social and economic groups) or proportional representation (whereby each political party gets legislative representation in ratio to its share of the total popular vote in an area) have never been used at the state level in the United States. In establishing geographical districts, Texas and the other states have usually followed the boundary lines of counties and other existing governmental units.

The Texas Constitution of 1876 stated that members of the House were to be elected from districts as nearly equal in population as possible. It also provided that senators were to be elected from districts having an equal number of qualified voters, with the limitation that no county could ever have more than one senator. In nineteenth-century Texas these rules, and practices thereunder, permitted substantial equality in representation on the basis of the "one man-one vote" criterion. But as the state increased in population and became more urbanized, the one-senator limit came to have a restrictive impact on populous counties. Then, in 1936 the constitution was amended to limit the number of representatives to the House from urban counties. No county could have more than seven representatives until its population reached 700,000; a county that exceeded that figure would receive one additional representative for each additional 100,000 population.

These constitutional limitations, legislative failure to redistrict after every federal decennial population census as required, and refusal of the legislature to provide as much equality under the rules as possible when it did act all resulted in substantial disparities in the populations of legislative districts. Thus, in 1961 the population of senatorial districts ranged from 157,000 to 1,243,000. The four most populous counties (Harris, Dallas, Bexar, and Tarrant) contained 35.7 percent of the state's population but elected only 4 senators, or 12.9 percent of the Senate. Another example: In accordance with the limitation on House representatives, Harris County had 12 representatives even though on a strict population basis it was entitled to 19. (Ideally, in 1961 each House member would have represented about 64,000 people, a figure obtained by dividing the state's population of 9,580,000 by 150.) In short, the situation was one of substantial inequality in legislative representation, with urban areas being under-represented and rural areas overrepresented—again using equal population size of districts, or the one man-one vote criterion, as the standard of judgment.

The Texas situation was not unique. Overrepresentation of rural areas was a nationwide phenomenon and indeed was much more severe in some other states, such as Florida and Georgia. In no state, it should be noted, were urban areas overrepresented. Many complaints were registered against this condition. It was argued that rural overrepresentation made state legislatures unresponsive to the problems and needs of urban areas, contributed to conservatism in public policy, gave an unfair electoral advantage to the political party or party faction dominant in rural areas, produced cynicism and distrust toward state government, and was generally unfair.[3] Those who benefited from rural overrepresentation were neither much disturbed by the situation nor convinced by the arguments levied against it. Redress would have required giving up some of their power, and those who possess power rarely yield it willingly.

For many years the efforts of those seeking to reform this situation were unavailing. In 1946 the U.S. Supreme Court held that legislative reapportionment was a "political issue" and hence was not something to be decided by the courts.[4] Other courts followed this lead, and the state legislatures were unwilling to act, being controlled by majorities that benefited from or approved of rural overrepresentation. Then, in 1962 a breakthrough occurred for the proponents of reform. The U.S. Supreme Court, in deciding a case entitled *Baker* v. *Carr,* overturned its 1946 rule and held that state legislative malapportionment raised an issue of equal protection (or treatment) of the laws under the Fourteenth Amendment and could properly be heard by the federal courts. (*Baker* v. *Carr* originated in Tennessee, where the state legislature had not been reapportioned since 1901 despite a constitutional provision requiring that it be done every ten years.[5])

As a consequence, many cases involving legislative malapportionment were rapidly brought to the federal courts. Two years later, in another case, the Court ruled that both houses of state legislatures had to be apportioned according to population (i.e., one man-one vote). The Court specifically rejected the federal analogy, or "little federal system," in which one house of the state legislature is based on population and the other on geographic units in the fashion of the U.S. Congress.

These decisions were brought home to Texas in 1965 in the case of *Kilgarlin* v. *Martin,* which originated in Harris County. A federal district court in Houston declared unconstitutional the provisions of the Texas Constitution that limit representation for urban areas, and the legislature was in effect directed to reapportion itself on a population basis. Its first effort at reapportionment in 1965 contained some substantial disparities in House districts and subsequently had to be revised in 1967 to meet constitutional requirements. (*Districting* refers to the drawing of the boundary lines of districts, while *apportionment* involves the allocation of representatives to districts. Although these terms are often used interchangeably with no great intellectual hurt, it is useful to keep in mind the two types of activity involved.)

Equality in representation has now become an established feature of the American constitutional system. It creates little controversy, unlike the situation of a decade ago.

REDISTRICTING IN THE 1970S: LAW AND POLITICS

In 1971 the legislature was confronted with the task of having to redistrict itself to reflect the population shifts revealed by the 1970 census. It is traditional for each house of the Texas legislature to redistrict itself without interference by the other. The Senate, for reasons that are not fully clear, never got around to redistricting itself before the 1971 legislative session was adjourned. The House redistricting was controlled by Speaker Gus Mutscher and his allies, who drew new district lines to the electoral disadvantage of as many members as possible of the "Dirty Thirty," a rather strange alliance of liberal Democrats, Republicans, and a few conservative Democrats who steadfastly opposed the speaker. The chairman of the House committee handling legislative redistricting was later quoted as saying that he had done his "dead-level best to eliminate liberal House members" and prevent reelection of many of the Dirty Thirty.[6] In the process many counties were split between legislative districts.

The House Redistricting Act of 1971 was immediately challenged in the state supreme court by some Republican party officials on the ground that it violated the Texas Constitution by unnecessarily dividing counties between legislative districts; their contention was upheld by the court.[7] Subsequently, the court ruled that new House districts would have to be drawn by the state Legislative Redistricting Board.[8]

As a consequence of the House's unconstitutional action and the Senate's inaction, redistricting of both houses became the responsibility of the Legislative Redistricting Board. Authorized by a constitutional amendment in 1949, the board is composed of the lieutenant governor, speaker of the house, attorney general, comptroller of public accounts, and commissioner of the general land office. If the legislature does not complete the task of redistricting in the first regular legislative session following the federal decennial population census, the board takes over the task. The year 1971 was the first in which action by the board was required; in 1951 and 1961 the mere threat of board action was apparently sufficient to produce legislative action.

The board, which was dominated in its proceedings by Lt. Gov. Ben Barnes, had little difficulty in producing a redistricting plan for the Senate. It protected the seats of most incumbent senators, a not uncommon practice in legislative redistricting. For the House, the board devised a plan providing for 11 multimember districts electing a total of 60 representatives and 90 single-member districts. Harris County was awarded single-member districts, as was demanded by most of the county's legislative delegation, while the other populous counties were given multimember districts.

Some words of explanation are in order here on the use of single-member and multimember districts. The members of the Senate have always been elected from single-member districts. The House used a combination of single-member and multimember districts, and in recent decades, as the state's population became concentrated in a few counties, it relied more heavily on multimember districts and the place system. In a multimember district a candidate runs for a particular seat, designated as Place 1, Place 2, and so on on the ballot, and each voter can vote for a candidate for each place in the district. To illustrate: Under the redistricting board's House plan, Dallas County, with its population of 1,327,321, was set up as a single district with 18 representatives (or one for each 74,645 persons, which was the ideal figure for a representative on the basis of the 1970 census). In the 1972 election Dallas County voters were entitled to vote for a candidate for each of the 18 seats (or places). The constituency of each representative was the entire county.

The use of multimember districts became increasingly controversial. Critics contended that multimember districts restricted electoral competition by necessitating large campaign expenditures and made districts so large that representatives could not be really responsive to their constituents. Further, the majority that elected one representative could elect all of them. This had the effect of denying representation to ethnic and political groups—blacks, Mexican-Americans, Republicans, liberal Democrats—who might be minorities on a countywide basis but would be majorities in some residential areas. The defenders of multimember districts contended that such districts promoted strong, united, civic-minded legislative delegations who would act for the good of the entire community. Moreover, single-member districts would polarize counties along racial lines.[9] In practice multimember districts favored the election of conservative Democrats, and they usually controlled the redistricting process, which became a source of political power.

The redistricting board's House plan was promptly challenged in the federal courts by Republicans, liberal Democrats, blacks, and Mexican-Americans on two grounds: (1) Multimember districts unconstitutionally discriminated against blacks and Mexican-Americans; the districts for Dallas and Bexar counties were especially criticized. (2) The deviation in population size was too great to be constitutional. With an ideal size of 74,645, districts ranged from 71,597 to 78,943 per representative, or from 5.8 percent overrepresentation to 4.1 percent underrepresentation. In January 1972 a three-judge federal district court agreed with both contentions, ordered single-member districts immediately for Dallas and Bexar counties, and directed the legislature to redistrict the entire House at its 1973 session.[10]

The state appealed the district court's ruling to the U.S. Supreme Court, which partly upheld and partly overruled the lower court.[11] The deviation in the population size of House districts was ruled not sufficient to make the redistricting unconstitutional because, in the Court's view, the constitutional standards for state legislature districts are not as strict as those for the U.S. Congress. (In another case, the Court upheld a districting scheme for Virginia that involved a population variance of 16 percent.[12]) The Court also said that multimember districts are not unconstitutional per se but must be shown to have a discriminatory effect. To sustain a claim of discrimination, it is not enough to show that the racial groups allegedly discriminated against do not hold legislative seats in proportion to their voting potential; rather, it is necessary to show that the potential process leading to nomination and election was not equally open to participation by particular racial groups. In sustaining the district court, the Supreme Court held that the lower court's order directing the abandonment of multimember districts for Dallas and Bexar counties was justified "in the light of the history of political discrimination against Negroes and Mexican-Americans residing, respectively, in those counties and the residual effects of such discrimination upon these groups."[13] The case was remanded to the federal district court for further action.

On the basis of the Supreme Court's decisions, single-member districts, as drawn by the federal district court, were in effect in Dallas and Bexar counties, as well as Harris County, for the 1972 elections. No action was taken concerning the constitutionality of multimember districts for the other nine counties, although the district court did retain jurisdiction over the matter.

The Texas legislature, in its 1973 session, took up the question of House redistricting but adjourned without taking any action. Conflict existed over what the legislature should do. Some especially wanted single-member districts for Tarrant County (Fort Worth), which—with a nine-member House delegation—seemed especially likely to be the subject of future court action; others wanted single-member districts on a statewide basis. Liberals were not strongly in favor of legislative action, believing that redistricting would be more in accord with their interests if done by the judiciary. As a consequence of the legislature's inaction, the judicial proceedings concerning the constitutionality of multimember districts were pushed toward completion. In January 1974 the federal district court ruled that multimember districts for Tarrant, Jefferson, Travis, El Paso, Neuces, Lubbock, and McLennan counties were unconstitutional because they discriminated against the electoral opportunities of minorities.[14] Multimember districts were upheld for Galveston and Hidalgo counties, each with two representatives, on the ground that sufficient evidence of discrimination had not been presented. Single-member districts for the seven aforementioned counties were prescribed for the 1974 elections. However, their implementation was suspended, on request of the Texas attorney general, pending appeal of the case to the U.S. Supreme Court. Before the court proceedings were completed, the Texas legislature in 1975 enacted a law providing single-member districts for all 150 house members. Although multimember districts still exist in some other states, they are a thing of the past in Texas.

As noted earlier, many contentions have been made concerning the impact of rural overrepresentation and multimember districts on state politics. What, now, have been the consequences of reapportionment in line with the one man-one vote criterion and the institution of single-member districts? One clear result is that urban counties now have more legislative representation than they had under the old system. Harris County, for example, now has 5 senators rather than one and 24 representatives rather than 13, as would have been the case under the old rules. Second, representation has been brought into line with the ethical standard of equality of representation by population, which many people have regarded as proper and desirable in itself, regardless of other effects. Third, single-member districts in large counties have contributed to the election of more black, Mexican-American, and Republican representatives. Those districts are the primary reason, for example, for the increase in black representatives from 2 in 1971 to 14 in 1979. Fourth, in populous counties, single-member districts have contributed to increased electoral competition, both in primary and general elections.[15] Fifth, so far as the nature of public policy is concerned, no drastic changes from past practices and policies appear to have been made by the legislature since 1967. Some before-and-after studies are needed to indicate with some precision what, if anything, has changed. It is our impression, however, that as of now the legislature has not become markedly more responsive to urban needs and problems.

MEMBERSHIP

The formal constitutional qualifications for membership in the legislature can be easily stated. To be eligible for the Texas House, one must be 21 years of age, a citizen, and a resident of his or her district for one year and the state for two years. For the Texas Senate, the standards are 26 years of age, citizenship, and one year of residence in the district and five years in the state. These are only the formal, minimal qualifications for legislative office, and few would contend that all who meet them really have an equal chance to be elected to the legislature. Many are eliminated by the unstated, informal qualifications that also exist. One formulation categorizes these informal qualifications under the headings of motivation, resources, and opportunity.[16] Some will in effect be disqualified because they are not motivated to seek a legislative seat, being uninterested in politics, unwilling to campaign for elective office, or whatever. Others who may be motivated may lack such necessary resources as money, time, or knowledge to realistically campaign for office. Still others may lack a meaningful opportunity to seek legislative office because of their socioeconomic characterisitcs. In many districts a person's race, sex, religion, or party affiliation may effectively disqualify him or her. For example, persons who are Republicans and who run for office as Republicans still operate at a decided disadvantage in most areas of the state, although change is occurring. Racial barriers severely limit the opportunity for blacks to gain office, and many people still do not regard politics as a proper sphere for women.

In respect to socioeconomic characteristics, the "typical" Texas legislator, like his counterpart in many other states, is a male, white, Anglo-Saxon Protestant—or WASP, to use the popular acronym. In 1979, of 181 members of the legislature, there were only 13 women, 14 blacks, and 17 Mexican-Americans. Twenty-six members were Republicans, which represented a substantial increase in their numbers from recent years. Over four-fifths were Protestants, and most were native-born Texans. Occupationally, lawyers were the largest group (68 percent in the Senate, 36 percent in the House), followed by businessmen (including insurance and real estate men) and farmers and ranchers. Industrial workers and union officials were scarce. Most of the legislators were between 30 and 45 years of age, with comparatively few under 30 or over 60. Most were also college graduates, with only a handful never having attended college.

What is the significance of all this? For one thing, it indicates that the legislature is clearly not comprised of a cross section of the state's population. Such groups as whites, Protestants, and higher socioeconomic-status persons are overrepresented in proportion to their numbers in society, while such groups as Catholics, blacks, women, and working-class people are underrepresented. Second, the data indicate that there are indeed informal qualifications for office. Other things being equal, a Texas-born, white, college-educated lawyer has a better chance of being elected to the legislature than does, for instance, a person born outside the state who has a high-school education and is employed in a factory. If he or she is a black or Mexican-American, the chances diminish even further. Third, the composition of its members probably helps give a broadly conservative orientation to the legislature. Most legislators are "successful" according to existing social standards and have a "stake" in existing social and economic structures. Consequently, they are indisposed toward making sweeping or radical changes in the existing order of things.

There has often been a substantial turnover in the membership of the legislature from one session to another. This has been a persistent characteristic of most state legislatures. On the average, in a given session of the Texas state legislature a quarter to a third of the members will be serving their first term. The rate of turnover has usually been lower in the Texas Senate than in the Texas House, perhaps because of the longer term of office and greater prestige of Senate service, and because many representatives view a House seat as a preliminary step toward another office.

The tenure (length of service) of members is fairly short, as the rate of turnover would lead one to predict. In a given session of the legislature, most members will have served six years or less, although senators tend to serve longer than representatives. In 1979 only a small fraction of the legislators had served ten years or longer. An exceptional case was Sen. A. M. Aikin, Jr., of Paris, who served continuously in the legislature from 1933 until he retired in 1978.

Partly as a consequence of rather rapid turnover and short tenure, many members of the legislature may be viewed as "amateurs." They lack the experience in the complexities of legislative procedure and in the rough-and-tumble of legislative politics and the knowledge of legislative issues—all of which often comes with continued service. This general condition probably serves to strengthen the position of the elected leadership, especially in the House, and of lobbyists, who are often more knowledgeable concerning both procedure and policy matters.

LEGISLATIVE STRUCTURE

SESSIONS AND COMPENSATION

The state constitution provides that the legislature shall meet in a regular biennial session, to last no longer than 140 calendar days, beginning on the second Tuesday in January in odd-numbered years. A particular legislature runs for a term of two years. Since Texas entered the Union, these terms have been numbered consecutively; thus, the legislature organized for the two-year term beginning in January 1977 was officially designated as the "Sixty-fifth Legislature."

Until the last decades of the nineteenth century, annual legislative sessions were the rule in the American states. However, growing public distrust of and dissatisfaction with the legislatures, which is well chronicled in histories of the late nineteenth and early twentieth centuries, led to the imposition of limits on the length and frequency of their sessions.[17] A common notion was that the less the legislature was in session, the less damage to the public welfare it could cause. A cynical definition of an "honest" politician during this era held that he was one who, once bought, stayed bought. By the mid-1940s only four states had annual legislative sessions. Since then the pendulum has swung in the opposite direction and now over 40 states have annual sessions, although many continue to regulate their length. Constitutional amendments authorizing annual sessions for the Texas legislature were defeated soundly by the voters in 1969 and 1972, however. Some assert that the legislature cannot deal adequately with the state's needs and problems on a limited, biennial basis; but others argue that it indeed can and, further, that annual sessions would lead to unnecessary legislation and increased costs for operating the legislature.

In addition to the regular biennial sessions, the legislature can be called into any number of special sessions, each limited to 30 days, by the governor. During special sessions the legislature may consider only legislation relating to topics specified by the governor. A total of 26 special sessions have been called during 16 of the 24 biennial terms of the legislature since 1930. Many take this as evidence that the legislature cannot adequately perform its work on a biennial basis.

The salaries of legislators in Texas are fixed in the constitution and traditionally have been low. A constitutional amendment adopted in 1975 raised salaries to $7200 annually (up from $4800). Legislators also receive an expense allowance of $30 a day for the first 120 days of a regular session and for the entire length of special sessions. Comparatively, among large urban states, Texas legislative salaries rank low. In 1977 California and New York had full-time legislators who earned annual salaries of $32,000 and $28,000, respectively.

A number of expense allowances in addition to the per diem allowance are available to legislators. These include a mileage allowance of 16 cents per mile for traveling to and from the capital, an allowance during sessions for secretarial assistance and contingencies (postage, stationery, telephone service, etc.), and interim expenses for when the legislature is not in session. During the 1977 regular session, for example, House members received $4000 per month for staff salaries and office expenses. Senators received $6500 per month for staff salaries; the limit on their office expenses was anything "reasonable and necessary." Except for the per diem, these allowances are set by the members of the two houses.

LEGISLATIVE LEADERS

The principal leaders in the legislature are the presiding officers of the two houses: the speaker of the house and the lieutenant governor. Although they are selected in quite different ways, each has available a substantial range of formal powers and informal means by which he can seek to control and direct the actions of his respective house. Included among their formal powers, which—it should be emphasized—are derived from rules adopted by a majority of each house, are the following:

1. Appointment of members to standing, special, and interim committees and designation of their chairpersons.
2. Appointment of members to conference committees.
3. Acting as presiding officers, which includes interpretation of their house's rules and decision of points of order, recognition of members who want to speak on the floor, the putting of motions to a vote and deciding voice votes, and so on.
4. Referral of bills to committees, which is especially significant when a bill comes within the jurisdiction of two or more committees.
5. Participation in debate and, for the speaker, voting on issues; the lieutenant governor can vote only in case of ties.
6. Substantial control of the agendas of their houses, that is, determination of what matters will be considered when, if at all.

These two leaders also benefit from the prestige attached to the positions they hold. Although they do derive much influence from their official positions, their influence also depends importantly on how skillfully they use their formal powers, their ability to bargain with and persuade both influential and rank-and-file members, the confidence they are able to evoke in their leadership, and the ideological composition of their respective houses. The last item is especially important for the lieutenant governor. A conservative lieutenant governor will undoubtedly have more influence and power if he is dealing with a conservative rather than a liberal majority. During the last two decades, a period during which much has been written about the power of the lieutenant governor, this condition has prevailed. During the 1973 legislative session, Lt. Gov. William Hobby, Jr., elected the previous fall as a reform candidate, early developed a close relationship with the veteran, mostly conservative, senators who dominated the Senate. Among other things, this helped him protect his formal powers against an effort at reduction by some liberal senators.

The lieutenant governor is elected by the voters in a statewide election for a four-year term (as of 1974). Most lieutenant governors have served in the Senate prior to their election, Hobby being a recent exception. Historically, the lieutenant governor has not always been an influential legislative leader. Prof. J. William Davis, a careful student of the office, states: "A weak lieutenant governor was anticipated by the framers of the Texas Constitution. . . ."[18] Even as late as the 1930s it was considered a position of honor and prestige but not one of power and influence. During the 1940s and 1950s the office was transformed into one of substantial power, especially during the tenures of Allen Shivers and Ben Ramsey, although the processes by which this happened remain unexplained. Thus, the Texas lieutenant governor stands in sharp contrast to the vice-president at the national level. Neither official is elected by or is formally a member of the body over which he presides. However, while the lieutenant governor has become an influential legislative leader, the vice-president is still essentially an outsider who has little impact on the operation of the U.S. Senate.

The speaker of the house is elected by the members of the Texas House at the beginning of each biennial session by majority vote on a secret ballot. The formal election of the speaker is the culmination of a lengthy campaign for the speakership and may only ratify what has already been determined by informal means. In 1969, for example, Rep. Gus Mutscher had clearly lined up enough votes to win the speakership before the session met. The other candidates had no real chance to be elected. In 1972, however, when Rayford Price was elected speaker at a special session following the resignation of Mutscher, the issue was in doubt until the formal House vote was taken.

Campaigns for the speakership usually begin at least two years before the time a candidate hopes to be elected and involve the expenditure of much time and many thousands of dollars. In the session preceding the one in which election will occur, candidates begin trying to obtain pledges of support from the present legislators. Since some of the legislators will not be in the legislature two years hence, speaker candidates may also involve themselves in the primary and general-election campaigns, seeking to help candidates favorable to their position to get elected and perhaps aiding the opposition of those who are unfavorable. The governor, lobbyists, pressure groups, and other political actors also become involved in the speakership contest because their political fortunes may be affected significantly by who is elected speaker. The important role played by the speaker in shaping House legislative action makes it clearly desirable to have a friend rather than an opponent in this position. It is not altruism that makes the lobby a major source of campaign funds for speaker candidates. Most persons selected as speaker since 1959 have served two terms.

Apart from the speaker and lieutenant governor, there are no other formally elected or designated leaders in the legislature. In each house, the presiding officer does have some trusted lieutenants—often referred to as "the team" or, less elegantly, "cronies"—who assist him in his leadership role, as well as a number of staff aides. Several representatives act as floor leaders for the speaker, helping to insure that things happen on the floor when the speaker wants them to happen (e.g., a motion being made at a propitious time or information being conveyed to the speaker's supporters as to his position on a given issue) and to line up votes in support of the speaker's position. In both the House and Senate, the chairmen of the powerful State Affairs committees will be close to the leadership, as will some of the other more influential committee chairmen.

THE COMMITTEE SYSTEM

Much of the work of the Texas legislature is done by the permanent standing committees in the House and Senate. On the basis of reform rules adopted in 1972 and 1973, the number of Senate committees was reduced from 27 to 9 and the number of House committees from 46 to 21. In 1975, however, speaker Bill Clayton increased the number of House committees to 28. About a third of the committees in each house have permanent subcommittees. The committees in existence during the Sixty-third Legislature are listed in Table 5.1.

The size of House committees is set by the House rules, with most committees having 11 to 15 members. In the Senate, committee size is left to the discretion of the lieutenant governor when he makes his appointments. Their size ranged from 7 to 13 in 1977. Along with the reduction in the number of committees came a reduction in the number of committee assignments for legislators. House members are limited to assignment on 2 committees. Senators were limited to 3 committee assignments and no more than one chairmanship each in 1977. This represents a considerable reduction from the average in 1971 of 5 committee assignments for House members and 11 for Senate members, which was criticized frequently as an impossibly large work load. It is not possible to say whether the reduction in committee work load has produced more careful and thorough committee action on legislation, but it is reasonable to assume that it should facilitate that end. A

TABLE 5.1 • TEXAS LEGISLATIVE COMMITTEES, 1977

House Committees		Senate Committees	
Agricultural and Livestock	(11)	Administration	(7)
Appropriations	(21)	Economic Development	(7)
Business and Industry	(11)	Education	(9)
Calendars	(9)	Finance	(13)
Constitutional Amendments	(9)	Human Resources	(11)
Criminal Jurisprudence	(11)	Intergovernmental Relations	(9)
Elections	(11)	Jurisprudence	(13)
Energy Resources	(11)	Natural Resources	(11)
Environmental Affairs	(11)	State Affairs	(13)
Financial Institutions	(9)		
Health and Welfare	(13)		
Higher Education	(11)		
House Administration	(9)		
Insurance	(11)		
Intergovernmental Affairs	(13)		
Judicial Affairs	(11)		
Judiciary	(11)		
Labor	(9)		
Liquor Regulation	(9)		
Local and Consent Calendars	(9)		
Natural Resources	(11)		
Public Education	(11)		
Regions, Compacts, and Districts	(9)		
Rules	(9)		
Social Services	(9)		
State Affairs	(15)		
Transportation	(13)		
Ways and Means	(13)		

The numbers in parentheses indicate the numbers of committee members in 1977.

fact to be kept in mind is that some committees have a heavier work load than do others.

In making committee assignments, the presiding officers and their top aides may take a variety of factors into consideration: for example, whether the legislator is a friend or supporter of the presiding officer, the preferences for assignments expressed by the legislator and perhaps his position on major issues that may come before the legislature, whether the legislator is of the same ideological bent (liberal or conservative) as the presiding officer, the legislator's preferences and support or opposition of lobbyists, the desire to maintain a geographical or rural-urban balance in assignments and provide ethnic-minority representation, and the apparent willingness of the legislator to cooperate with the presiding officer and his team. Experience indicates that a legislator who is a trusted friend or supporter of the presiding officer, and who shares his ideological leanings, is likely to fare much better in getting desired committee assignments or chairmanships than is the legislator who does not. Thus, in 1969 and 1971 Speaker Gus Mutscher, a conservative, appointed conservatives as chairmen of nearly all the committees and largely ignored liberals, who constituted a substantial minority of House members. By contrast, in 1973 Price Daniel, Jr., distributed committee chairmanships fairly evenly among liberals and conservatives and, on the whole, was evenhanded in making committee assignments. In the 1973 Senate, dominated by conservatives, most committee chairmanships went to conservatives.

In 1973 the House adopted rules which provided for a limited seniority system. Under this system, up to half of the members of most committees are selected on the basis of seniority (years of cumulative service in the House). At the beginning of a regular session, in order of seniority, each representative selects a preferred committee. If half of the committee positions have not already been filled by seniority, the representative gets a place on the committee. This continues until each member has picked a committee. The remainder of the positions on the committees, including the chairmen and vice-chairmen, are appointed by the speaker. Exempted from the seniority system are the Local and Consent Calendars, House Administration, and Rules Committees; all their members are appointed by the speaker. These four committees are important internal legislative management committees, control of which helps the speaker control the House. There is no seniority rule in the Senate.

From one session of the legislature to another, there has been a substantial turnover of both committee members and chairmen, even when they are reelected; in the U.S. Congress, by contrast, the seniority system provides much stability in committee membership. Instructive here are the findings of Prof. William Oden concerning assignments to nine important Texas House committees and eight important Texas Senate committees during the six sessions meeting from 1947 through 1957. In the House, "70 percent of the committee members had no previous experience on that committee, while 22 percent had one previous experience [or term] on that committee." In the Senate, "35 percent . . . had no previous assignment on the committee while 31 percent of them had had only one previous experience on that committee."[19] The situation does not appear to have changed greatly since Oden's study. Thus, Melvin Hairell found that 70 percent of the members of all committees, for the 1959–1969 period, had no previous experience on their committees.[20] Committee chairmen are more likely to have had previous experience on the committees they chair, and Senate chairmen are more likely to be experienced than are House chairmen. For the 1959–1969 period, 47.5 percent of the House chairmen had no prior experience on their committees.[21] Whether greater continuity in committee membership develops as a consequence of the reduced number of committees remains to be seen.

The various House and Senate committees differ significantly in terms of their importance, prestige, and legislative work loads. Some, such as the State Affairs, Appropriations, Finance, and Ways and Means committees, are powerful and prestigious, handling most of the important legislation coming before the legislature. Others, such as the House Agriculture and Livestock, Liquor Regulation, and Transportation committees, handle few bills and rank low in prestige. In 1973 four House committees (judiciary, intergovernmental affairs, state affairs, and education) handled over 52 percent of all bills dealt with by the House.[22]

Although some committees are not very important in the handling of legislation, they may still serve useful purposes when viewed from other perspectives. A committee chairmanship or vice-chairmanship, even of a relatively inactive committee, may be desired by members for prestige and to aid their reelection. From the leadership's point of view, committee assignments and chairmanships are, to use Odom's phrase, "coins of the political realm" that can be used in promoting its programs. Lesser committees may be used as "dumping grounds" for those out of favor with the leadership.

The fate of bills introduced in the legislature depends greatly on the committees and their chairmen. The committee chairmen have significant power over the operation of their committees, including the appointment of subcommittees (except permanent Senate subcommittees, whose members are designated by the lieutenant governor), the conduct of committee meetings, determination of the committee agenda and whether public hearings will be held on bills, referral of bills to committee, and selection of the committee staff. The power exercised by chairmen over their committees is what makes their selection such an important prerogative of the leadership. In exercising their power, chairmen have customarily been responsive to the leadership; an indication by the speaker to a committee chairman that he wants a particular bill killed, for example, usually is sufficient to cause it to be forgotten in a subcommittee. In 1977, speaker Bill Clayton chose not to reappoint Rep. Craig Washington as chairman of the Criminal Jurisprudence committee because of his opposition to the speaker's position on anticrime legislation.

All bills are referred to a committee following introduction, and there they are discussed, evaluated, amended, sent to the floor for action, or killed. Much of the deliberative work on legislation is done by the committees, floor action often being perfunctory. Of course, committee action on bills may also be perfunctory, with only a few minutes, or less, being spent in consideration of some bills. The committee system permits a division of legislative work and should facilitate the development of specialization so that the legislature will have its own policy experts or specialists to handle the various types of legislation that come before it. Also, it is obviously not physically or intellectually possible for each member of the legislature, or the legislature as a whole, to fully examine and master the hundreds of bills considered in a single session.

Although the Texas committee system provides for a division of legislative work, it is conjecturable as to what extent it actually does provide the legislature with policy experts or specialists. The short duration of legislative sessions, the lack of professional staff assistance for most committees, and the rather large turnover of members all work against the growth of expertise. Consequently, the Texas legislative committees lack the expertness and influence of their counterparts in the U.S. Congress. Their lack of expertness, the high turnover of members, appointment by the presiding officers, and the lack of a seniority system also prevent them from becoming independent sources of power in the legislature. To put it another way, the committee system does not disperse and decentralize political power, as does the committee system in Congress.

LEGISLATIVE AIDS AND ASSISTANTS

The modern legislator is harried for time, confronted by a variety of demands and pressures, and faced with the task of having to consider, make sense of, and vote on hundreds of issues, many of which are quite complex or technical. If he is to act somewhat rationally, he sorely needs information, advice, and assistance in the performance of his duties. Some sources of assistance for Texas legislators are surveyed in this section.

Personal and committee staffs. Each legislator is given funds for hiring a personal staff. Although much of a staff's time is devoted to secretarial and clerical work (e.g., handling mail from constituents), many legislators do have assistants to help them keep track of legislation, brief bills, research particular problems, and perform other duties related to the business of legislating. Because such jobs are often of a part-time nature, given the legislature's limited sessions, they tend not to attract really professional people or afford good opportunities for professional development. Many legislators draw on the student body of the University of Texas, especially the Law School, for staff assistance.

Since 1975 a loosely knit coalition of several dozen representatives (mostly liberals) known as the House Study Group has existed. Members have pooled some of their expense money to hire staff to analyze legislation and thereby increase their legislative effectiveness. Some Study Group members, however, believe that the group's staff has been too active in lobbying against what the staff considered bad legislation. This also caused some consternation among the House leadership, who had the House rules rewritten in an effort to curb such lobbying activity.

Most of the committees have clerks but not professional staffs, that is, staff members who have special knowledge or skill in particular substantive policy areas. (Notable exceptions are the House Appropriations and Senate Finance committees, which receive assistance from the staff of the Legislative Budget Board, and the House Committee on Revenue and Taxation, which draws on the staff of the Texas Research League, a private, business-supported organization.) Thus, the average legislator can expect little aid from his committees in the performance of his duties. The committees' lack of professional staff is probably another factor reducing their legislative importance in that it deprives the committees of the power that staff knowledge and expertness could bring to their dealings with lobbyists, administrators, and others.

The Texas Legislative Council. Created by legislation in 1949, this council is headed by a joint committee of ten representatives and five senators; the speaker of the House and lieutenant governor, who appoint the members from their respective houses, serve ex officio. The lieutenant governor serves as chairman of the council, which has a full-time executive director, a research staff, and an annual budget of several hundred thousand dollars. The council's principal purpose is to conduct studies of public problems, prepare reports thereon, and make pertinent legislative recommendations. In recent years the council has studied such topics as constitutional revision, local legislation, county government, municipal annexation, juvenile delinquency, and state insurance laws. In addition to its research activity, its staff does much of the drafting of bills and resolutions for legislators. Also, for a few years now the council has conducted a short orientation program for new legislators to help inform them on such matters as legislative organization and procedure.

The Legislature Reference Library. Perhaps the major task of this library is to maintain an up-to-date, computerized legislative history of all bills and resolutions introduced in the legislature. Run by a professional library staff, it also maintains a large collection of state documents and other materials pertinent to the legislative process. Although the library is an invaluable source of information, it should be emphasized that it is primarily a place in which to do research rather than a source of research assistance, producing studies of public problems for harried legislators.

The Legislative Budget Board. This board is given detailed consideration in Chapter 10. Composed jointly of members from the House and Senate, the board, with the assistance of a full-time director and staff, prepares a state budget for legislative consideration. It also is authorized to make evaluations of state programs. During sessions, members of the board's staff serve as the staffs of the legislative appropriations committees.

Interim committees. During each legislative session, many interim committees, to consist of a few House and Senate members, are authorized at the behest of legislators. These interim committees (so named because they meet between legislative sessions) are set up to investigate particular policy problems on matters of legislative concern, for example, tax-exempt charitable foundations, the vending machine business, public school financing, and water districts. The House in 1977 authorized 139 interim studies to be conducted by its 28 committees, such as a study by the Energy Resources Committee of possible legislative remedies "should the federal government enact energy measures particularly punitive to Texas."

Interim committee studies can be a fruitful source of information on public problems, and they have on occasion recommended important legislation.[23] For example, the legislature in 1969 passed a series of antipollution bills recommended by an interim committee on land use and environmental control. The attention of an interim committee may also be a means of keeping an unsuccessful piece of legislation "alive" from one session to another. Nonetheless, the usefulness of these committees is limited by inadequate planning of their activities, insufficient staff assistance, and poor attendance by members (who do receive travel and per diem expenses when attending committee meetings). Some committees seem to be largely a means for the political advancement of individual legislators or, as some allege, an excuse to be in places like Austin and College Station on football weekends.[24] The validity of the latter allegation is in dispute, especially by legislators.

LEGISLATIVE PARTICIPANTS AND THEIR INFLUENCE

In addition to those officially elected as legislators, there are many other participants in the legislative process. Although the formal power of decisions on proposed legislation resides with the legislators and the governor by virtue of his veto power, various individuals and groups interact with and seek to influence or control legislative decision making. They provide advice and information, exert pressure, and otherwise seek to influence the conversion of demands into policy outputs. Collectively, the legislators plus these individuals and groups comprise the legislative system. While it is impossible to state precisely how much impact particular groups or participants may have, we can at least indicate their patterns of activity.

POLITICAL PARTIES

Because of the almost total domination of the Texas legislature by the Democratic party until the 1970s, party influence in the legislative process has been practically nil. It is difficult to be partisan when there are few, if any, persons against whom to be partisan. This situation is beginning to change as the number of Republicans increases, especially in the House. In 1969 there were 2 Republicans in the Senate and 7 in the House; in 1979 there were 4 in the Senate and 22 in the House. Currently, neither house is organized along party lines, although in 1973 the House Republicans did operate generally as a cohesive voting bloc. In 1977 the House Republicans operated as part of the Coalition supporting Speaker Clayton and two Republicans chaired House committees. Partisanship was avoided because, as one Republican representative put it: "anything smacking of partisanship might land us right back where we were under Gus Mutscher and his predecessors: junior members of the Poet Laureate selection committee, not even able (in the Texas legislative idiom) to pass gas."[25] If the Republicans really mean what they say concerning the desirability of two-party politics in Texas, they cannot continue to avoid partisan organization and action in the legislature.

To date, the absence of meaningful party organizations and partisanship in the legislature has probably had the effect of increasing the impact of pressure groups in the legislative process. In one-party systems the party loyalties and influences that would compete with and lessen the influence of pressure groups are largely nonexistent, leaving groups with a more hospitable context in which to operate.

There are liberal and conservative factions within the Democratic party, with most legislators being identified with one or the other.

Since 1950 the conservative faction has been dominant, except in the Senate, for a couple of sessions; its ratio of strength has varied from two-to-one to three-to-two. These factions are rather loose and amorphous, however, and tend to lack continuity and leadership. Moreover, many issues that come before the legislature do not lend themselves to liberal-conservative conflicts: for example, liquor regulation (where wets and drys struggle), highway construction, fish and game regulation, and most local legislation. Factional alignments are most likely to be visible and important on such matters as taxation, civil rights, welfare, and labor legislation. Even on these, the individual legislator may be influenced by gubernatorial pressure, constituency interests, public opinion, or the leadership of his house to vote other than his ideological orientation would indicate. Factionalism, in short, appears important on only a portion of the legislation considered in a session, albeit an important portion, and even then it may be only one of many factors that help shape the legislator's voting decision.

Nonideological factions may also develop, perhaps forming around a major issue or in opposition to the leadership. An illustration of the first is a grouping known as the "Immortal 56," which blocked the enactment of a sales tax in the early 1940s. The Dirty Thirty of 1971, held together by its distaste for and opposition to the heavy-handed leadership of Speaker Mutscher and his team, is an example of the second (see p. 108). Each displayed considerable unity in voting.

THE GOVERNOR

The twentieth-century Texas governor has become an important source of major policy proposals and initiative in the legislative process. What he recommends will usually receive serious consideration and what he opposes will often not be enacted. Although the Texas legislature clearly does not serve as a rubber stamp for gubernatorial initiatives, legislators are typically concerned to know the governor's position on major issues (if, one must add, he has one). This is one clue they can use in assessing the importance of legislation and evaluating the support or opposition for it.

His formal powers better equip the governor to act as legislative leader than as chief executive. Further, the public's evaluation of him depends more on his successes and failures in the legislative arena than on his skill or finesse as an administrator. Both the public and the legislature have come to expect him to lead; this is part of his official role. He possesses a variety of tools for leadership, some authorized by the constitution, others informal in origin.

The constitution authorizes the governor to send messages to the legislature recommending the enactment of legislation. His "State of the State" message at the opening of a regular legislative session is customarily delivered in person to a joint meeting of the two houses and is well reported by the press. In this message the governor appraises the problems confronting the state and recommends a general program for dealing with them. The details of his program will subsequently be spelled out in written messages sent to the legislature as the session moves along. The impact of these messages will depend on such factors as the popularity of the governor, the timeliness and political acceptability of the messages, the governor's relationship with the legislative leadership, and the skill and effort with which he works for their adoption. One of the most prolific users of the message power was Gov. W. Lee (Pappy) O'Daniel (1939–1941).[26] He enjoyed comparatively little success, however, because of sharp political differences between him and the legislature. Prof. Fred Gantt, Jr., has commented that, over the years, "Results would seem to indicate that the legislature resents too frequent a display of 'gubernatorial influence' through exercise of the message power."[27]

The constitution also empowers the governor to call special sessions of the legislature. Each special session is limited to 30 days' duration, but the governor can call as many as he wishes. The governor's influence is enhanced during special sessions, as the legislature can consider legislation only on topics he specifies. The legislature does possess all of its other powers during these sessions. In fact, it was during a special session called in 1917 to deal with appropriations for the University of Texas that the legislature impeached, convicted, and removed Gov. James E. ("Pa") Ferguson from office.

The items most frequently specified for consideration by special sessions include appropriations, taxation and revenue, education, and liquor regulation.[28] A call for a special session, after indicating the main tasks for which the session is being called, usually includes as a final item "to consider and act on such subjects and questions as the governor may submit from time to time." This open-ended item lays the basis for bargaining by the governor with the legislature. He may seek to win support for measures on which he wants action in turn for agreeing to open the session for consideration of matters of interest to legislators. Variations in the use of this power are illustrated by Gov. Price Daniel, who called eight special sessions during six years in office, and Gov. Dolph Briscoe, who called two special sessions during an equal period in office. In 1959, following the regular session, Governor Daniel called three consecutive special sessions and kept the legislature in Austin the entire summer before it was induced to pass a tax bill to meet a large budget deficit.

The governor also has the veto power. The constitution provides that before any bill passed by the legislature can become law it must be submitted to him for consideration and approval. While the legislature is in session, the governor has 10 days after he receives a bill in which to exercise his veto. If a bill comes to him during the last 10 days of a session or after the legislature has adjourned, he has 20 days in which to take action. In either instance he must take action if he wants to veto a bill; otherwise it will become law without his signature. The governor has no pocket veto, as does the president. If the veto power is exercised while the legislature is in session, the governor must return the bill—along with a veto message setting forth his objections—to the house that first passed it. If the bill is repassed by a two-thirds vote in each house, the governor's veto is overridden and the bill becomes law. Of course, when the legislature has adjourned before the governor acts, his veto is absolute because there is no opportunity for the legislature to reconsider. This is when a large portion of the bills passed by the legislature reach him.

In practice, however, the governor's veto in recent decades has been final, no matter at what point it is exercised. During the long period from 1876 through 1968, only 25 out of a total of 936 vetoes (or less than 3 percent) were overridden by the legislature. Moreover, not since 1941 has the legislature overcome a veto.[29] Among the reasons given for vetoes are that the bills in question were against public policy, uneconomical, unconstitutional, unnecessary, and defectively worded. Cutting through the verbiage, this essentially means that the governor disagrees with the judgment of the legislature.

Included in the veto power are the item veto and the threat to veto. On appropriations bills, the governor can veto particular items while accepting most of the bill's provisions. This serves to enhance his power in the area of finances. Probably at least as important as the actual use of the veto is the potentiality of the threat of a veto. The enactment of some bills can be prevented by the governor's indication that he will veto them if passed. More positively, the governor may seek to influence the content of a bill by threatening to veto it should it contain, or not contain, particular provisions. Such action, if skillfully done, will often produce the desired changes because most legislators are more interested in passing bills than provoking vetoes. Thus, many observers believe that the legislature in 1969 would not have passed a one-year appropriation bill, which was vetoed, had Governor Smith clearly indicated he would veto it if passed. In 1971 he confounded the legislature by vetoing the entire second year of the Appropriation Act.

These three constitutional powers—messages, special sessions, and veto—constitute only a portion of the total legislative power available to the governor. Many informal or extralegal means are open to use. For one, the governor may seek to influence the selection of the speaker of the house in order to have a speaker with whom he can work effectively. This must be done circumspectly, as too strong or overt action on his part could antagonize the legislature. Second, the governor may use his power of appointment to reward or bargain with legislators for support of his legislative goals. An alternative use of this device was made in 1965 when Governor Connally appointed Speaker Byron Tunnell to a Texas Railroad Commission vacancy; he thereby seemingly cleared the way for selecting his friend and supporter, Ben Barnes, as speaker. Third, informal conferences, breakfast meetings, social gatherings, and other meetings may be used to win legislative support. Professor Gantt reports that "without exception, governors, staff members, and legislators say they consider a conference to be one of the most successful and most frequently used techniques in the legislative process."[30] Fourth, the governor can use the communications media, especially radio and television, as means of appealing directly to the public for grass-roots support for his legislative proposals. Fifth, executive liaison men may be used to lobby and communicate with, and persuade legislators. Sixth, the governor may use influential persons to bring pressure to bear on legislators. These can include pressure-group representatives or important residents in the legislator's district (e.g., bankers, businessmen, local party leaders, or important campaign contributors). Contacted by the governor or his staff, such persons may act to urge or otherwise induce legislators to do the governor's bidding. Lastly, the influence the governor enjoys because he is the state's chief elected official should not be ignored. The office confers high status upon its occupant.

The governor thus has available for his use a considerable bag of leadership techniques. Much of his success will depend, however, on his personal and political standing and the deftness with which he uses the tools available. Heavy-handedness or excessive timidity in their use may diminish his influence, as may an inadequate sense of what is politically timely or possible. Gov. John Connally is generally regarded as having been more successful as a legislative leader in his second term than in his first, an important difference being the skill and experience he had acquired in this role. In contrast, Gov. Dolph Briscoe often seemed uninterested in acting as a legislative leader. Party affiliation became an important factor in 1979 when Republican Bill Clements became governor.

INTEREST GROUPS

Although interest groups have already been discussed at length, reiteration of their importance in the Texas legislative process is appropriate. Scores of organized groups use a variety of methods to influence legislative activity. Group representatives lobby, or communicate directly, with legislators in an effort to secure desired policy decisions. Besides providing selective information to legislators, lobbyists reason, persuade, exhort, cajole, and occasionally threaten in trying to bring legislators around to their position. Organized groups wine, dine, and entertain; provide opportunities for legislators to legally supplement their meager public salaries, as by retainer fees for lawyers; and frequently intervene in the electoral process in support of friends and in opposition to enemies. Though it is difficult to measure with precision, interest-group activity undoubtedly has a substantial impact in the legislative arena. The consequences of that impact are in dispute.

Defenders of interest groups and their lobbying tactics point out that any group in Texas is entitled to bring its views to the attention of the state legislature. Group activity provides a two-way channel through which citizen demands can be presented to public leaders and leadership positions can be communicated to the members of various groups. Additionally, these groups make available much needed, if sometimes biased, information to underinformed legislators and stimulate public interest and participation in politics.

Critics rejoin that the tactics groups utilize in securing influence in the legislature are expensive and thus usually available only to the more affluent or well-organized groups. They argue that the host of favors, preferments, and campaign contributions available to legislators inevitably obligates the members who accept them and undermines their independent judgment on public issues that are of special interest to those bestowing the favors. The ultimate result is that the legislature, which is publicly responsible for making policy decisions, ends up rubber-stamping policies covertly decided on by group representatives outside the legislative halls.

Achieving a balanced view of the role of interest groups is difficult. There are cases, like the 1969 Workmen's Compensation Act, in which the legislature simply approved a bill that had been worked out in advance by representatives of business, labor unions, and the plaintiff attorneys. Bills creating local water districts may be quietly passed, with little public awareness, in response to requests from real estate developers. But there are many instances where the legislative output is determined by a complex set of factors, of which interest-group activity is only one. Comparatively, interest groups are probably more important in the Texas legislative process than they are in the U.S. Congress or most other state legislatures. The absence of a strong state executive and a competitive party system, coupled with underpaid, understaffed, part-time legislators and little media publicity on lobby activities, all combine to increase the impact of interest groups.

ADMINISTRATIVE AGENCIES AND OFFICIALS

State agencies and officials become involved in the legislative process if for no other reason than because it is the source of their legal authority and appropriations. Bills introduced in the legislature frequently originate in the agencies, and agency officials appear before legislative committees to defend or oppose legislation in which they are interested. The bill that eventually became the Texas Clean Air Act of 1965 was drafted by two employees of the State Health Department, the agency which at the time had responsibility for pollution control; it was introduced by a state representative acting at their request. The two employees said they wanted to both make state pollution control more effective and avoid federal control, as provided by the national Clean Air Act.[31]

Agencies may also engage in lobbying, legislative liaison, and related activities on behalf of their legislative goals. The University of Texas has attracted considerable attention to its lobbying activities in recent years in support of larger budgets and expanded operations. To a great extent, agencies have to take care of their own interests before the legislature as best they can. Because of their substantial independence from the governor, because of the many demands on his time, and because he may hesitate to become embroiled in some controversies, agencies do not depend very greatly on him for support. Indeed, they may oppose him on some legislative matters.

Two officials of notable importance to the legislative process are the attorney general and the comptroller of public accounts. The attorney general's department gives legal assistance to legislators in bill drafting and, upon request, provides legislative committees and others with opinions concerning the constitutionality of actual or proposed state legislation. Although these opinions are not legally binding, they are almost always complied with. (In 1973 Atty. Gen. John Hill was an especially active legal adviser to the legislature.) The comptroller has a constitutional duty to certify whether funds are available under existing laws to finance appropriations. Appropriation acts cannot be passed until he certifies that funds are available. (See Chapter 10 for further discussion.) In sum, these two officials help provide the legal framework within which the legislature operates and, in so doing, affect legislative outputs.

THE COURTS

The state courts, particularly the appellate courts, must be counted as occasional participants in the legislative process. Through exercise of their powers of statutory interpretation and judicial review, they help determine the meaning and impact of laws and, upon proper challenge, their constitutionality. We have already seen how the Texas Supreme Court declared the 1971 Legislative Redistricting Act unconstitutional. As another illustration, the state courts have declared a number of "bracket laws" unconstitutional. These are specific laws dealing with local governments that are so drafted as to have the appearance of generality and thereby avoid the state constitutional prohibition on local legislation. A bracket bill might be drafted to apply to all counties falling between specified upper and lower population limits, while in actuality only *one* county does so. Many such laws are passed at the request of local officials and groups; they continue in effect because they are needed and no one tests them in the courts.

The legislature may be influenced in the drafting and enactment of laws by anticipation of what the courts may do in interpreting their meaning or passing on their constitutionality. Long a commonplace reflection of this was the "severability clause" that was included as a matter of routine in many laws. The clause provides that if one part of a statute is declared unconstitutional, the validity of the remainder of the statute shall not be affected. In 1973 the legislature sought to deal generally with this "problem" by adopting a statute that declared all statutes, past or future, "severable" unless otherwise specially provided.

The federal courts may also affect the state legislative process, as by the chain of decisions from 1962 to 1976 that led to and provided guidelines for the reapportionment of state legislatures. Sometimes, too, substantive state laws are declared unconstitutional, as was one that levied a tax on natural gas sold in interstate commerce. The appeal of such a tax was that its burden would be "exported" to the citizens of other states. Generally, considerations of constitutional authority are more significant for the state legislature than the U.S. Congress.

LEGISLATIVE PROCEDURE

The primary concern of this section is the formal rules and procedures by which bills become law. (Technically, when introduced, a legislative proposal is called a bill; after its passage, it is designated as an act. Unless vetoed it becomes law and is legally binding on those affected.) For purposes of brevity and ease of understanding, only the major stages in the process will be sketched, beginning with action in the Texas House of Representatives.

INTRODUCTION OF BILLS

The formal introduction of bills and resolutions is a privilege reserved for members of the legislature. (Resolutions are used mainly for formal expressions of legislative opinions, as on busing or a legislator's birthday, or for internal legislative matters; however, joint resolutions are used to propose amendments to the state constitution and to ratify amendments to the U.S. Constitution.) Customarily, a bill is introduced in the House when a representative gives four copies of it to the clerk of the House. There is no limit on the number of bills that representatives can introduce, but realistically only a few will probably have much chance for consideration. Constitutionally, bills concerned with taxation or revenue can originate only in the House, and resolutions for the approval of gubernatorial appointments are solely a matter for the Senate. Bills and resolutions dealing with all other matters can be introduced initially in either the House or the Senate, or they can be introduced concurrently in both houses in an attempt to speed their adoption.

According to constitutional prescription, no bill may deal with more than one subject. This may seem like a technical detail and, in a sense, it is. However, those who cannot block the passage of a bill may subsequently challenge its constitutionality on the ground that it deals with more than one subject. A successful challenge renders it null and void. This is another illustration of how formal rules can be used for political advantage.

What has been said thus far relates to the formal introduction of bills. Their actual origin or birth is another matter. Probably few bills are conceived by the legislators who introduce them. Most will trace their origins elsewhere—to the governor, state agencies, local governments, interest groups, private citizens—and will be introduced as an accommodation to such parties. Whether the legislator actually works for their passage is another matter. Bills are not infrequently introduced and then quietly forgotten.

Bills not passed during the session in which they are introduced die when it ends. To be considered during the next session, they would have to be reintroduced and started again at the beginning of the process. Some controversial bills may be dealt with in several sessions before they are finally enacted into law. Bills concerning state regulation of public utility companies were before the legislature for many years prior to the enactment of legislation in 1975 setting up a Public Utility Commission.

COMMITTEE ACTION

Once introduced, all bills are referred to a committee for consideration. If there is a question as to which House committee should receive a bill, the speaker makes the assignment on the basis of the rules defining committee jurisdictions. These leave him considerable discretion, which he may exercise to the advantage of the interests he favors. In

"Some bills never see the light of day."

the Senate, the lieutenant governor has similar power; moreover, the
Senate rules make no attempt to define committee jurisdictions. Once
referred to a committee, the fate of a bill depends greatly on the actions
of the committee chairman and members. Many bills are pigeonholed
and never heard from again. In 1965 House committees failed to report

out 481 of 1184 bills (40.5 percent) referred to them. In comparison, Senate committees did not report out 138 of 584 Senate bills (23.7 percent).[32] Legislative committees in several other states, unlike Texas, are required to report on all bills sent to them.

Quite a few bills, because of the importance of their subject matter, the controversy they create, or the influence of their proponents, are given a public hearing at which witnesses (e.g., lobbyists, officials, private citizens) appear and give testimony on their merits, possible impact, and the like. Hearings are often poorly publicized and poorly attended. A notice tacked on a bulletin board five days prior to the hearing often constitutes "public notice." The House rules provide for the electronic recording of testimony, but no printed transcripts are readily available; this obviously reduces the value of hearings as a source of information for those not in attendance.

It is not necessary, however, for a bill to be given a hearing before it is reported out of committee, and many are not. Committee action, but not necessarily a committee hearing, is part of standard legislative procedure. Sometimes committee action can take such perfunctory form as a hastily called meeting of committee members in a corner of the legislative chamber. In other cases, committees may simply ratify decisions made by the leadership of their house.

The House committee (or subcommittee thereof) considering a bill may make changes in it during the "marking-up" process, as detailed treatment is called. All changes or amendments in a bill made at the committee stage must be approved by a majority vote of the House when the bill comes before it. A committee can circumvent this requirement by adopting and reporting out a complete committee substitute (a "clean bill," in legislative parlance) in place of the original bill. It may possess little similarity to the original bill, and legislators have been known to disown or abandon bills after committee treatment, or floor an amendment for that matter. Bills are reported out of committee and sent to the floor of the House for consideration either by a majority vote favoring the bill or by a minority report signed by two to four members, depending on the size of the committee (a majority vote on the floor is subsequently needed to place it on a calendar). The minority-report procedure is infrequently used because a bill that cannot get majority support in committee will usually have little chance of passage.

CALENDAR STAGE

Bills reported favorably from a House committee go to the Calendar Committee for assignment to one of the House calendars. The speaker can have the final say here because he appoints and controls the

Calendar Committee. (There are also calendars for resolutions and for minor and congratulatory resolutions; these are not included in this discussion.) The six calendars, listed in the order of their priority, are these:

1. *Emergency calendar.* All bills requiring immediate action, bills submitted as emergency matters by the governor, all tax bills, and the general appropriations bill.
2. *Major state calendar.* All bills of statewide effect that involve major developments or changes in state policy, excluding any on the first calendar.
3. *Constitutional amendments calendar.* All joint resolutions proposing amendments to the Texas Constitution or ratification of amendments to the U.S. Constitution.
4. *General state calendar.* Bills of statewide effect and secondary importance and bills that apply to more than one, but not all, counties.
5. *Local calendar.* Bills that apply to single-named counties, such as those involving game or fish regulations, excluding bracket bills.
6. *Consent calendar.* Bills that are not expected to have opposition regardless of their extent or scope, as recommended by the appropriate standing committees.

Bills are usually placed on the appropriate calendars in the order in which they are received from the committees, although the Calendar Committee has "full authority to make assignments to calendars in whatever order is necessary and desirable . . . to insure adequate consideration by the House of important legislation." The rules further provide that the calendars, except those for local and consent matters, shall be taken up in the order we have listed. The Calendar Committee prepares and distributes printed calendars at least 24 hours before they will be considered. (The lead time is 48 hours for the state and local calendars, which are under the jurisdiction of a separate committee on Local and Consent Calendars.)

Under House rules, Senate-passed bills and resolutions are given priority on Wednesdays and Thursdays. As the House usually does not meet on Fridays and Saturdays, this leaves Mondays and Tuesdays as the main days for consideration of House bills and resolutions. This schedule is fairly flexible, however; on Senate days when no Senate bills are pending, the various House calendars can be taken up. Local and consent bills may be taken up as the volume of business warrants and convenient openings in the schedule appear. Toward the end of a session, as the volume of floor business increases, the House may meet on Fridays, and perhaps even Saturdays. Also a suspension of the rules procedure permits a bill to be brought up for consideration out of its regular order. The speaker has discretionary authority to recognize a member to make a motion to make the bill a special order, which then requires an affirmative two-thirds vote of the members.

FLOOR ACTION AND DEBATE

Once a bill comes out of committee and reaches the floor for consideration, its chances for passage are fairly good. For example, Prof. Wayne Odom reports that in 1965 in the Senate 341 of the 447 bills reported out of committee achieved floor passage. House committees reported out 291 of the 341 Senate bills referred to them, of which 273 were passed by the House.[33] These data show that much of the real consideration and screening of bills, to the extent that such takes place, is handled by the committees. On the other hand, this should not be taken to mean that once a bill clears a committee the worries of its sponsor are largely over. Support must be actively sought to insure passage, especially if a bill is of major importance, and amendments intended to cripple or substantially alter the bill must be fought off. Some amendments may have to be accepted to pick up support for the bill. Occasionally a bill will be so altered by floor amendments that its sponsor withdraws it from consideration.

When debate occurs on "major" bills (i.e., those on the first four calendars listed above) it is rather restrained, at least in duration, by the House rules. Each speaker is limited to 10 minutes, except that the representative in charge of the bill is permitted 20 minutes to open and 20 minutes to close debate. Under the rules, debate can be terminated by majority vote (on a motion to call the previous question), which enables a majority to easily forestall filibustering. Some delaying activity, called "chubbing," may be permitted by the speaker if he desires to delay a vote or consideration of a matter for some reason. Commentators seem agreed that the debate on bills is often not of high quality and that it may do little to inform or enlighten on the merits of legislation; but it may generate some heat, as attested to by the fact that physical altercations are not unknown on the floor of the Texas House. An exceptional debate was one conducted on the appropriations bill in 1973; it covered seven days, involved the consideration of scores of amendments, and examined the content of the bill rather thoroughly. (In contrast, the Senate passed its version of the $9.5-billion bill after 84 minutes of unfocused debate.)

Many bills, especially those on the local and consent calendars, are quickly and quietly passed with little or no debate, and many representatives will be uninformed as to their content. In a single session in May 1977, the House passed some 150 bills listed on the local and consent calendars. A representative has provided the following description of the House in action on "local and consent calendar day":

> Facing us is a long list of bills that are theoretically "uncontested"—though several are at least as important as others we've debated for hours on the regular calendar. The impetus is to move the bills through all the necessary motions—fast—with members lining up to give only one-sentence "explanations" of each measure.
>
> Clayton is a master of the auctioneer's patter required for this show, and he has developed a rhythmical slapping of the gavel that almost demands that the pace not be broken. Once today when a colleague was a little slow in coming to the front mike (in the House chamber), the Speaker barked unhappily, "C'mon members! Let's keep rolling!"
>
> As well as I can make them out, these are the magic words that the Speaker intones to move bills on "L&C" to third reading and final passage:
>
> "Clerkill readabill." (The clerk starts to read the bill's title but is interrupted a split-second later by the smack of the gavel.) "Izzair jection? Passterd reading."[34]

The legislature tends to move at a somewhat leisurely pace during the early weeks of a session. Daily sessions are short and adjournments for three-day weeks are not uncommon. Activity picks up as the end of the session looms, and a substantial portion of the bills passed by the legislature are put through during the closing days. During this end-of-the-session rush, lack of time and pressure for adjournment (which must occur by midnight on the 140th day of the session) causes even major bills to be considered often in a perfunctory manner.

The Texas Constitution requires that a bill must be "read on three several days" before it can be passed by either the House or the Senate. The first reading, by caption only, takes place after introduction and before referral to committee. The second reading occurs when the bill is taken up for consideration on the floor, at which time the bill is subject to debate and amendment. Approval of the bill, together with any amendments made to it, is by majority vote at this stage. The third reading takes place when, on a different legislative day (which may or may not coincide with a calendar day), the bill is taken up for final passage; this also requires a majority vote. As a consequence of a constitutional provision obviously intended to help insure adequate consideration of legislation before adoption, all of this means that each house must formally give its approval to a bill twice before passage. The formal requirement is often complied with in mechanical fashion. Also, it is possible for the House to suspend the rules by a four-fifths vote and vote on the final passage of a bill immediately following the second reading.

Voting in the House is done electronically. Each representative has on his desk a voting button that is connected to a large electronic board at the front of the House chamber. This records whether a legislator votes yea or nay on the issue at hand and permits quick and visible, if not always fully accurate, votes to be taken. Although it is in violation of House rules, members occasionally cast votes for other members who are absent from the floor temporarily, or even out of Austin, by merely pushing their voting buttons. This has become an accepted practice, and it may be done with or without the permission of the absent member. Despite the publicity sometimes given the practice by the press, nothing has been done to discipline those involved. Questions to ponder are whether it is ethically or politically desirable for a representative to cast votes for another and whether the practice is justifiable given our beliefs about representation.

SENATE PROCEDURE

As some comparisons between House and Senate procedures have already been made, only a few unique features of Senate procedure are commented on here.

Bills can be reported out of Senate committees only by a favorable majority vote of the committee members unless the Senate directs otherwise. Once reported out, bills are placed on a single Senate calendar in the order in which they come out of committee and without regard to their content or importance. The Senate rules provide that bills shall be taken up for consideration in the order listed on the calendar. However, the rules also permit the suspension of the calendar by a two-thirds vote to enable bills to be considered out of their regular order. This has become the customary manner in which bills, especially those of some importance, are brought before the Senate. The lieutenant governor has considerable discretion in deciding whom to recognize to make a motion to suspend the calendar and take up a bill. Those wanting to make such motions usually informally arrange to do so in advance with the lieutenant governor, who is more likely to favor his friends or supporters than others in making such agreements. Thus, while a bill can be passed by majority vote, it normally takes a two-thirds majority vote to bring it to the floor. Conversely, one-third of the Senate can block consideration, thereby making possible minority control over what bills are considered. In 1973 a mandatory oil and gas field unitization bill, strongly backed by the major oil companies, was killed because its Senate supporters, while in the majority, were unable to muster the two-thirds vote needed to take it off the calendar.

Debate in the Senate is conducted under looser rules than in the

House. A senator is generally permitted to talk on a bill as long as he desires or is physically able to keep talking. In 1977, Sen. Bill Meier (Euless) spoke for 43 hours against a bill, which was passed as soon as he quit the floor. (For those interested in such matters, this set a Texas and world record for a one-person filibuster.) Debate can be limited by simple majority vote, which eliminates the possibility of lengthy filibusters such as those that occasionally occur in the U.S. Senate, where a two-thirds vote is required to close off debate. Filibusters in the Texas Senate are thus comparatively short-lived. They are most likely to be effective in the closing days of a session, when every hour counts and a few hours' delay can prevent consideration of important matters. Then a filibuster may have the desired effect of preventing consideration of a bill or getting agreement from the leadership to bring up a particular bill. A filibuster in 1969 was unable to prevent the Senate from passing, by a 15-to-14 vote, a bill extending the sales tax to groceries. The filibuster did have the effect of publicizing the issue and provoking a flood of complaints from the taxpayers. The bill was subsequently defeated 147 to 0 in the House.

During the first 60 days of a legislative session, a four-fifths vote is required to pass most bills in the Senate; after that, a simple majority suffices. Voting is usually done by roll call.

CONFERENCE COMMITTEES

Different versions of a bill are often passed by the House and Senate for various reasons: for example, the interests of particular members, different constituency interests, and response to pressure groups. When this happens, the house that first passed the bill is usually requested to accept the changes made by the other house. If this is done, the bill is sent on to the governor. If this tack fails, the house that made the changes may be asked to reconsider its changes. Customarily, however, the differences between the two houses will be resolved through the use of a conference committee to devise a compromise version of the bill acceptable to both.

A conference committee is an ad hoc committee composed of five members from each house who are appointed by the presiding officers. Usually a conference committee's members are drawn from the standing committees that originally handled the bill; a majority of the conferees are supposed to represent the majority position on the bill in their respective houses. Nonetheless, it is not unknown for a presiding officer to appoint a majority of conferees hostile toward a bill passed by their house. A conference committee deals only with a single bill and, during a session, there will be as many conference committees as bills in dispute. A single member, especially if in favor with the leadership, may serve on several conference committees.

In adjusting the differences on a bill, the conferees from each house act as a unit, which means that anything done by the conference committee must be acceptable to a majority of the conferees from each house. Conference-committee action well illustrates the dealing and bargaining characteristic of the legislative process. Once the conference committee agrees on a compromise version of a bill, it is sent to the two houses for approval. If the conference committee cannot reach agreement, a new conference committee may be appointed or the bill may simply be abandoned. Although a conference-committee bill can be disapproved by either house, this rarely happens. The pressure of time (conference-committee reports often come up near the end of a session), the desire "to have a bill," and the lack of ready alternatives all work toward acceptance of the conference committee's handiwork. (The rules prohibit amendment of conference-committee bills.) The alternatives, in short, are often the conference-committee bill or no bill, and to many the latter is unacceptable.

FINAL ACTION

A bill that has been passed in the same form by both houses is then enrolled (put into final, official form), signed by the presiding officers, and transmitted to the governor for his action. Gubernatorial approval or disapproval marks the final stage of the formal legislative process. With the exception of general appropriation acts, which become effective at the beginning of the fiscal biennium, acts go into effect 90 days after the legislature adjourns. If, however, an act is deemed an "emergency matter" (by virtue of a statement to that effect being included in it) and if it is passed by a two-thirds vote of those elected to each house, it goes into effect as soon as it is signed by the governor.

Enactment of Local Legislation

Members of the Texas legislature are often called upon to help local governments in their districts with local problems. Henry Allee represents the 98th House district, which is located in eastern Harris County and includes the cities of Galena Park and Jacinto City. In 1977 these cities wanted legislation to authorize the Texas Water Rights Commission (now part of the Department of Water Resources) to regulate sales of water to them by the city of Houston. Representative Allee introduced a "bracket" bill (see text) to authorize this.

In getting such legislation passed, Representative Allee comments, "nothing is done automatically." The sponsor of the legislation needs to get the relevant committee chairman to schedule a hearing, round up witnesses, work the committee for support, and do the other work necessary to move the bill to passage. A strong committee vote in favor of the bill is especially desirable, as this will enhance its likelihood of approval on the floor.

Representative Allee decided to leave his own bill in committee and help secure enactment of a similar bill introduced by a Dallas representative who was in better favor with the speaker of the house. This bill was "watered down" to meet some of the objections of the City of Houston and passed after brief House debate.

In the Senate, the bill was combined with a similar bill pushed by Sen. Chet Brooks, who thus became its Senate sponsor (another needed source of support) and whose Senate district also lies in eastern Harris County. This bill was enacted into law as an amendment to the legislation setting up the Department of Water Resources.

After much effort and in rather circuitous fashion, Representative Allee thus helped some of his constituents deal with a problem confronting them. This, he says, is an important responsibility of legislators. Being able to pass such legislation is also a measure of one's effectiveness.

THE IMPORTANCE OF PROCEDURE

The ostensible purpose of the formal rules and procedures by which the legislature operates is to make the legislative process fair, orderly, and predictable. Without stable, agreed on rules it would be difficult for legislators to make decisions on the hundreds of bills and resolutions coming before them during a session. In the absence of rules, chaos would reign. Although the rules of the Texas legislature are not as complex as those of the U.S. Congress, they will contain many technicalities and ambiguities and may prove to be quite baffling, especially to new members. Other things being equal, more experienced members are likely to have greater knowledge and ability to use and manipulate the rules and consequently have an advantage.

Knowledge of rules and procedure is one skill a legislator must have to be effective in passing bills. But, as a former member of the legislature has written, a legislator soon "learns that a knowledge of the formal steps that a bill must go through between introduction and final passage merely provides him with a road map. It is not a means of transportation." Each of the formal steps required by the constitution and rules is "more like a roadblock than a gateway for the author of the bill."[35] Eleven major points or "roadblocks" through which a bill must pass before becoming law can be listed: committee (and perhaps subcommittee) action, scheduling, and floor action in the House; committee action, scheduling, and floor action in the Senate; conference committee; House and Senate action on the conference report; and gubernatorial approval. At any one of these points a bill can be killed by its opponents (or perhaps die of indifference). When a bill passes any one of these points, it may mean only that its supporters can go on and try to navigate the next point. Bargaining, compromise, and modification of a bill are often necessary to clear it through the various points. The legislator who wants to get his bills passed must actively work to garner support for them.

A major conclusion that can be drawn is that current legislative procedure tends to give an advantage to those seeking to prevent the enactment of certain legislation or bring about a weakened version of it. This, indeed, is the desire of many pressure groups, especially business and conservative groups, operating in Texas politics. Those who are skilled in the manipulation of procedures have an added advantage.

NOTES

[1]Texas Legislative Council, *Accomplishments* (a report to the 64th Legislature, Austin, 1975).

[2]Gordon E. Baker, *The Reapportionment Revolution* (New York: Random House, 1966), p. 20.

[3]For further discussion, see ibid.

[4]Colegrove v. Green, 328 U.S. 549 (1946).

[5]Baker v. Carr, 369 U.S. 186 (1962).

[6]William C. Adams, "The Introduction of Single-Member House Districts in Harris, Dallas, and Bexar Counties: Some Implications for Texas Politics" (paper presented at the annual meeting of the Southwestern Political Science Association, Dallas, March 1973), p. 4.

[7]Craddick v. Smith 471 S.W. 2d 375 (Tex. 1971).

[8]Mauzy v. Legislative Redistricting Board, 471 S.W. 2d 570 (Tex. 1971).

[9]*Houston Post,* January 9, 1972, Section A, p. 9.

[10]Graves v. Barnes, 343 F. Supp 704 (W.D. Tex. 1972).

[11]White v. Register, 412 U.S. 755 (1973).

[12]Mahan v. Howell, 410 U.S. 315 (1973).

[13]White v. Register.

[14]Graves v. Barnes, Civil Action No. A71CA142 (1974), U.S. District Court.

[15]Adams, op. cit.

[16]James D. Barber, *The Lawmakers* (New Haven: Yale University Press, 1965), pp. 10–15.

[17]See, for example, Rupert N. Richardson, *Texas: The Lone Star State,* 2nd ed. (Englewood Cliffs, N.J.: Prentice-Hall, 1958), chaps. 12 and 13.

[18]J. William Davis, *There Shall Also Be a Lieutenant Governor* (Austin: Univeristy of Texas, Institute of Public Affairs, 1967), p. 92.

[19]William E. Oden, "Tenure and Turnover in Recent Texas Legislatures," *Southwestern Social Science Quarterly* 65 (March 1965): 373.

[20]Melvin Hairell, "The Politics of Committee Assignments in the Texas House of Representatives" (Master's thesis, University of Texas at Austin, 1971), pp. 173–180.

[21]Ibid., pp. 177–180.

[22]Citizens Conference on State Legislatures, *A New Order of Business* (a report to the Texas Legislature, April 1973), pp. 26–27.

[23]For a description of the operation of the 1971 Senate Interim Committee on Urban Affairs, see Delbert A. Taebel, "Administering the Interim Committee: A Case Study," *Public Affairs Comment* 17 (January 1971).

[24]*Houston Post,* September 30, 1973, Section A, p. 3.

[25]*Texas Observer,* 69 (June 17, 1977), p. 11.

[26]Fred Gantt, Jr., *The Chief Executive in Texas* (Austin: University of Texas Press, 1964), p. 212.

[27]Ibid., p. 218.

[28]Fred Gantt, Jr., "Special Legislative Sessions in Texas: The Governors Bane or Blessings," *Public Affairs Comment* 16 (November 1970), p. 2.

[29]Fred Gantt, Jr., "The Governor's Veto in Texas: An Absolute Negative?" *Public Affairs Comment* 15 (March 1969), pp. 1–4.

[30]Gantt, op. cit., *Chief Executive in Texas,* p. 245.

[31]G. Todd Norvell and Alexander W. Bell, "Air Pollution Control in Texas," *Texas Law Review* 67 (June 1969): 1089–1092.

[32]Wayne Odum, "The Functions of Standing Committees in the Texas Legislature" (paper presented at the Southwestern Political Science Association Convention, Dallas, March 1967).

[33]Ibid., pp. 8–9.

[34]Chase Untermeyer, "The House Is Not a Home," *Texas Monthly* (September 1977): 112.

[35]Dick Cherry, "The Texas Legislature from Within," in Fred Gantt, Jr., Irving O. Dawson, and Luther G. Hagard, Jr., eds., *Governing Texas: Documents and Readings* (New York: T. Y. Crowell, 1966), p. 119.

The Chief
Executive

The twentieth century is sometimes called the "century of the executive." Americans traditionally have thought of their governments as consisting of three branches—the executive, legislative, and judicial—with the executive consisting of those institutions that comprise the administrative, or "doing," side of government, that is, those that have direct contact with the populace in carrying on the day-to-day work of government. The executive branch is ordinarily headed by a chief executive—the president, governor, or mayor. However, this concept of the executive branch is of limited value in understanding modern politics and is not very descriptive of political reality. A more realistic view of modern government in the United States might describe it as consisting of four branches, with the chief executive and his administrative team comprising a separate entity from the administrative agencies that conduct the programs of the government. The twentieth century has witnessed an increase in the prestige and power of both the chief executive and the administrative agencies, with the focus of attention in the political process centering increasingly on the chief executive.

The foundation of the position of chief executive is his authority to direct the administrative apparatus of the government. Article II of the U.S. Constitution establishes such a position for the president by vesting the executive power in the office and then providing it with tools designed to make the power effective. The president, however, has become much more than the administrative head of the government; he may appropriately be referred to as chief legislator, commander in chief of the armed forces, ceremonial head of the government, leader of his political party, and leader of public opinion. The presidency has become the center of the process through which policy is formulated, adopted, and executed. The same is true for most chief executives throughout the world, for the position has become the focus of attention and the major center of power in most governments.

Three factors have combined to contribute to the increased importance of chief executives in modern governments. First, the development of the welfare/regulatory state has tended to make the programs of government more complex, requiring that legislation be adopted in general terms, leaving more discretion in the hands of those who carry out policy. This strengthens the chief executive vis-à-vis the legislative body because he usually has first call on the loyalty of the administrators. Second, the long series of crises that have characterized every decade of the twentieth century have contributed to the enhancement of the chief executive because crises usually result in at least temporary increases in executive power. Third, the decline in power and influence of legislative bodies has been a contributing factor; with their divided and fragmented patterns of leadership, legislatures have tended to have trouble mastering the complexities of modern policy and programs.

The preceding comments on chief executives have been couched in general terms more relevant to chief executives in nation-states than in states in the United States. But despite the existence of formidable obstacles, the development of a broad and inclusive role in the policy process for the chief executive has also occurred in the American states. The evolution of the governorship has aptly been described as moving from figurehead to leadership.[1]

A trio of factors combined to make governors of the eighteenth and nineteenth centuries resemble figureheads more than chief executives. First, the colonial experience left Americans with a fear of excessive executive power; the result was that the early state constitutions generally provided for a dominant legislature and a weak governor. The legacy of the colonial years was short terms in office, restrictions on reelection, and restraints on the governor's power to appoint and remove. Second, the Jacksonian era of popular democracy resulted in the election of a multiplicity of administrative officials over whom the governor potentially had little influence. Third, a widely accepted goal of depoliticizing administration resulted in the creation of boards and commissions to head agencies. The governor's influence over such agencies often was quite limited, for the members usually served overlapping terms and were removable only for narrowly specified cause.

The enfeeblement of governors began to end in the latter years of the nineteenth century as they began to assert themselves as the political leaders of their states, and the growth of the importance of the governorship has continued into the twentieth century. Several factors have contributed to the rise of the governorship. The general factors that contributed to the rise of chief executives have been at work. Additionally, an "administrative efficiency" movement supported by good-government reform groups became active in the states. Efficiency was equated with coordinated government having central administrative responsibility placed in the hands of the governor as chief executive. Constitutional revisions and administrative reorganizations supported by the movement resulted in increased powers for many governors. Finally, the development of universal suffrage and political parties tended to strengthen the governor's political position by making him head of his political party in the state. The consequence was that the governor's role as chief executive expanded.

THE OFFICE OF GOVERNOR

The forces of national scope that worked to reduce the governorship to a position of impotency and then restored it to a position of leadership have also been at work in Texas. The Texas governorship historically traces to the office of President of the Republic of Texas, but the present framework was created by the Constitution of 1876. The executive branch of government established by Article IV reflected general distrust of strong executive leadership.

> The Executive Department of the State shall consist of a Governor, who shall be the Chief Executive Officer of the State, a Lieutenant Governor, Secretary of State, Comptroller of Public Accounts, Treasurer, Commissioner of the General Land Office, and Attorney General.

While naming the governor chief executive officer of the state, the constitution thus established an executive branch of which he was only first among equals in a group of elected officials. The constitution then proceeded to further limit his authority by not allowing him to exercise various tools commonly granted chief executives.

POLITICS AND THE GOVERNORSHIP

The Constitution of 1876 provided for the selection of the governor by the qualified voters of the state for a term of two years, with the winner required to receive only a plurality of the votes cast. However, the constitution was amended in 1972 to provide four-year terms for the governor and other elected state officials, and in 1974 the gubernatorial term became four years. The governor must be at least 30 years of age, a citizen of the United States, and a Texas resident for at least five years preceding the election.

The formal qualifications leave a sizable portion of the population legally eligible for the governorship. Political realities, however, serve to limit the number who realistically can aspire to the office. Although the office does not carry a label stating that Jews, Catholics, blacks, and Mexican-Americans need not apply, past governors have been white, Anglo-Saxon, and mainstream Protestant. Additionally, other political requirements seem to be imposed; a would-be governor has a much better chance of success if he is in his 40s or older and has accumulated a record of substantial achievement in some field of endeavor. While it is not always necessary to have served in lesser political office, most governors have done so. Only two true political novices (Miriam Ferguson in 1924 and W. Lee O'Daniel in 1938) have won the governorship in this century: the first ran as a proxy for her politician-husband, who was legally ineligible for the office because of his removal through impeachment; the latter was a well-known salesman-entertainer. All governors since World War II except John Connally and Bill Clements have held at least one lesser elective office prior to becoming governor.

Other factors also serve to limit access to the governorship. Party and factional identification play a vital role. Prior to the election of Republican Bill Clements in 1978, all governors since World War II were conservative Democrats. An analysis by Fred Gantt, Jr., of the governors from 1906 to 1964 indicates the pervasiveness of the dominance of Democratic conservatives. All 17 governors were Democrats, only 1 was considered consistently liberal, and 3 were moderately liberal; the remainder were conservatives.[2] Liberal Democrats have regularly contested the Democratic nomination since World War II (8 of the 16 elections from 1946 through 1978 were seriously contested), but they have not been successful. Republicans began presenting serious challenges in the 1960s (5 of the 7 elections from 1962 through 1974 were seriously contested), but not until Clements's victory in 1978 were they successful.

The conservative faction of the Democratic party, however, is an amorphous group without a clear organizational structure. There are various hues of conservatism and a variety of groups within the conservative faction. Interfactional divisions occur because of personality, regional, and ideological considerations. Gantt distinguishes between moderate and rigid conservatives and classifies only 2 of the 14 conservative Democratic governors in the 1906–1964 period as rigid; the remainder are considered moderates.[3] His classification does not include Dolph Briscoe and Preston Smith. Smith was generally considered quite conservative before he took office, but his performance was not as conservative as anticipated. Briscoe was considered moderate-to-liberal during his service in the legislature in the 1950s, but his performance in office, with his emphasis on law and order and opposition to revenue-raising, makes him the most conservative governor since Allen Shivers, who left office in 1957.

Electoral considerations encourage Democratic conservatives toward a moderate rather than right-wing orientation in the governor's office. The growth of the Republican party in Texas meant that the Democrats were not assured of election; Democratic conservatives, in need of votes from supporters of their liberal primary opponents, consequently have tended to develop moderate programs that appeal to liberal groups. The Clements victory in 1978 was partially attributable to the low turnout of such traditionally liberal voters. The conservative orientation of Texas Republicans and Governor Clements probably will further incline Democratic gubernatorial candidates toward moderate policies. Paradoxically, the election of a conservative Republican governor may result in less conservative Democratic gubernatorial candidates.

Some of the more intangible qualities for a would-be governor are an outgoing personality, skill in interpersonal relations, and above-average intelligence. A successful candidate probably must possess a combination of great ambition and tremendous drive and energy. The amorphous nature of factional and party organization increases the demands on would-be governors, since the absence of effective party machinery makes for greater demands on personal campaigning than might otherwise be the case.

A rough profile of the successful candidate can be drawn. Typically, he is a businessman or lawyer with a background of political activity, moderately conservative in his politics, a member of the Baptist or Methodist church, born in Texas, and probably educated within the state. Often he has been an incumbent being sworn in for another term, for governors ordinarily have been reelected to at least one additional term. With four-year terms, however, possible opponents may be less willing to concede a second term.

THE FORMAL OFFICE

The salary and fringe benefits of the governor are, in comparison with other states, moderately attractive; the salary, which during fiscal year 1979 is $71,400, compares especially well with salaries in other states. Other benefits accompany the office, including a residence and an allowance for operating it, offices in the capitol building, a limousine, and an executive-type airplane.

The governor is also provided a staff. The development of a

gubernatorial staff was slow, however; Gantt recounts that near the end of the second decade of this century the governor's staff numbered only 4 people. By the end of the 1940s the number had risen to around 30, up from about a dozen 10 years earlier.[4] By the beginning of Preston Smith's first term as governor the number of employees in the office of the governor had risen to over 100, and by the end of his term there were almost 400. The rapid increase in the number of employees under Smith is somewhat misleading, however, since it did not for the most part involve his personal assistants.

Although staff organization varies from governor to governor, there are certain essential functions staffs perform: program development, media relations, scheduling appearances and otherwise planning the governor's schedule, appointments to office, political and party affairs, liaison with other governmental bodies, and supervision of staff services. The development described by Gantt largely concerns these functions. The growth under Smith, which actually was under way when he came into office, was different. Largely under the impetus of federal requirements and often supported by federal funds, a number of units of the governor's office that were established have responsibility for planning and coordinating programs of state and local governments.

Some of the planning-coordinating adjuncts to the governor's office have little to do with the essential functions of executive leadership, and they tend eventually to be separated from the office. Thus defense and disaster relief and comprehensive health planning divisions have been transferred to state agencies with similar responsibilities, and federal-state relations and community affairs have been converted into separate state agencies. Although Dolph Briscoe was very committed to governmental retrenchment and actually abolished Smith's Office of Information Services, which was supposed to coordinate and develop a master plan for utilizing electronic data processing and telecommunications in state government as well as to develop a model of the Texas economy, the growth in planning/coordinating responsibilities was continued during his term in office. New divisions concerned with migrant affairs, equal employment opportunity, and cultural affairs in South Texas were attached.

The governor of Texas may be removed only through the process of impeachment and conviction. The process specified by the Texas Constitution provides that impeachment (indictment) must be by a majority vote of the House of Representatives and conviction by a two-thirds vote of the Senate. Impeachment is not as restricted under the Texas Constitution as under the U.S. Constitution; the Texas Constitution does not specify grounds, whereas the U.S. Constitution states that impeachment may be only for high crimes or misdemeanors. Even so, a governor has been removed only once.

That removal constitutes one of the most interesting episodes in

Texas political history, In 1917 Gov. James Ferguson became embroiled in a conflict with officials at the University of Texas and eventually vetoed the appropriations for the university. Impeachment proceedings were begun at the subsequent special session called to consider another appropriations bill. The charges centered around misapplication and diversion of public funds and the acceptance of large sums of money from a source the governor refused to identify. Ferguson was convicted and removed, making him permanently ineligible to hold state office; but he subsequently made a successful comeback by securing the election of his wife as governor. Cynics commented that bedfellows make strange politics and that Texas had two governors for the price of one.

The constitution provides that the lieutenant governor shall exercise the power and authority of the office in case of death, removal from office, inability or refusal to serve, or impeachment of the governor. If the lieutenant governor is unable to serve, the president pro tem of the Senate is next in line of succession, and succession beyond that point is determined by statute. At present the order of succession is the speaker of the House, attorney general, and the chief justices of each of the 11 civil appeals courts, based on the numbers assigned to the courts for purposes of identification.

As a legal matter the lieutenant governor becomes governor when the governor is out of the state; lieutenant governors normally have several such opportunities to act as governor. Governors ordinarily arrange their excursions outside the state in such a manner that important gubernatorial decisions are not made during their absence, a policy attributable to the rivalry that ordinarily exists between two influential and ambitious politicians with differing interests. The constitutional framework of separation of powers and checks and balances has the consequence of encouraging conflict between the legislative and executive branches. Furthermore, although the Texas Constitution provides that the lieutenant governor is a member of the executive branch, the important functions of the office are essentially legislative. Consequently, conflict inevitably occurs between the lieutenant governor and the governor. A classic example of such conflict and of the triumph of political realism (the lieutenant governor as legislative official) over constitutional formalism (the lieutenant governor as executive official) was Gov. John Connally's veto in 1965 of a bill making the lieutenant governor a member of the Building Commission. Connally explained that the principle of separation of powers would be violated by making the presiding officer of the senate a member of an executive agency.

THE GOVERNOR AS CHIEF EXECUTIVE

The office of governor of Texas is a product of the framework established by the Texas Constitution as modified by statutes, traditions, and popular expectations. The result is that the office has a multiplicity of responsibilities and duties, accompanied by a somewhat less impressive collection of powers to be used in carrying out those responsibilities.

GUBERNATORIAL RESPONSIBILITIES

The duties of the governor are varied and complex, leading him to engage in such diverse activities as shepherding his policy proposals through the legislature, naming the members of the boards that make policy for economic regulatory agencies, promoting the state's agricultural and indistrual products, and heading his party's delegation to a national convention. For purposes of analysis, the duties can be grouped into five types: administrative, legislative, political, intergovernmental liaison, and ceremonial. But beyond the five there exists a miscellany of responsibilities.

Administrative responsibilities. The Texas Constitution provides that the governor shall be the chief executive officer of the state and shall cause the laws to be faithfully executed. This constitutional provision has combined with popular expectations to place responsibility on the governor for the operation of the agencies that constitute the executive branch of government.

Legislative responsibilities. Popular expectations and constitutional provisions also combine to place considerable responsibilities on the governor in the area of legislation. The constitution establishes the governor's legislative responsibilities through five provisions: (1) He may present information to the legislature on the condition of the state at the beginning of each session and at the close of his term of office. (2) He may recommend legislation he thinks desirable. (3) He is required to present to the legislature at the beginning of each regular session an estimate of the amount of money required to be raised by taxation. (4) He may veto bills (and items of appropriations within appropriation bills) that have been passed by the legislature. (5) He may call the legislature into and specify the purpose of special sessions. Beyond the constitutional provisions, expectations have developed that the governor will pursue the office by presenting a program designed to improve the condition of the populace or the operations of state government. In consequence, the governor is expected to present an extensive program to the legislature for its consideration.

Political responsibilities. The legislative and administrative responsibilities of the governor have a constitutional basis. And, although the governor's political responsibilities are not founded on constitutional provisions, they are just as imbedded in the political structure of the state. He was always considered the leader of the Democratic party and dominated the party organization. The importance of this is limited, however, by the negligible role that the official party plays in the policy-making process. His role as party leader has been of real significance only in presidential election years, when traditionally the governor has led the state's delegation to the Democratic National Convention. Changes mandated at the national level in the delegate selection process designed to insure more proportional representation have weakened the control of the governor over the membership of the delegation, however, and not since 1968 has a governor actually dominated the delegation.

Governors Smith and Briscoe have experienced difficulty in maintaining control of the State Democratic Executive Committee, for the defacto veto over the membership exercised by earlier governors has been lost; the tendency of precinct conventions to attract only the ideologically committed, combined with the tendency of conservatives to lose interest in the Democratic party, has resulted in the selection of committees which are more liberal than the governors. Both have struggled to maintain control, for even if the party is not of crucial importance, opponents could use it to harm the governor politically. For example, an opponent in the chairmanship could oppose gubernatorial policies; such opposition would be deemed newsworthy and embarassing.

The relationship between a Republican governor and the state Republican party can only be a matter of conjecture, but it is probable that it will be similar to that of Democratic governors. A conservative governor probably will have little difficulty in asserting his influence, but a moderate probably would face challenges from conservatives who dominate the party at the precinct level.

Intergovernmental-liaison responsibilities. The constitution provides that the governor shall in the manner prescribed by law conduct all intercourse and business of the state with other states and with the United States. By tradition and expectation the governor also serves as liaison officer with political subdivisions of the state. Although some of the activities conducted under the intergovernmental-liaison responsibilities are not new (for manyyears governors have had responsibilities for extradition of fugitives and have served on interstate boards and commissions), the growth of national programs of grants-in-aid to state and local governments has greatly increased the importance of this role.

Many of the programs provide that governors are responsible for coordination of the program within their states. Texas governors have assumed these responsibilities and have created units in their offices to handle specialized tasks. Special divisions, later made separate departments with directors appointed by the governor, were created in the late 1960s to handle relations with national and local governments. The Criminal Justice Division provides assistance and evaluates grant applications in the field of criminal justice. Most of the activity involving federal grants, however, centers around the Office of Budget and Planning, which provides policy guidance, technical assistance, and financial aid to the regional councils of governments. The regional councils, in turn, must approve grant applications from local governments. Budget and Planning also reviews and comments on all grant applications acted upon by the councils prior to their official submission to the federal agencies.

Ceremonial responsibilities. The governor is the symbol of state government. Probably every government has a ceremonial figure who symbolizes in himself the government, hopefully bestowing dignity and majesty; in the United States this responsibility is usually placed on the chief executive, and Texas is no exception. The governor issues decrees and proclamations, signs documents and issues certificates of office, acts as the goodwill ambassador of the state, and greets notable visitors (often making them honorary Texans or even admirals in the Texas Navy).

Miscellaneous activities. The governor undertakes many additional activities that over the years have accumulated around the office. Some of the more important of these are his military and judicial responsibilities. The Texas Constitution makes him commander in chief of the military forces of the state (as such, he may call out the national guard to execute the laws, repel invasions, and suppress insurrections and may assume command of the state police during public disasters, riots, and insurrections). The constitution also bestows limited judicial responsibilities on the governor; He may grant pardons, but only on the recommendation of the Board of Pardons and Paroles, and he appoints some judges, but only to serve out the remaining portions of incomplete terms. The governor may also grant one 30-day reprieve in a capital case at his own discretion.

GUBERNATORIAL POWERS

The Texas Constitution declares that the governor is chief executive; the public identifies him as responsible for the administrative activities of state government; he is the leader of his political party; and he is expected to develop a legislative program that will become the focus of attention in the legislature. If he is to operate effectively as the chief executive, however, he must have the necessary tools. Such tools are of a political as well as legal nature, for the chief executive needs both formal authority and persuasive ability to accomplish his objectives. Political scientists believe that the formal tools needed by any chief executive include the power to appoint, remove, and direct the activities of lesser executive officials and to prepare and oversee the execution of the budget.

Appointive powers. The constitution provides that unless otherwise provided by law and with legislative positions excluded, vacancies in state and district offices are filled by appointment of the governor with the consent of the Senate. The governor appoints the heads of most of the administrative units in the executive branch, including, with the exception of the Board of Education which administers the state's program of aid to local school districts, the ones that control the essential functions of health, welfare, education, and highways. Although the exact number of positions filled by gubernatorial appointment is not known, it apparently numbers in the thousands. One report indicated that in his first three years in office Dolph Briscoe made over 1700 appointments, and that early in a single year over 600 terms expired.[5]

While the governor appoints the heads of most of the state agencies that are essential to his interests, three important factors serve to dilute considerably the influence that he derives from that authority.

First, a two-thirds majority in the Senate is necessary to confirm most appointments, and this constitutes a formidable barrier. Additionally, a tradition of senatorial courtesy allows a senator to veto appointments of residents of his senatorial district who are personally objectionable, thereby forcing the governor to check with a senator from a potential nominee's district before making the appointment.

Second, the necessity of considering the desires of an agency's clientele before making appointments serves to limit a governor's choice. This occurs for two reasons: the governor may be politically indebted to the clientele, or the clientele may be able to muster the necessary votes in the Senate to prevent confirmation.

Third, the administrative structure of most of the state agencies, which are headed by boards or commissions whose members serve six-year staggered terms, limits the governor's influence. Ordinarily, one-third of the membership is appointed by two-year intervals. As a result, a governor potentially could serve for two years and still have appointed only a third of the membership of a board. That third may have been appointed at the end of the two years, not the beginning. Under existing interpretation, the terms of some board members expire on December 31, and new governors are not sworn in until late in January. An outgoing governor thus has an opportunity to fill those positions. (John Connally and Preston Smith made such appointments to the Board of Regents of the University of Texas, perhaps the most prestigious positions filled through gubernatorial appointment.)

The Appointment of UT Regents

Appointments to the nine-member Board of Regents of the University of Texas System are the most prestigious made by Texas governors. Regents usually are prominent businessmen, lawyers, or bankers with political ties to the governor and longtime involvement with the UT system, especially UT Austin. In 1975 Gov. Dolph Briscoe made his first appointments, all of whom were major financial contributors to his campaign. The nominees were typical regents: Dan Williams of Dallas had varied financial interests and was a director of a major insurance company; Walter Sterling was the son of a former governor and past president of the Petroleum Club in Houston; and attorney Thomas Law was president of the Fort Worth Chamber of Commerce. All three had extensive prior involvement with UT as students, fund raisers, members of advisory committees, and officials of alumni organizations.

During the 1975 legislative session Governor Briscoe, out of a concern shared by all recent Texas governors for inefficient proliferation of programs and buildings at the state's colleges and universities, supported legislation giving the coordinating board authority to approve campus construction projects. The administrators of the UT system vigorously opposed the legislation as an unwise restriction on the school's endowment and were supported in that position by the regents, including the three new appointees. With the aid of other state schools, Briscoe's construction policy was successfully frustrated.

In 1977 Briscoe again made three regental appointments. The 1977 nominees were similar in social and economic background to his first appointees but differed in that all had close personal relationships with Briscoe (included were his chief fund raiser Jess Hay; his hometown physician Sterling Fly; and a longtime family friend Jane Blumberg) and two of the three lacked extensive, intimate involvement with UT.

Briscoe's defeat in the Democratic primary in 1978 came before further inevitable regental-gubernatorial conflict developed. He may make three "lame duck" appointments in January 1979; if his nominees are approved by the Senate, his appointees, barring unexpected resignations, will constitute a majority on the board until 1985. The governor inaugurated in January 1979 will name his first regents in 1981.

The turnover rates on some boards probably allow the governor to appoint a majority of their members somewhat earlier than might otherwise occur. Nevertheless, a governor may be confronted with a key board in which a majority of the members were appointed by his predecessor(s).

Removal power. The governor's removal power is very limited. The Texas Constitution does not bestow on the governor any power to remove administrative officials and in fact imposes crippling limitations. Article XV provides for the removal of elected state officials and judges of state district and appellate courts through the process of impeachment and trial; it also provides for removal for actions not sufficient for impeachment of the judges by the governor on address after a two-thirds vote of each house. The article also states that the legislature shall provide by law for the trial and removal from office of all officers of the state for whom a removal process is not specified in the constitution. The terms *trial* and *removal* are of great importance; the requirement of a trial means that removal by executive action of a state official is prohibited. This does not mean that all employees of the state must be tried in a judicial proceeding before removal, for the legislature can classify most jobholders as "employees" rather than "officers." It can also provide that an appointee holds office at the pleasure of the appointing authority rather than for a fixed term. While the constitution does not confer removal authority on the governor, the legislature could confer such authority by allowing him to appoint administrative officials or board members to serve at his pleasure. The legislature, which usually has no desire to increase the power of the governor, has not done so, and with a few minor exceptions the governor is without authority to remove executive officials outside his own staff.

Directive power. While the Texas Constitution provides that the governor shall be the chief executive officer of the state and directs that he shall cause the laws to be faithfully executed, it does not provide him with power to carry out its imperatives. The Constitution further provides that the governor may require reports from all administrative officials, but he has no authority to direct their activities beyond his limited authority in the law enforcement field during emergency situations. Even the governor's power to compel reports is somewhat impotent, for he is not given any means to compel compliance and is not authorized to take any action on whatever might be reported. Other governors have undoubtedly shared John Connally's lonely lament: "Nobody works for the governor. They all work for their boards. Administrators won't volunteer anything—I never know anything except by hearsay. They volunteer nothing." [6] A governor who desires action from administrative officials must resort to political maneuvering rather than the issuance of administrative directives.

Budgetary powers. The governor's role in budgeting is discussed in greater detail in Chapter 10, but for the moment it is necessary to note that the influence he derives from his budgetary responsibilities is probably as restricted as that of any governor of an American state. While the governor is authorized to prepare a budget encompassing a spending plan for state government, the legislature has diluted his influence by establishing a Legislative Budget Board to prepare a competing budget. This reduces legislative dependence on the governor for information. Additionally, Texas has not provided the governor with authority similar to that of the president and many other governors for overseeing the execution of the budget.

Informal avenues of influence. Joseph Schlesinger developed a general rating of the formal powers of the governors of the 50 states based on four measures of strength: budget powers, appointive powers, tenure potential, and veto powers. Governors were rated on each of the four factors and assigned a score from 1 to 5. Under this rating system the governors of New York, Illinois, and Hawaii were rated the most powerful, receiving 20 points, and the Texas governor was last, with only 7 points.[7] While such a rating system has certain weaknesses, it does serve to indicate the comparative weakness of the formal powers of the Texas governor.

Real power is not always formally conferred by constitutions or statutes; formal power may be little more than a legal clerkship, while real power may be exercised through political influence rather than legal delegation of authority. The Texas governor possesses various informal bases of power that enable him to influence the actions of others, even though he may not possess legal authority over their actions. Inherent in the governorship are factors that potentially provide the governor with great influence. The governor can use his position as leader of his political party to attain his objectives; he can use his prestige as the symbol of state government and most widely known official in the state to command public attention and build support for his position that will exert pressure on other officials; and he can use his power to appoint to obtain support from groups interested in securing favorable appointments. Under such conditions his power is the power to persuade, not to direct. Ultimately his success depends on his persuasive ability with the legislature. The governor is dependent for success on securing legislation that will make his objectives law, for his position in the executive branch does not allow him to direct the activities of administrative officials.

The real importance of the Texas governorship thus lies in its legislative role. The evolution of the office has been such that the governor is expected by popular attitudes to assume leadership in formulating and steering to enactment the program presented in his campaign. The success or failure of a governor's administration is thus likely to be determined by his success or failure in dealing with the legislature and, consequently, is more dependent on the variations in his political fortunes than on his legal powers. Thus, the degree to which the governor is in fact an effective chief executive hinges on his personal political influence and prestige and varies greatly from governor to governor and even from year to year within a governor's term.

INDIVIDUAL STYLES OF TEXAS GOVERNORS

Many things determine the success of Texas governors, but four factors seem to be of predominant importance. First, the successful governor needs to possess a considerable store of personal and poltical skills, including articulateness and persuasiveness with both small groups and mass audience; knowledge of when to offer rewards or threaten punishment and when to push on or retreat; and ability to attract and utilize a capable staff. Second, the governor's standing with the electorate affects his performance. His margin of victory may be of importance, but current popularity is probably of greater significance. Third, relations with the legislature, especially in presiding officers, are of great importance, for a recalcitrant legislature can thwart a governor almost completely. Fourth, the governor's attitude toward the office may contribute to success or failure.

In respect to the last factor, two attitudes are identifiable. An aggressive attitude on the part of a governor leads to the development of an extensive legislative program, broad and intensive interest in the policies of administrative agencies and pursuit of objectives with all the tools at his disposal. A deferential attitude leads to a more passive role: a limited legislative program, with what is offered treated merely as suggestions that others are free to accept or reject, and acceptance of the independence of the administrative agencies. Of course, a particular governor would never be aggressive at all times on all issues and, given the expectations that have arisen around the office and the drive necessary to become governor, wholesale adoption of a deferential attitude is improbable. Nevertheless, some governors are much more aggressive than others, and in some a tendency toward a deferential attitude is detectable. Generally, a governor who adopts an aggressive rather than a deferential approach is more likely to be considered successful. A governor who sets out to accomplish little and does so might be considered a success, but the expectations of the public and political analysts require a record of positve accomplishment.

JOHN CONNALLY: PROTOTYPE OF THE AGGRESSIVE GOVERNOR

Even though a decade has passed since he left the governorship, John Connally remains one of Texas' best-known politicians.[8] He served as Secretary of the Treasury, left the Democratic party to become a Republican, was considered for appointment to the vice-presidency of the United States and was mentioned as a possible nominee for president and vice president by the Republican party, and was acquitted of Watergate-related bribery charges. However, when he began his campaign for governor in 1962 he was unknown to most Texas voters. Connally had not previously sought elective office, and his only official position had been a short term as secretary of the navy during the first months of the Kennedy administration in 1961. He was politically experienced, however, having been active for many years in the campaigns and other political endeavors of Lyndon Johnson and having served as a lobbyist before the Texas legislature and the U.S. Congress, where in 1955 he had been one of the leaders in an attempt to have national controls on the price of natural gas removed.

Connally's first term as governor was at best only modestly successful. The most important aspect of his program involved improvement of the higher education system. He lost a battle with the Appropriations conferees on the importance of construction projects at mental hospitals and schools for the retarded vis-à-vis operating funds for colleges and universities. The members of the conference committee offered and Connally rejected a compromise; Connally then made the most extensive use of the item veto in recent Texas history to eliminate numerous appropriations, including several construction projects at the hospitals and special schools. He did achieve such secondary objectives as the merger of the separate parks and game and fish agencies into a unified Parks and Wildlife Department and the creation of a "blue ribbon" committee to study education beyond high school.

Overall, Connally's relations with the legislature were not friendly. As was to be true throughout his governorship, he did not care for intimate, day-to-day contact with rank-and-file legislators, who found him inaccessible and aloof. He preferred to work through the presiding officers and key members, but his influence over those figures during the 1963 legislative session was not great.

Some factors that were to account for his later success were already identifiable in Connally's first term. He demonstrated his tenacity by refusing an unacceptable compromise on appropriations and his willingness to exact a price for opposition through the use of the item veto. Throughout the dispute he insisted that the proper role of the governor in budgeting be recognized. His explanation of the vetoes on statewide television was articulate and persuasive. During the remainder of his first term he moved to extend his influence over the bureaucracy, even becoming involved in a minor scandal when he prevented the University of Texas regents from selecting a Republican architect to design a building.

Many, but not all the conditions necessary for success were present during Connally's first term. Although not of decisive importance, some observers thought that his staff, while bright, was a bit inexperienced and occasionally guilty of errors and cavalier treatment of legislators. An example of poor staff work was Connally's explanation of his appropriation vetoes. He said that the vetoed expenditures would provide a contingency fund for higher education should additional money be badly needed. Since some of the items vetoed were constitutionally or statutorily "earmarked" for specific purposes, his statement was misleading in that the money could not be diverted to the colleges and universities. Good staff work would have prevented the misleading explanation, which was seized upon by critics.

More importantly, Connally was not an overwhelming political figure; he had been elected by a narrow margin, and he confronted a legislature presided over by strong and independent politicians who were not inclined to look to the chief executive for leadership.

Events between 1963 and 1965 were to change Connally's political position drastically. First, he took the opportunity presented by the debate in the U.S. Congress on civil rights legislation, which was to become the historic Civil Rights Act of 1964, to separate himself from the liberalism of the national administration by denouncing the public accommodations section of the bill, thereby firmly establishing himself as the leader of the state's conservative Democrats. Second, President John Kennedy was killed and Connally wounded by an assassin in Dallas in November 1963. The two developments combined to improve Connally's electoral standing, and he was overwhelmingly renominated and reelected in 1964. As the legislative session of 1965 approached his position was improved, but he faced, as he had in 1963, a legislature in which each house was headed by a strong and independent presiding officer who was expected to oppose major portions of his program. A vacancy suddenly occurred on the Railroad Commission, and Connally appointed the speaker of the house, Byron Tunnell, to the position. Ben Barnes, who had been a Connally campaign worker in 1963 and was considered a protégé of the governor, was then elected speaker, thus insuring that at least one of the two houses would be led by an ally.

Connally enjoyed great success in securing desired actions by the legislature in 1965. He secured approval of the main features of his budget proposals, including generous appropriations for the colleges and universities. Other legislative successes included reorganization of the state's programs for coordinating higher education, tuberculosis control, and water resources and the authorization of comprehensive community mental health programs. His staff, with some changes in personnel and two years of experience, seemed to work almost flawlessly (several were later to join President Johnson's administration in important positions), and the House—under Barnes's leadership—did not present any obstacles. Lt. Gov. Preston Smith, who was eyeing the governorship and definitely was not a political ally, seemed hesitant to oppose Connally; he did not even create the expected havoc when Connally vetoed a prized medical school for his hometown of Lubbock.

By the beginning of his third and final term in 1967, Connally had established his reputation as a successful and aggressive governor. Many of the policy initiatives during the final term, however, seemed to belong to Barnes, who continued to serve as speaker. Smith became a major obstacle, forestalling a Connally/Barnes attempt to have the Senate accept without change the House version of the appropriations bill, which would have prevented Smith from appointing and influencing the Senate conferees. Smith also prevented the Senate from giving its consent to a constitutional revision effort, forcing Connally and Barnes to proceed with only the approval of the House. Even the House largely ignored his budget and revenue proposals, but his overall influence remained so strong that he was able to dominate the Texas delegation to the 1968 Democratic National Convention, even though his successor as Democratic nominee for governor had been chosen.

There is room for disagreement about the accomplishments of John Connally as governor. Professor Clifton McCleskey considers Connally a strong, skilled, political practitioner who frittered away his talents and finally wrought nothing more majestic than a circumscribed coordinating board for higher education.[9] Admirers claim a more substantial list of accomplishments, including reorganization of the agencies administering the state's water resources, tuberculosis control, and parks and wildlife programs, and initiation of comprehensive community mental health programs. Most of the acomplishments involve organizational and managerial changes, not initiation of new programs or alteration of power relationships. Critics question how successful many of the changes have been: The water agencies were again reorganized in 1977; the Parks and Wildlife Department has had a stormy existence; and the coordinating board at times appears ineffectual. The limited success of the reorganizations may be attributable to a tendency alleged by some critics to become interested in a challenge, arrive at a solution, and then lose interest rather than provide the continuing support necessary for long-range accomplishments.[10]

PRESTON SMITH: DEFERENTIAL EX-LEGISLATOR

Preston Smith became governor in 1969 after serving 12 years in the legislature and 6 years as lieutenant governor. He contrasted sharply with his predecessor, John Connally, in that he was not as articulate or photogenic. The center of his political strength was in the rural areas, towns, and small cities. He was not particularly popular with the middle-class voters of the larger cities and their suburbs, and he did not enjoy the close relationship experienced by Connally with the major business and financial leaders of the large cities.

Smith was able to assemble a very experienced staff, drawn largely from former legislators, campaign aides, and associates in state government. His staff was competent and diverse, and he tended to grant its members considerable discretion. On some occasions the discretion may have been too great, for in some instances he was badly served by his staff. For example, in 1969 Smith appointed two campaign contributors to the Board of Examiners of Psychologists; he quickly withdrew the appointments after the nominees were criticized as not having the required qualifications. One nominee, the operator of a marital counseling service, was accused of being a medical quack whose degrees were awarded by a degree mill. Good staff work would have revealed the backgrounds of the nominees before the appointments were made.

Smith's victory margins in the 1968 primary and general elections were comfortable if not overwhelming; but he was regarded as somewhat unproven electorally, since many observers felt that his primary victory was more an indication of the weakness of his liberal opponent, Don Yarborough, than of his strength. Additionally, Ben Barnes, now widely regarded as a handsome, articulate young politician with a bright future, was overwhelmingly elected lieutenant governor, and inherited much of Connally's organizational and economic support.

Smith's performance as governor reflected both the weakness of his political position and his ambivalence toward the role of the governor. He presented a legislative program that was surprising in its ideological moderation, given his reputation as a staunch conservative. The program emphasized improvement in the state's vocational/technical education program, development of new medical schools in Houston and Lubbock, and enactment of a state minimum wage. He pledged support for constitutional amendments to increase the compensation of legislators and lower the voting age to 18. His budget proposals consisted essentially of Legislative Budget Board recommendations plus increases for selected programs, but he did recommend sources for the additional revenue needed to finance his spending recommendations.

Smith pursued his recommendations with mixed diligence. A few were actively and successfully supported (e.g., new medical schools and occupational education), but most seemed to receive little attention from either Smith or the legislature. His tax recommendations were disregarded. When it appeared that agreement on taxes would be difficult, the legislative leadership decided to appropriate funds for the first year only of the biennium, for which funds were adequate, and delay action until a special session a year later on second-year appropriations and taxation. Smith did not indicate objections to this procedure, but when the appropriations bill reached his desk he vetoed it and announced that he would recall the legislature to consider a biennial appropriation act.

A similar disinclination to press his view occurred in 1971, when he allowed a tax bill to be approved that contained an unacceptable increase in the gasoline tax and then announced that he would veto the bill if the gasoline provisions were not removed. Both incidents apparently resulted from the governor's hesitancy to "dictate" to the legislature. The same motivation may have influenced his position in 1969 when he indicated, during legislative consideration of removing the exemption of food from the sales tax as part of an omnibus tax bill, that he would accept whatever bill the legislature approved.

Smith's second term as governor was marred by allegations that he was involved in the Sharpstown Bank scandal. The allegations were revealed in 1971 near the beginning of the term, and he became a political lame duck. An indication of his difficulties was his inability to secure senatorial confirmation for appointments to the Insurance Commission, whose rate-setting policies were under criticism. His relations with the legislature were complicated by Barnes's active but eventually unsuccessful pursuit of the governorship.

Smith left office in 1973 with only a limited record of accomplishments. He did not propose as much as Connally, and he did not have as aggressive a concept of the governorship. Nevertheless, he was not willing to adopt a completely deferential approach; he eventually intervened on crucial matters, even though the timing served to reduce the impact of his efforts. Perhaps the most important development during his administration was the establishment of the planning-coordinating apparatus in the governor's office, which potentially had profound consequences for national-state-local relations; but that development is largely attributable to decisions at the national level.[11] That potential appears not to have been exploited by his successor.

DOLPH BRISCOE: UNAGGRESSIVE PERSONALITY

Dolph Briscoe became governor in 1973 with a background very different from that of his politically experienced predecessors. Briscoe had served in the legislature in the 1950s and in 1968 had unsuccessfully sought the Democratic nomination for governor; he also had engaged in some activities of concern to his business interests, including support for a state-sponsored screwworm eradication program. Otherwise, he was not especially politically active. During the period he was out of public office, he had accumulated great personal wealth (he is rumored to be the state's largest individual landowner), and to a considerable degree he personally financed his unsuccessful 1968 and successful 1972 campaigns. Perhaps as a consequence of this method of campaign finance, he entered office with few programmatic commitments. Among those he did have were opposition to increased taxation and support for strengthening the criminal laws and law enforcement, and those themes have remained the cornerstone of his policy proposals.

Briscoe seemed almost tentative in taking control of the governorship. After the general election in November he returned to his South Texas ranch, but the usual announcements of staff appointments were slow in coming. When he took office his staff was only partially complete; several members of Smith's staff were invited to remain on in a temporary basis, and some eventually remained permanently. The new appointees tended to be former campaign workers who had little experience in state government.

Briscoe's legislative program and budget recommendations were revealed slowly and were not very extensive. He did recommend a temporary two-year plan for improving the system for financing the public schools, but it was not released until after the education committee of the House had favorably reported a different plan. He successfully resisted a tax increase, but his spending proposals were delayed until after both the House and Senate had completed hearings on the general appropriations bill.

The featured aspects of Briscoe's legislative program dealt with law enforcement, including restoration of the death penalty for certain crimes, denial of bail to habitual criminals, toughening of drug laws, legalized wiretapping, and expanded use of oral confessions. A drug reform law, which received considerable attention because of its reduction of marijuana possession penalties, was enacted. Four years later a constitutional amendment was adopted authorizing denial of bail to habitual criminals, but the desired wiretapping and oral confession legislation remains unenacted.

Although there are occasional exceptions, strong, aggressive leadership has not characterized the Briscoe governorship. He played a negligible role in the constitutional convention of 1974, and in 1975 and 1977 he did not vigorously pursue extensive legislative programs. He did present numerous suggestions in his state-of-the-state address, but tended to leave them with the legislature and not work vigorously for their enactment; much of the legislation similar to his recommendations that was enacted appears to owe its passage to factors other than the governor's support.

Public school and highway finance are examples of policy areas where Briscoe's influence has been more apparent than real. In 1975 he recommended a new system for distributing state aid to local schools, and the legislature eventually enacted a temporary plan which increased the amount of state aid. In 1977 a similar situation occurred, except that a permanent plan eventually was enacted. Highway interests had worked vigorously throughout 1976 to secure additional funding for highways construction, and Briscoe recommended a plan to the 1977 legislative session for providing additional funds. The legislature eventually approved additional funds, but the amount was considerably less than that recommended by Briscoe and the method of providing it was different.

Overall, Briscoe's relationship with the leaders of the legislature were very friendly. During his first-term relations with Speaker Price Daniel, whom many thought an ally of Atty. Gen. John Hill, a prospective opponent for the governorship, were cool, but Daniel was succeeded by Bill Clayton, a conservative West Texan much closer to Briscoe. Lt. Gov. Bill Hobby was also considered a possible gubernatorial opponent, but he eventually made clear that his plans did not include a challenge to Briscoe, and relations between the two were cordial.

Briscoe's good relations with the two presiding officers were not converted into great influence with the legislature. His popular support appeared broad, but not intensive, and such support did not lead legislators to fear popular retribution if they opposed him. At the same time, he did not make active, effective use of personal contact to persuade legislators to support him and his programs.

Dolph Briscoe did not dominate the Texas political scene as have some governors. Apparently his major accomplishment in both his and the voters' perception was the total absence of revenue-raising legislation. Otherwise, his legislative accomplishments have been sparse. However, he did not appear philosophically to accept a deferential role for the chief executive. He undertook such aggressive actions as threatening to veto revenue-raising legislation and indicating in a special message delivered during the final minutes of the 1973 session that he would refuse to call a special session to deal with public school finance if the legislature failed to approve a bill during the regular session. Such assertiveness was not characteristic of Briscoe. Bo Byers, an experienced and able journalistic observer of Texas government, concludes that Briscoe preferred to propose plans and then allow the legislature to settle issues without much pressure from the chief executive's office. He reported that lawmakers and lobbyists gave low ratings to Briscoe's staff, whom they found not very knowledgeable about the legislative process, and concluded that the staff's "lack of push" was a result of Briscoe's approach to the governorship.[12]

Another conclusion might be that, given the occasional outbursts of aggressiveness, Briscoe's nonaggressive attitude was derived more from an unaggressive personality than from a philosophical approach to the role of the governor. Byers noted that Briscoe has always had an image of aloofness, rarely holding press conferences for the capital press corps, seldom socializing in Austin, and frequently departing Austin for relaxation at his Uvalde ranch, and concluded that he cared little for the day-to-day drudgery of governing. Regardless of whether his lack of assertiveness was philosophical or psychological, Byers' summation of Briscoe's governorship seems accurate: Briscoe was honest, well meaning, and cautious, but neither an imaginative nor a strong leader.[13]

THE GOVERNORSHIP IN RETROSPECT

There are inherent difficulties in evaluating the Texas governorship and the individuals who have occupied it in recent years. The foregoing description of the individual styles of the three most recent occupants of the office are not particularly flattering, but the problem may be as much in the standards and expectations applied as in the personality, skills, leadership style, and political situation confronted by the governors. The expectation is that the governor will develop and institute a program designed to improve either the condition of the populace or of the state government, but a particular governor may not do so either because conditions beyond his control prevent him from doing so or because he does not choose to do so.

Allen Shivers and John Connally are undoubtedly the strongest governors in the post-World War II period, if strength is measured by the force of their personalities, respect from legislators, and accomplishing what they desired. Sam Kinch and Stuart Long, longtime Texas journalists and biographers of Shivers, contend that he acquired the greatest power a Texas governor ever had.[14] Shivers may in fact be the most successful postwar governor. He came to the office well-prepared (he was the lieutenant governor when he became governor on the death of Gov. Beuford Jester, and prior to his election to that office he was the "dean" of the Senate), was expert in his relations with the legislative leadership and individual legislators, had a well-developed concept of executive leadership, and effectively used his standing with the voters and the economic leadership of the state to achieve his objectives. Nevertheless, his programmatic accomplishments do not appear great: He made extensive recommendations to the legislature on taxing, spending, labor law, and school segregation, and was able to achieve the enactment of many of his recommendations—but his lasting accomplishments of great magnitude are but two. He secured a much-needed modernization of the facilities and treatment methods at the state's mental hospitals and schools for the retarded, and made Republicanism respectable and helped bring competitive two-party presidential politics to Texas by supporting Eisenhower for president.

The absence of greater programmatic accomplishments was, more than anything else, the result of his philosophy, which essentially was conservative. Many of his recommendations, rather than attempting to secure improvements, were designed to maintain existing conditions. Notably this was the case with school segregation, where he favored the use of the discredited doctrine of interposition to preserve segregation, and labor law, where he supported many antiunion measures designed to maintain the low level of unionization in the state's work force.

In one other area Governor Shivers favored policies which, if adopted, would have left a permanent imprint on Texas government. Shivers believed in a strong and unified executive; specifically, he favored a four-year term and greater appointive and removal power for the governor. He supported a constitutional amendment which provided four-year terms for elected state officials that was approved by the legislature but defeated by the voters; otherwise, Shivers did little to strengthen the formal powers of the governorship, perhaps because the possibility of success was negligible.

The impact of Texas' other "strong" postwar governor, John Connally, is quite similar to that of Shivers. Most of his accomplishments were managerial and organizational, not programmatic, and the long-term success of most is questionable. The limited nature of his success is attributed by some critics to his tendency to neglect them after an initial success. A more fundamental cause may be that his approach was organizational and managerial because he was not disposed to challenge basic programs and power relationships. If the new organizations were to have a lasting impact, they needed his continuing interest and support; the problems faced by the old organizations were more than just managerial, but instead reflected a balance of influence among competing groups. An obvious example is Connally's first triumph, the Parks and Wildlife Department.

When the Parks and Wildlife Department was created in 1963, the state's parks, administered by a parks board, were underfinanced and poorly located, whereas the Game, Fish, and Oyster Commission had ample funds from dedicated sources but was a poorly run agency whose leadership was buffeted by pressures from competing sports, landowning, and commercial interests and often overrode the advice of its professional staff. The creation of a new agency did not change the basic problem. In a compromise accepted by Connally to make the legislation more acceptable to sportsmen, game and fish funds can not be used for parks. Conflicts continued among the competing sports, landowning, and commercial interests. park funds are still dispersed among many locations which have been determined more by historical and political factors than by the needs of the state's population.

The fundamental cause of Connally's failure to leave a more substantial record of accomplishment is the same as with Shivers—his essentially conservative philosophy led him not to challenge existing conditions, not to chart new programs and press for their adoption. A major exception would appear to be the creation of the comprehensive community mental health and mental retardation program, but the impetus for this program actually came from the national government, which in response to new attitudes of programmatic specialists favoring noninstitutional care had established a grants-in-aid program for community mental health and mental retardation centers.

Modern Texas governors have not been dominating political figures who leave great permanent imprints on the state. Yet state government has changed tremendously in the period since World War II. The state provides many more services, regulates more activities, and is more responsive to urban and minority interests. Clifton McCleskey attributes the changes primarily to outside forces such as the national government or the marketplace, rather than conscious public choice or public directive.

> One would be hard pressed to name a single significant new policy that has originated in Texas in the past 20 years; to the extent that state policies have been changed it is the result of pressure from the national government, or of tinkering with pre-existing policies, or of belated borrowing from other states.[15]

McClesky concludes that there has been little political leadership in recent Texas history. In modern government much of the responsibility for political leadership lies with the chief executive, but when an institutionally weak office is combined with individuals whose basic conservatism leads them not to challenge the existing distribution of power and the programs that have evolved thereby, absence of leadership appears inevitable.

NOTES

[1]Leslie Lipson, *The American Governor from Figurehead to Leader* (Chicago: University of Chicago Press, 1939).

[2]Fred Gantt, Jr., *The Chief Executive in Texas* (Austin: University of Texas Press, 1964), p. 327.

[3]Ibid.

[4]Ibid., pp. 92–104.

[5]*Austin American Statesman,* December 31, 1974, p. 8.

[6]*Texas Observer,* October 4, 1968, p. 5.

[7]Joseph Schlesinger, "The Politics of the Executive," in Herbert Jacob and Kenneth Vines, eds. *Politics in the American States,* 2nd ed. (Boston: Little, Brown, 1971), p. 232.

[8]The following discussion of Connally's governorship draws heavily on Ann Fears Crawford and Jack Keever, *John Connally* (Austin: Jenkins, 1973).

[9]Clifton McCleskey, "Some Changes for the Better," *Texas Observer,* December 27, 1974, pp. 58–59.

[10]Crawford and Keever, op. cit., p. 39.

[11]For a report by Smith on his accomplishments as governor, see *Programs for People* (Austin: Executive Department, 1973).

[12]*Houston Chronicle,* April 10, 1977, p. 10, section 1.

[13]Ibid.

[14]Sam Kinch and Stuart Long, *The Pied Piper of Texas Politics* (Austin: Shoal Creek, 1973), p. 5. The following comments on Shivers are based on this biography.

[15]McCleskey, op. cit., p. 58.

The Administrative System

Although the press, the public, and social scientists often concentrate their attention on electoral politics, the chief executive, the legislature, and—somewhat less often—the superior appellate courts, the day-to-day work of government is performed in administrative agencies. Chief executives, legislatures, and courts may make decisions, but the task of carrying out those decisions is performed by the administrative agencies. They enforce laws, provide services, and regulate various activities; it is with the administrative units that most citizens have almost their entire experience of direct personal contact with government.

An infinite variety of arrangements exists for structuring the overall organization of the administrative units of government. Analysts have long identified two types of structures, however, and most administrative systems resemble one or the other. Students of administration have generally favored the integrationist model: this model calls for an administrative structure that is headed by a chief executive and has all the activities of the government grouped into a small number of departments, each headed by a single person who is appointed and removable by the chief executive. The weak-executive model provides for a chief executive who has limited influence over the administrative units; agency heads are not subject to appointment or removal by him, and authority is not centralized in the chief executive.

The weak-executive model existed without challenge in most state governments well into the twentieth century. The governor more often than not was designated chief executive but had little control over the administrative agencies, which were headed by elected officials or boards and commissions whose members served overlapping terms. Those agencies often acted independently of and even contrary to the wishes of the governor; his influence on agency decisions was exercised, if at all, through informal political means. Professional students of administration and citizen reform groups look with disfavor on the weak-executive model, and a long-standing reform movement has attempted to force revision of the administrative structure of state governments.

The integrationist model aims at strengthening the governor's influence over the state's administrative agencies by granting him formal authority over their decisions. Proponents argue that such action would reduce the proliferation of independent agencies, eliminate the depulication of work that accompanies such proliferation, and overcome the diffusion of authority and responsibility inherent in the weak-executive model.

The reform movement in the past half century has scored impressive if partial victories in a number of states. When major changes are made by conventions or legislatures, they tend toward the integrationist model. Nevertheless, neat administrative hierarchies that make the governor responsible for the management of the executive branch do not exist in most states. The usual pattern is for a large number of administrative units, some of which enjoy autonomy from the governor, to exist. The failure of even the states so inclined to develop integrated systems is attributable to the complexity of governmental programs, which develop through a general accretion of new functions. The tendency is to adopt the most readily available administrative solution when a new problem arises: creation of a new agency. Thus, even states committed to the integrationist model have difficulty meeting their commitment. For example, New York, a reformed state, has constitutionally limited the number of its departments to 21, but it uses one as a catchall for unrelated functions.[1]

The structure of the executive branch of government in Texas is a classic example of the weak-executive model. Three factors combine to make Texas an exaggerated case of the fragmentation of executive power.

First, there is a tremendous number of separate administrative entities. An exact count of the separate units is difficult, if not impossible, to obtain; it is difficult even to define what constitutes a separate administrative unit. There are departments, agencies, officials, boards, commissions, advisory boards, and advisory commissions. If one limits the count to agencies or officials having operating or ministerial responsibilities who are not subordinated to a higher authority other than the governor or the legislature, the number of agencies apparently exceeds 160. Additionally, there are several agencies that enjoy a statutory existence but are currently inactive: examples include the Pink Bollworm Commission and the Stonewall Jackson Memorial Commission. Others apparently are on their last legs. For example, the Board of Tuberculosis Nurse Examiners was created to license specialized tuberculosis nurses, but since the last school in the country graduating tuberculosis nurses was closed in 1961, the board is restricted to issuing annual renewal licenses. Table 7.1 presents an approximate tabulation of the administrative agencies, grouped by predominant function, as of the beginning of 1977.

Table 7.1 presents an image of dispersion that is somewhat misleading, for many of the agencies perform activities of little consequence. For example, the 24 agencies in the "general government" category include not only the departments headed by the attorney general and comptroller, but also the Board to Approve Contracts for Fuel and Public Printing and the Board to Calculate the Ad Valorem Tax Rate, which have ministerial responsibilities for the performance of very routine functions. Among the 55 agencies classified as "economic regulatory and promotional" are over 30 licensing-examining boards; like numerous others, the Structural Pest Control Board and the Board of Polygraph Examiners are important to

TABLE 7.1 • ADMINISTRATIVE AGENCIES IN THE TEXAS STATE
GOVERNMENT BY FUNCTION AND TYPE OF CONTROL, 1977

Type of agency	Total	Appointed by governor	Ex officio	Elective	Appointed by others	Mixed
General government	24	8	5	5	0	6
Public safety and correction	13	7	2	0	0	4
Health and hospitals	9	6	2	0	0	1
Education	23	18	4	1	0	0
Welfare and employee benefits	14	10	0	0	1	3
Economic regulatory and promotional	58	44	1	2	1	10
Conservation, recreation and culture	19	18	0	1	0	0
Transportation	3	1	1	0	0	1
Total	163	112	15	9	2	25

SOURCE: The information for this table is drawn largely from *Guide to Texas State Agencies*, 4th ed. (Austin: Lyndon B. Johnson School of Public Affairs, University of Texas, 1978).

limited segments of the population but do not loom very large in the overall operations of state government. Also included in the tabulation as state agencies are the Texas members of interstate compacts; in several instances (e.g., compacts on juveniles, mental health, and parole), state officials who perform related duties have been designated compact representatives from Texas.

The second factor contributing to the fragmentation of executive power is the existence of nine elective officers and boards having administrative responsibility. The Constitution of 1876 provided for the popular election of not only the governor but also the lieutenant governor, comptroller of public accounts, treasurer, attorney general, and commissioner of the General Land Office. In 1891 an amendment provided for the election of the three members to the Railroad Commission. In this century the legislature has provided for the election of the commissioner of agriculture (1907) and the members of the State Board of Education (1949). Additionally, the legislature in 1939 provided for the selection of five members of the Soil Conservation Board by conventions held in each of the five districts created by the Soil Conservation Act. In most states the creation of new elective state offices ended in the past century, but Texas has continued the practice into the twentieth century.

The third and most important factor contributing to the fragmentation of executive authority is the means of control the legislature has devised for the agencies not headed by elective officials (Table 7.1). Fifteen of these are headed by boards at least some part of whose members serve ex officio because they occupy other positions. A couple have heads appointed by someone other than the governor. Of the remaining agencies, most have heads appointed by the governor; but over 20 are headed by boards and commissions appointed in a mixed manner (in most instances, the governor appoints part of the membership and the remainder are appointed by other officials or serve ex officio).

Of the agencies whose heads are appointed by the governor, almost all are headed by boards and commissions whose members serve overlapping terms. In the entire executive branch only about a dozen agencies are headed by single officials, and that figure includes the elective officials (but excludes the representatives on interstate compacts). Most of the members of the boards serve on a part-time basis, and agency activities are directed by a chief administrative officer.

The governor thus appoints over 100 boards to head administrative agencies. Included in this number are most of the largest and more significant state agencies. But the governor's ability to influence the boards is limited by the existence of overlapping terms for board members, restrictions on his freedom to select his appointees, and the absence of removal authority.

A variety of factors have contributed to the fragmentation of executive power, including Jacksonian Democracy and the goal of depoliticizing administration, but three additional factors of a peculiarly Texas nature have been at work. First, the Reconstruction experience left many Texans with a distrust of governmental power, especially of concentrated executive power. Second, the Texas legislature is a traditionally independent body whose members have distrusted executive leadership. Legislative politics have operated in a manner that produces two strong leaders, the lieutenant governor and the speaker, who are competitors with the governor for power and influence. Finally, the politics of the administrative process is such that the fragmentation of executive power works to the advantage of various groups concerned with administrative policymaking, and they have exerted their influence to prevent reforms aimed at developing an integrated executive structure.

MAJOR ADMINISTRATIVE AGENCIES

A description of the activities and responsibilities of the over 160 administrative agencies of the Texas state government would be difficult and dull, for many of them perform minor or perfunctory tasks. Others, however, are of broad and general interest; still others, while little known, perform important functions in state government or carry on activities of importance to limited segments of the population. The following sections, using the classification of governmental activities presented in Table 7.1, describe some of the more important state agencies and their responsibilities.[2]

GENERAL GOVERNMENT

Of the 163 agencies tabulated in Table 7.1, 24 were classified as "general government." Their responsibilities are of a varied nature, involving the management of the government or responsibilities for services to other governmental agencies. A majority—including the Surplus Property Agency, Board for Lease of University Lands, Commission on Uniform State Laws, and Board to Approve Contracts for Fuel and Public Printing—are of little consequence. Among the more significant agencies are those responsible for fiscal, legal, and administrative services.

The comptroller of public accounts and the treasurer. These two agency heads are responsible for the operation of the state's fiscal services. The comptroller's responsibilities fall into three areas: (1) central accounting, under which his department maintains the accounts for all appropriations made to state agencies and audits and approves, in advance of payment, all expenditures to be made from state funds; (2) tax administration and enforcement, under whic most but not all of the state's tax laws are administered; and (3) revenue estimating, involving the estimation—for the legislature and the governor—of the amount of money that will be available for expenditure for each fiscal year and certification that the amounts approved in appropriations bills will in fact be available.

Although the office of the comptroller is elective, for all practical purposes, it was a career position for Robert Calvert, who served as comptroller from 1949 to 1975, but he did not seek reelection in 1974 in the face of a difficult primary campaign in which his age and minority hiring practices were to be attacked. Calvert was succeeded by Bob Bullock, who undertook a highly publicized campaign to collect delinquent taxes. Bullock is unlikely to be a career comptroller. In 1978, in an unusual step for an elected state official, he actively participated in the Briscoe-Hill gubernatorial primary in support of Governor Briscoe, who, had he been successful, would not have sought a fourth term in 1982 when Bullock was to run for governor.

The treasurer heads a department having responsibility for receiving state funds, acting as their custodian, and paying obligations upon authorization by the comptroller. He has custody of securities owned by several state investment funds as well as those required by law to be deposited by various businesses. Essentially, the treasurer is the state's banker, but as such most of his activities are routine, even clerical. The political significance of this office is enhanced, however, by the treasurer's membership on the State Banking Board and the State Depository Board (the banking commissioner is also a member of the two boards, and the governor appoints a third member in each). The banking board must approve charters for new state banks, a potentially juicy form of patronage. The depository board selects the banks in which funds held by the treasury are deposited, and such deposits may be a form of patronage. The treasurer's influence on the depository board is enhanced because his department also administers matters relating to the depositories. His position is thus of greater significance than the otherwise routine functions might indicate. Like the comptroller, the treasurer is an elective official, but the office became a career position for Jesse James, who held it from 1941 until his death in 1977.

The attorney general. As the state's lawyer, the attorney general heads an office responsible for two primary functions: representing the state in civil litigation and giving legal advice in the form of opinions to public officials. In civil litigation, the attorney general serves as the lawyer for state agencies and acts independently in direct legal representation of the state. The furnishing of legal advice in the form of opinions is at least as important as the representation of the state and its agencies. Only authorized public officials (a sizable group, including the heads of state agencies, the chairmen of legislative committees, and numerous local officials) may request opinions, and opinions may not be issued on matters of strictly private concern. The opinions are of great significance: many of the problems that are the subject of opinions are never litigated, and the opinions are simply accepted by other public officials as the law; although the opinions are not binding onstate courts, the courts regard them as persuasive. The position of the attorney general is quite prestigious, and incumbents usually try to use it as a stepping-stone to higher office.

The Board of Control. This board provides other agencies of state government with a varied range of administrative services, the most important of which is purchasing supplies, equipment, and other material. In its role of central purchaser, the board receives and consolidates estimates of supplies needed by state agencies and advertises for bids on quantity purchases, awards contracts, and then orders the items as needed; items not under contract are purchased on the open market on a competitive bid basis. The Board of Control has several other responsibilities, the most significant of which are the sale of surplus property and the care and custody of state property in Austin, including a state cemetery. The board is composed of three members appointed by the governor with the consent of the Senate; an executive director acts as chief administrative officer.

PUBLIC SAFETY AND CORRECTION

Of the 13 agencies in this category, the most significant are the Department of Public Safety (DPS), Department of Corrections, Youth Council, and Adjutant General's Department.

The Department of Public Safety. The DPS has broad responsibilities for crime suppression and control, motor vehicle transportation management, and civil defense and disaster relief services. In the area of crime suppression and control, the department maintains an extensive set of police records and operates a statewide police-communications system and laboratories that are available to local law enforcement officials. The famous Texas Rangers are the most famous division of the DPS responsible for field services in the law enforcement area; their field of operations is broad: protection of life and property, suppression of riots and insurrections, apprehension of fugitives, and investigation of major crimes. The DPS, however, also maintains enforcement units concerned with criminal intelligence and organized crime, narcotics, and vehicle theft.

In the area of vehicle transportation management, the most important DPS responsibilities involve patrolling the state's highways, administering the motor vehicle safety inspection program, and licensing drivers. The DPS's primary responsibility in disaster relief is for coordination of activities and assistance to local authorities. The department is headed by a director who operates under a three-member commission appointed by the governor with the consent of the Senate.

The Department of Corrections. This department, headed by a director responsible to a nine-member board appointed by the governor with Senate concurrence, operates the state's prisons. The Texas prison system is an extensive agricultural and industrial operation, encompassing over 100,000 acres of land, and several factories and repair and manufacturing plants. A construction program utilizing inmate labor performs all construction work for the system. The agricultural and industrial products are used within the system or sold to other tax-supported agencies. The prisons' physical plants are comparatively modern, and the system is proud of its rehabilitation and educational programs, although some critics contend that the heavy emphasis in vocational programs on agriculture and on industries with consumable end products does not provide inmates with saleable skills when they reenter the job market. Texas has largely avoided the riots and protests experienced by prisons in other states, although there are occasional allegations of brutality.

The Youth Council. This agency administers programs intended to rehabilitate and reestablish in society children adjudged delinquent by courts. Historically, the programs have centered around care and treatment in state training schools, which eventually came under criticism for brutality and emphasis on incarceration and not rehabilitation and education. A federal lawsuit resulted in a ruling which closed the system's maximum security unit, ordered the creation of community-based programs for delinquents whose needs could be best met in their community, and recommended institutionalization only when necessary. In response to the order, a variety of community-centered programs have been created: the council operates five small residential facilities in cities around the state, contracts with various entities for residential care, and provides grants for local probation programs for youths who might otherwise be committed to the state institutions.

The Youth Council had additional legal difficulties. It was determined through a series of cases that admissions had been made without providing the accused with due process of law, and over 500 students were eventually released. The population of the training schools dropped from over 2100 to less than a thousand, but it has again climbed to about 1400.

The Youth Council is composed of six members appointed by the governor with the consent of the Senate; day-to-day operations are the responsibility of an executive director. The council is also responsible for the operation of the state's three homes for dependent and neglected children.

The Adjutant General's Department. The adjutant general is appointed by the governor with Senate concurrence, and his department is responsible for the operation of the National Guard. Since a large part of the mission of the guard is a national responsibility, financing of the units is national and many of the training requirements are established by the national government. The state, nevertheless, is responsible for command, administration, recruitment, and training. During peacetime the guard may be called upon in emergencies to assist in the maintenance of order. There are almost 170 army and air force units of the Texas National Guard with an authorized strength of over 20,000 men.

HEALTH AND HOSPITALS

The Department of Health. Several state agencies carry on important programs in the health field. The Department of Health conducts the most inclusive range of programs. It inspects dairies, bedding manufacturing and renovation plants, and poultry plants; and enforces the state's food and drug laws and approves public water supplies. The Health Department maintains the state plan for construction of hospitals under the federal hospital construction program and is responsible for maintaining a comprehensive state health plan and for aiding area-wide health planning groups. It also operates the state's tuberculosis-control program, including the state chest hospitals, and participates in immunization campaigns and several educational programs. Direct public health services for the most part are provided by health units responsible to local government, but the department operates 10 regional offices which provide services in 178 counties without local organized health services. The chief administrative officer is a director who is responsible to an 18-member board appointed by the governor with the consent of the Senate. By statute the board includes 16 members of health-related professions and 2 public members.

The Department of Mental Health and Mental Retardation (MHMR). This department administers programs for the care and treatment of the mentally ill, the mentally retarded, and aged, alcoholics, and drug addicts. The department's predecessor agency, the Hospital Board, was primarily concerned with the operation of the state's schools for the retarded and mental hospitals. The creation in 1965 of MHMR supposedly signaled a change in philosophy that emphasized continuity of the patient's home community rather than institutionalization. Under authorization of the 1965 legislation, comprehensive community mental health centers, which are established by local governments, receive grants-in-aid as well as federal and local funds. The centers must receive approval from the department for their plans for services, which include diagnosis and evaluation, inpatient and outpatient treatment, halfway houses for persons recently released from institutions, special education, rehabilitation, and specialized programs for children, alcoholics, and drug abusers. Centers are in operation in all major population areas, and outreach services from the hospitals and schools for the retarded have been established in some areas.

Despite the development of community services, the bulk of MHMR's budget is still devoted to the operation of the institutions under its control. Included are nine hospitals or centers for the mentally ill with resident populations of over 6,000. The resident population is declining, despite an increase in the number of individuals admitted each year; improved treatment techniques, most notably improvements in the drugs available to treat the mentally ill, have resulted in much shorter periods of institutionalization. The 13 schools for the retarded have over 10,000 residents. Over 1,100 patients and students are enrolled in four prototype day care facilities called "centers for human development." The department also operates a research facility in Houston, the Texas Research Institute of Mental Sciences, and a small rehabilitation center in Leander in central Texas.

MHMR and the appropriating authorities have been consistently criticized for their priorities among the programs conducted by the department. Only a little over 10 percent of the MHMR budget is devoted to community centers. The critics, who desire greater emphasis on community programs, suspect that the tendency of entrenched bureaucrats to support growth in their programs and of legislators to support construction projects that are physical proof of their endeavors in behalf of their districts accounts for the underemphasis on community services. Defenders of the department point out that the costs of the intensive treatment of the severely ill and retarded who need institutionalization are very high, and that many of the hospitals and special schools are old and in need of repair.

Air Control Board. Concern with ecological health has resulted in programs administered in several agencies intended to maintain a healthy environment and one agency whose sole responsibility is a healthy environment. The Air Control Board, composed of nine members appointed by the governor with Senate concurrence, has responsibility for controlling or abating air pollution. The board, through its executive director and his staff, measures air quality throughout the state and samples emissions from various pollutant sources in order to determine discrepancies between existing air conditions and acceptable standards. Legal action may be taken against sources which fail to comply with regulations. Prior to 1977, when it was combined into a Department of Water Resources with two other water-related agencies, Texas had a Water Quality Board with responsibilities in the water area similar to those of the air board for air. Both agencies have been attacked by environmentalists, who contend that the boards are proindustry and tend to give greater weight to economic considerations than to a cleaner environment. The efforts of the two boards have resulted in the abatement of some pollution, but critics contend that their efforts have been due to pressures from federal agencies, which provide funds and in some instances could undertake enforcement of federal requirements if state actions are inadequate. Environmentalists have proposed a variety of measures designed to clean up the environment, including creation of an umbrella agency with responsibility for coordinating all environmental efforts. But industrial interests, led by the Texas Association of Business and Industry, have either defeated or weakened what were regarded as the most important measures.

EDUCATION

The Central Education Agency. Texas has undertaken responsibility for maintaining a program providing every student with an opportunity to obtain a minimum level of education. The Central Education Agency (CEA) administers state aid for basic programs, services, and controls that constitute the foundation school program, and the local school districts operate the schools. The agency is headed by a commissioner who is responsible to the State Board of Education, which is composed of 24 members elected on the basis of 1 member from each congressional district.

The CEA operates schools for the blind and deaf in Austin, and it also serves as the agency responsible for administering a variety of federal grants-in-aid programs. The most important of the federal programs is the vocational/technical education program, which has expanded rapidly in recent years as the amount of federal aid and state-appropriated matching funds has increased. Much of the increase has been in the occupational education programs at community colleges. Almost 115,000 students are enrolled in courses costing over $130 million each year. While vocational/technical education once meant agriculture and homemaking, the greatest increases in enrollment have occurred in distribution, marketing, and office occupations and in industrial, technical, and health-related fields.

The foundation school program has been criticized as not providing an adequate minimum program, much less equality of educational opportunity. Historically, the program required local school districts to offer a minimum or foundation program. Costs of the program were shared between the state and the districts, with the state contributing a statewide percentage. The percentage contributed by each local district varied according to its ability to pay, with ability determined by a multifactor economic formula. The districts could, however, levy ad valorem, or property, taxes that raised more than its required share, thus providing services at levels above that required by the state. Such enrichment, along with inequities in the multifactor formula, resulted in considerable variation in the quality of the districts' programs.

The entire financing system was declared unconstitutional in a federal district court, but the U.S. Supreme Court overturned the decision. The suit did, however, arouse interest in reform of the school finance system, and in 1975 and 1977 legislation was enacted which significantly revised the system. Essentially, the system shifted from the multifactor index to market value of property for determining a school district's taxing ability and thus its share of the foundation programs cost. At the same time, the number of programs and services eligible for state aid were expanded, thereby increasing total state expenditures and, coincidentally, insuring that most school districts received more (and no district less) under the new system than under the old. The problems with the new system are: (1) Accurate district-by-district information on property values is not available. (2) The value of property may not be a good guide to the ability of a district's residents to pay taxes. The system of state support remains a major political issue.

Higher Education. The state's institutions of higher education are governed by a variety of governing boards, usually called boards of regents, appointed by the governor with the consent of the Senate. Several of the state's universities (there are 32 general academic campuses) have boards that are responsible for the operation of individual schools, but in other instances boards are responsible for the operation of multicampus systems. The Board of Regents of the University of Texas is responsible for the operation of its several general academic branches, medical and dental schools, and special institutions. The Board of Directors of Texas A&M University oversees the operation of the main university and two other general academic institutions, the Texas Maritime Academy, and a variety of agricultural and engineering agencies. The Board of Regents, Texas State University System, governs, four of the small-to-medium-sized state universities. The Board of Regents of Texas A&I University is responsible for the operation of three branches of that school. The Board of Regents of the University of Houston is responsible for the four campuses of that university.

The Coordinating Board, composed of 18 members appointed by the governor with Senate concurrence, directs a staff headed by a commissioner of higher education. The board has responsibility for coordinating higher education policy and for administering the state grants to public junior colleges (which are operated by special junior college districts), the Texas Opportunity Loan Program, a program of tuition equalization grants for students attending private colleges and universities, and various federal grants-in-aid programs.

Another component of the state's higher education system is the Texas State Technical Institute, a four-campus system with over 5000 students governed by a nine-member board appointed by the governor with the concurrence of the Senate. Courses of study are offered in specialized vocational/technical areas, involving not only such conventional programs as farm and ranch operations and heavy truck mechanics but also programs dealing with newer areas such as nuclear systems technology.

WELFARE AND EMPLOYEE BENEFITS

The state operates a number of welfare programs that are administered by special agencies (included are the programs of the Commission on Indian Affairs, Commission for the Blind, and Veterans Affairs Commission) and several retirement programs. But the most important programs are conducted by the Department of Human Resources, Employment Commission, and the Commission for Rehabilitation.

The Department of Human Resources. This department, formerly the Welfare Department, had administered the four major public assistance programs—old-age assistance, aid to the needy blind, aid to families with dependent children, and aid to the permanently and totally disabled—until 1974, when all but the dependent children program became the responsibility of the national government. The state continues to have responsibility for providing medical assistance/under the Medicaid program for persons in all four categories. The department also administers programs of social services to children, the aged, and the disabled.

Child-related services include licensing of child care facilities; protective services to dependent, neglected, and abused children; assistance to children in conflict with the law; aid to the physically and mentally handicapped; adoption placement; aid to unmarried mothers; foster and day care services; and, in cooperation with the Employment Commission, a work incentive program to find jobs for unemployed adults receiving assistance under the aid to families with dependent children program.

The social services program for the aged and disabled involves protection from hazardous conditions, special assistance to encourage recipients to remain in or return to their homes, assistance in securing health services, and aid in improving opportunities for participation in social activities. The department also administers the federally aided food-stamp program. It is headed by a three-member board appointed by the governor with Senate concurrence; day-to-day operations are directed by a commissioner named by the board.

The Texas Employment Commission (TEC). This commission administers the state's program of unemployment insurance, under which contributions are collected from covered employers and benefits are paid to the justifiably unemployed. The costs of administering this program are paid from federal unemployment tax receipts. The entire program operates under considerable control by the U.S. Bureau of Employment Security, although the state has some control over standards of eligibility for benefits. The TEC also operates a system of free public employment offices to serve employers and workers throughout the state and conducts programs funded through federal grants directed toward the training and job placement of the hard-core unemployed. The three commissioners, who occupy full-time positions, are appointed by the governor with the consent of the Senate.

The Texas Rehabilitation Commission. The commission is composed of six members appointed by the governor with the consent of the Senate; it is responsible, through its executive director, for the administration of two programs: (1) The disability determination program, which is funded entirely through federal grants, determines eligibility of the disabled for social security. (2) The vocational rehabilitation program attempts to rehabilitate the handicapped, including the mentally ill and retarded, alcoholics, adult and juvenile offenders, the hard-of-hearing, persons suffering from respiratory diseases, drug abusers, migrants, epileptics, public assistance recipients, and the physically handicapped. Services provided include evaluation to determine work potential; guidance and counseling in confronting problems and selecting vocational goals; medical treatment to remove disability; the purchase of such assistance devises as artificial limbs, braces, wheelchairs, and hearing aids; provision of financial assistance during training periods at schools or rehabilitation centers; and job placement. Most of the funds for the rehabilitation programs are provided under federal grants, but the state must provide some matching funds.

ECONOMIC REGULATORY AND PROMOTIONAL

Although more state agencies are classified as "economic regulatory and promotional" than are included in any other category, this group does not contain a large number of the more significant state agencies. Perhaps this is because the state's economic regulatory and promotional activities have only a marginal influence on the economy. The most significant economic policies are made by the national government, while state regulation tends to be of particular activities or industries. The state regulates a number of professions and occupations: Over 30 of the agencies classified as economic regulatory and promotional are licensing and/or examining boards, ranging from the Board of Landscape Architects to the Board of Veterinary Medical Examiners. The state also regulates a somewhat smaller number of industries, among the more important being the liquor industry, regulated by the Alcoholic Beverage Commission; state-chartered banks, by the Banking Department of the Finance Commission; and insurance by the Board of Insurance. The regulation of industries tends to be for the purpose of preventing abuses (or, in fact, to promote the well-being of those being regulated), and the overall economic impact is relatively small.

The Railroad Commission. The most important exception to the contention that state economic regulation has only a marginal economic impact is the regulation of the oil and gas industry by the Railroad Commission. This commission was established to regulate railroads, and eventually its authority was expanded to include regulation of express companies and trucks and buses. Of course, the most important regulation of transportation occurs at the national level, and state regulation is restricted to economically less significant intrastate activity.

The Railroad Commission, however, has been assigned responsibility for regulation of the production of petroleum and natural gas. The commission regulates not only various technical matters relating to production but, of greater significance, the volume of production to conform to market demand with the purpose of maintaining a favorable price structure. Since Texas is by far the largest producer of petroleum among the 50 states, Railroad Commission decisions have had a significant impact nationally on the volume produced and the price of petroleum. Changes in the 1970s in the domestic petroleum industry from conditions of excess productive capacity to scarcity have reduced the impact on prices, since essentially the commission's decisions now restrict production only for conservation reasons. The three commissioners, who are elected officials, have been closely allied with the petroleum industry.

Public Utilities Commission. The legislature in 1975 created the Public Utilities Commission and gave it authority to regulate all intrastate telephone service and electric, water, and sewer operations in unincorporated areas. Incorporated areas may choose to have the commission regulate the latter services, and most have done so. The creation of the commission culminated a long campaign by consumer advocates who charged that regulation by individual municipalities was inadequate, but the immediate impetus for the action was recent price increases for natural gas and electricity, much of which was generated from natural gas. The gas industry, however, was successful in its efforts to have responsibility for natural gas remain with the Railroad Commission, and the well-head price of intrastate natural gas remains unregulated.

The Public Utility Commission is composed of three full-time commissioners appointed by the governor with the consent of the Senate. A director is responsible for administrative management. The commission's first major decision, on a telephone rate case, did not satisfy consumer groups but fell far short of the company's request, perhaps an indication that it will be neither an aggressive proponent of consumer interests nor a mere advocate of the interests it was established to regulate.

Promotional agencies. A number of state agencies are responsible for activities that are promotional in nature. The Tourist Development Agency promotes tourism; the Poultry Improvement Board promotes poultry, and the Industrial Commission promotes Texas as a favorable location for industrial development. Other agencies combine promotional activity with regulatory or service functions: The Department of Agriculture undertakes numerous regulatory, research, and educational activities in addition to promoting the marketing of agricultural products, and the Department of Water Resources, in addition to promoting and financing the development of water resources, regulates the taking of water by impoundment. It also is responsible for controlling water pollution.

CONSERVATION, RECREATION, AND CULTURE

Included among the agencies in this category are several river compact commissioners who represent Texas on interstate compacts designed to conserve (or exploit) interstate rivers and a mixed group of other minor agencies. The most important agency in this classification, however, is the Parks and Wildlife Department. This department is headed by six commissioners appointed by the governor with Senate concurrence who, in turn, name an executive director responsible for directing agency activities. The department has two major responsibilities: game and fish management and park management. In the management area it conducts management and research programs and is responsible for the enforcement of state laws regulating hunting and fishing in most of the counties and the development of policies regulating the sale of sand, shell, and gravel from public waters and streams.

The department is responsible for the opeation of the state park system, which in 1977 consisted of 93 recreation, scenic, and historical parks. Admissions are charged at some of the more popular and heavily used parks, with proceeds used for the acquisition and development of new parks. In 1971 legislation was enacted dedicating one cent of the state cigarette tax for the acquisition, planning, and development of state parks and historic sites. The state parks system, which was almost undeveloped into the 1960s but has made considerable progress since the present department was created in 1963, receives about $13 million yearly from this source.

TRANSPORTATION

The Department of Highways and Public Transportation. The Texas highway system is administered by the Department of Highways and Public Transportation, which is headed by a three-member commission appointed by the governor with the concurrence of the Senate; a state highway engineer is responsible for administration of the department. The department has two primary responsibilities: maintenance of existing roads and construction of new highways. The existing system contains over 71,000 miles of highways, including 3,200 miles of interstate highways, about 27,000 miles of primary (U.S. or state-numbered) roads, about 40,000 miles of secondary (farm- and ranch-to-market) roads, and over 20,000 bridges. The department performs its own maintenance operations, which include picking up litter, repairing damages, and providing various traffic services. Maintenance also involves beautification of highway right-of-ways, and the department plants and maintains more than 800,000 acres in grass and wild flowers.

Highway construction, however, is performed by private contractors selected through competitive bidding, although plans are drawn by the department's engineers. More employees participate in maintenance than construction, but construction accounts for almost three-fourths of the department's budget. The highway program is financed from three-fourths of the state gasoline tax, and department officials have consistently opposed use of the proceeds for other transportation purposes, including urban mass-transit systems. Generally, the leadership of the department works closely with the Good Roads Association, an organization dominated by highway contractors but including other groups committed to "good" highways. Even the critics who charge that the department's policies are too oriented to the automobile concede the excellence of the Texas highway system.

In 1975 the legislature abolished the Mass Transportation Commission and assigned its functions to the Highway Department, which was renamed the Department of Highways and Public Transportation although it is still widely known by its former name. The Mass Transportation Commission had some planning responsibilities but had been underfunded and inactive. Along with these functions the Highway Department was assigned responsibility for administering a new public transportation fund of $15 million. Sixty percent of the funds must be spent in urban areas with more than 200,000 in population and the remainder in smaller cities and rural areas. The fund constitutes only a minor portion of the department's overall budget, and the depth of the department's interest in mass transportation is questionable.

The Aeronautics Commission. The Aeronautics Commission until recently was a noncontroversial agency whose most important responsibility was the administration of grants to aid airport development in the state's smaller cities. The commission was also responsible for intrastate commercial air services and certified and regulated intrastate airlines, but there was not much interest in intrastate air service. In recent years, however, several commuter carriers have begun, with the active encouragement of the commission, to offer services between the larger cities. The interstate carriers object that the commuter services are "skimming off" their most profitable routes.

THE PERSONNEL SYSTEM

The personnel system of the Texas state government is decentralized, with the operating agencies being largely responsible for personnel management. Decentralization is practiced to such a degree that a study conducted by the Texas Research League concluded that in a very real sense there are no state employees, only employees of particular agencies.[3] Much of the following account of the personnel system is dependent on this study.

The legislature does establish some basic policies, either through statutes or rider provisions of the appropriations act. Certain conditions of employment have been established, including a 40-hour workweek. There are prohibitions on conflict of interest, publicizing individuals, attempting to influence the outcome of an election or the passage or defeat of legislation, and specified forms of nepotism. Discrimination on the basis of race, religion, color, sex, national origin, and age (for those between 21 and 65, with exceptions for such positions as law enforcement officers) is prohibited. Veterans or their widows and orphans are entitled to a preference in employment over other applicants not having better qualifications. The state laws governing conditions of employment, however, are not part of an integrated general framework of personnel policies; they are a hodgepodge of provisions enacted over time to deal with particular problems.

The policies established by the legislature governing employee benefits are more comprehensive and consistent than those affecting conditions of employment and employment practices. State employees are provided at least 13 paid holidays, vacation and sick leave, and retirement and group insurance. The group insurance program varies from agency to agency, with differing costs and benefits. Separate policies on holidays, group insurance, and retirement apply to the units of the higher education system.

Prior to 1961 wage and salary administration was not uniform, and rates of pay and qualifications for similar employment often varied from agency to agency. In that year the legislature approved a position classification plan designed to establish classes of work for most positions and to assign each job class to a pay grade within a salary-classification schedule. Agency administrators are responsible for determining that employees are properly classified, and the state auditor has authority to determine that the classifications are correct. The positions comprising the salary plan are listed in the general appropriations act, and the legislature occasionally reclassifies positions or reallocates them to other salary groups. The legislature can also exempt positions by specifying the salary in a line-item appropriation, and most sensitive policy positions and many professional positions are exempt. Units of the state system of higher education are not covered by the plan. Limited responsibility for administration of the position-classification system is vested in a classification officer appointed by the state auditor. His office maintains a current listing of all classified positions; provides descriptions for new positions; aids state agencies in the application of the plan; and conducts studies for and makes recommendations to the budget offices, governor, and legislature on the operation of the plan and on salary rates in other governmental units and industry.

Each general appropriations act (passed biennially) sets out a salary schedule applicable to positions included in the classification plan, which covers about 80 percent of non-higher-education employees. The salary schedule establishes salary groups to which all positions are assigned, and within each group a series of steps provides for different salary levels. At present there are 20 groups and 8 steps within each group. Generally, there is a differential between groups of 6.8 percent and a difference of 3.4 percent between steps within groups. In recent years the legislature has regularly increased the salaries of state employees by revising the schedule upward, usually by either 3.4 or 6.8 percent. For one biennium, however, the middle groups were increased more than others because of high turnover of middle-management personnel; on another occasion, the lower-paid groups were increased more than others because their need was allegedly greater.

Most state employees are either on the first or second steps of their group, primarily because the legislature has not provided authorization and funds for the awarding of step (or merit) increases. The adequacy of the salary schedule is a matter of dispute. The Texas Public Employees Association, the dominant state employee association, which is actively antiunion and is committed to furthering the interests of state employees through traditional lobbying tactics, regards it as inadequate. There are other indications that state salaries are competitive. Salaries paid by state government in Texas compare favorably with salaries paid in neighboring states; they are also apparently competitive in the Texas labor market, with the possible exception of high labor-cost areas such as Dallas and Houston. During the inflationary periods of the late 1960s and early 1970s, salaries increased faster than the rate of inflation.[4]

Within the context of the policies established by the legislature, the major responsibility for personnel management resides with the state's operating agencies, where there is great variation in personnel practices. Some agencies have developed sophisticated personnel management staffs having responsibility for recruiting and testing prospective employees, developing and coordinating agency training programs, and counseling employees on personnel matters. Others, including a few of the large agencies but predominantly those with a small number of employees, leave all personnel activities to supervisory officials. A majority of state agencies, including those that employ an overwhelming percentage of employees, do use such procedures as qualifying tests, orientation programs, probationary periods for new employees, and exit interviews at the time of separations; but many, including a few large agencies, do not.

Since there is not a central contact point, such as a state personnel office or civil service commission for prospective state employees, the agencies resort to a variety of sources for finding applicants. Many use the Employment Commission, but others use private employment agencies and college placement centers. Still others depend on walk-ins or employee referrals. Employment patterns have led to complaints that several agencies discriminate against women and ethnic minorities, which is forbidden by state and national laws. The U.S. Equal Employment Opportunity Commission tends to regard organizations with nonsystematic recruiting methods as practicing discrimination if the work force is overwhelmingly white, a situation that has forced some agencies to formalize their recruitment and promotion policies. In an effort to prevent discrimination in state employment, an Equal Employment Office was created in the governor's office in 1973 to which state agencies must submit affirmative action plans. In 1975 another step toward opening up state employment to all persons was taken through a requirement that all openings for jobs with state agencies in Travis county be listed with the EEO and the Employment Commission.

Policies also vary in other areas of personnel management. Most major state agencies have formalized procedures for handling employee complaints, but the majority of the smaller agencies do not. Almost three-fourths of the state agencies do not have formal systems of performance evaluations, but the fourth that do employ 70 percent of non-higher-education employees. Even the application of legislative policies within the agencies is uneven. For example, the state policy on nepotism provides that an agency head may not employ a relative within the second degree of affinity (marriage) or the third degree of consanguinity (blood); but a number of the state agencies apply a policy that prohibits the employment of any related individuals.

Exceptions to the decentralization of personnel administration are the agencies participating in the Merit System Council. The council consists of three members appointed by the members of the Employment Commission, with the consent of the heads of participating agencies. It was created in response to federal laws that condition the receipt of grants-in-aid upon the administering agency's participation in a merit system of personnel administration; it is headed by a director appointed by the members of the Employment Commission upon recommendation by members of the council. At present about a dozen agencies (or divisions of agencies) are members of the council, but the only major agencies have most of their employees covered by the merit-system regulations are the health and welfare departments and the Employment Commission.

The Merit System Council operates much like civil service commissions in other states, but without as much authority to make binding decisions. The council actively conducts recruiting campaigns for its member agencies and tests all applicants for positions. When a vacancy occurs, the member agency sends a requisition to the council and the council certifies the names of the five highest-ranking eligibles. The vacancy must be filled by a person on the list, or another certification list must be requested. Employees of merit-system agencies may be dismissed for cause (negligence, inefficiency, and most other reasonable grounds for dismissal are justifiable causes) or because of lack of funds, curtailment of work, or reinstatement of former employees upon their release from military service. An employee serving in a position subject to merit-system regulations may appeal to the council any action involving his disqualification from examination, examination rating, removal from a register, discrimination, dismissal, suspension, or demotion. The decision of the council on an appeal involving a dismissal, suspension, or demotion is advisory, and the agency head retains the authority to make the final decision; but council decisions on matters involving examination, registers, or discrimination are binding.

Three problems are identifiable with the personnel system of Texas state government. First, there is no system to protect most state employees from political pressures and removal without cause for "spoils" purposes or to protect the public from use of state employees by politicians to enhance their chances for reelection. Such a system is provided in the national government and in many states through civil service systems, usually administered by an independent commission. But there is little interest in or support for a civil service system for state employees in Texas. The Texas Public Employees Association concentrates primarily on employee benefits and has not supported extension of the merit system to all state agencies.

In its report on personnel management in state government, the Texas Research League concluded that a merit system was unnecessary because the use of the independent board system to head most state agencies provided an insulation from political pressure for state employees. Furthermore, the league concluded that the flexibility the

Texas system now provides should not be exchanged for a more authoritarian system that might produce a cadre of personnel unresponsive to public needs, not accountable for job performance, and consequently inefficient and indifferent.[5]

Although the insulation from political pressure afforded by the independent board system can be overstated, most state agencies do not have higher turnover rates of rank-and-file employees attributable to changes in political control. There are occasional examples of the spoils system at work. For example, employees of agencies headed by elected officials often are expected to contribute to or participate in their campaigns, and several years ago an employee of a unit of the higher education system was fired after her husband began a campaign against a powerful state legislator. But for the most part Texas has escaped the more flagrant spoils-system abuses.

The second problem with the personnel system involves the administration of the salary system. A sound salary system recognizes meritorious performance by awarding salary increases, with increases not limited to promotions to more responsible or difficult positions but awarded for continuous performance on the same job. The Texas system recognizes this principle by providing for a series of eight steps within each salary group; an employee can thus be rewarded with step increases. The legislature, however, has only sporadically provided both the authorization and the funds for awarding merit increases, and most employees are in the first two steps of their salary groups. In effect, the state does not have a mechanism for rewarding proficiency. Agency heads tend to try to have the positions of employees whom they desire to reward for meritorious performance reclassified to higher salary groups; this provides higher salaries but defeats the principle, equal pay for equal work, upon which the classification plan was based.

The failure to provide merit salary increases is a result of the process by which the salary program is established. Since riders to the general appropriations act establish the salary schedule and provide for the administration of the system, the salary program is subjected to fiscal rather than administrative review. This violates a principle of public personnel administration that while salary levels (the amount of salary increases) necessarily depend on the overall fiscal situation, the elements of salary administration (who gets raises) should not be so related. The legislature tends to favor awarding across-the-board increases since such increases are more likely to be attributed by the employees to the beneficence of the legislators. The Texas Public Employees Association is less than enthusiastic in its support of merit salary increases, preferring that what funds are available be used for increases for all employees.

Support for the merit principle is provided, if at all, by top-level administrators. But forcing them to make choices among employees complicates their task, and some agency heads are not enthusiastic about merit increases. The Texas Research League report cites one instance in which funds for merit increases were available but were not used by an unnamed agency head because the amount was inadequate to provide all employees a raise. This attitude, of course, is a denial of the merit principle.[6]

The third problem with the state personnel system is the absence of a focal point in administration. There is no center of responsibility concerned with where the state is going in terms of personnel: with the number of employees needed in future years, where they will come from, and what skills they will need. There does not appear to be any serious movement to develop a mechanism for developing and coordinating state personnel policy.

THE POLITICS OF THE ADMINISTRATIVE PROCESS

A long-held ideal in the United States was that politics and administration should be separated. Politics was identified with the process of determining what goals were to be pursued by governmental policies and the content of those policies; administration was thought of as the process of carrying out those policies. Ideally, goals and policies should be established by those who are politically responsible (the chief executive and the legislative body), and administration should be by those who are technically competent (officials in the administrative agencies). Students of public administration now recognize, however, that in most situations this ideal is not attainable. The application of policy almost inevitably involves making policy choices, for policy is almost never enacted in a form that anticipates all policy questions. In many instances policy is left deliberately vague, and on other occasions legislatures delegate policymaking responsibility to administrative agencies. Further, administrative officials regularly participate in the formulation of policy; they have knowledge that other participants feel should be used, and they are individuals with their own views and preferences.

Administration actually is a process diffused with politics, and participants in the administrative process are engaged in making policy choices, promoting group interests, struggling for power and influence, and maneuvering for partisan advantage. Political scientists used to advance a formalistic perspective that viewed administration as dominated in policy matters by the top-level, politically appointed administrators. But they have come to view administration as a process in which agencies interact with their entire environment, including not only the chief executive, the legislature, and the courts, but also the general public, party and factional groups, other administrative agencies, and the clientele. Agencies are faced with situations in which the policy choices they make are to the greater advantage (or lesser disadvantage) of certain elements of their environment than to others. To cite a contemporary problem faced by a Texas agency, the Public Utility Commission is confronted with such a choice. It can approve higher electric rates and thereby provide capital for federally mandated conversion of gas-generated plants to other fuel and/or for construction of new plants, thereby pleasing electrical utilities and chambers of commerce who need to assure sought-after industries of guaranteed sources of power. Or it can hold rates down, thereby pleasing current residential customers. The situation is complicated in that the choice will be made, at least partially, not only on the basis of what constitutes a fair rate of return on investment, but also on the relative weights assigned to original and current cost in the determination of value of invested capital.

ADMINISTRATIVE POLITICS IN TEXAS

Agencies respond differently to various groups in the community. In Texas, administrative agencies exist in a political environment that encourages their response to follow well-established patterns. The administrative process operates within a governmental structure and political context that fragments authority and is conducive to the dominance of policymaking by the organized clienteles of agencies. More often than not the most influential elements of agency clienteles are conservative business groups. The governor is in a relatively weak position; although the office is the most important in the state and a strong and popular occupant conceivably could dominate the policy process, decisive gubernatorial influence is more the exception than the rule.

The legislature is a strong contender with the governor for influence in the administrative process, but it suffers from the weakness of fragmentation and division that are common to legislative bodies in providing policy leadership. While the presiding officers are influential, neither the speaker nor the lieutenant governor is selected through a process that encourages the development of extensive legislative programs. Effective initiative in policy development lies elsewhere than with the legislature and its leaders; for the most part administrative agencies and organized interest groups provide such leadership.

Throughout the United States the interests of the administrative agencies and spokesmen for pressure groups tend to converge, and administrative agencies develop close relationships with the representatives of organized groups interested in their activities. This tendency is abetted in Texas by the governmental structure and the pattern of politics.

The governmental structure encourages close relationships between administrative agencies and clientele groups by placing the agencies in positions that insulate them from the general political process. The agencies headed by elective officials tend to be unnoticed by the public unless a scandal occurs or those segments of the public with which the agency has day-to-day contact voice criticisms. Incumbents are ordinarily reelected and in effect have career positions unless they attract a great deal of unfavorable publicity; only personal scandal and clientele dissatisfaction threaten their security. If the organized groups that constitute an agency's clientele are content, they provide campaign support for the incumbent, and opposing candidates find it difficult to develop an effective base of support for their campaigns.

The only elected agency heads defeated for reelection in the past 20 years were Land Commissioner Jerry Sadler in 1970 and Atty. Gen. Crawford Martin in 1972. Sadler was accused of bungling a contract with a firm recovering treasure from a shipwreck off the Texas coast and of consequently misleading the legislature about the nature of the contract, as well as chocking a newscaster who was investigating the story. Martin was accused of not pursuing his investigation of the Sharpstown Bank scandal with sufficient vigor; but he also suffered from poor health, which prevented an active campaign.

To maintain their positions, then, elected agency heads tend to be very responsive to their clienteles: for example, the Railroad Commission to the transportation and petroleum industries, the Treasury Department to banking and the Agriculture Department to farm groups.

For somewhat different reasons the agencies headed by boards enjoy similarly close relationships with their clienteles. Pressure groups take an active interest in gubernatorial appointments, attempting to influence the governor in his selection and the Senate in its approval. The two-thirds requirement for Senate approval affords an influential clientele a reasonable opportunity to block the appointment of a nominee it views with disfavor. Thus, Gov. Preston Smith's repeated efforts to appoint an alleged consumer advocate to the insurance board were frustrated by opposition from the insurance industry, which helped prevent his nominees from receiving the required two-thirds vote in the Senate. Segments of the industry supported Smith, however, and other factors contributed to the defeat of the nominations; these included personal antipathy between Smith and his nominees and Lt. Gov. Ben Barnes.

The consequence of both the system of election and appointment of agency heads is that the leadership of Texas administrative agencies is very friendly to those the agencies serve or regulate; this is especially the case for those elements of the clienteles that command enough resources to organize and pursue their interests. An example of such agency-clientele relations was revealed in the 1960s in a report by the attorney general on the activities of the Liquor Control Board (LCB), which has since been reorganized and renamed the Alcoholic Beverage Commission. The report, which accused the LCB of an extremely lax attitude toward enforcement of the liquor laws, contained allegations that staff conferences were conducted by the lobbyist for the Wholesale Beer Distributors of Texas; that favorable and irregular treatment was accorded accused violators by top agency officials; that industry representatives participated with the administrator in the selection and promotion of lesser agency officials; and that acceptance of gifts from the regulated industry was widespread. The report concluded:

> There is considerable evidence that the Texas Liquor Control Board, insofar as its administration is concerned, has been, in a large measure, controlled by the very industry it was designed to regulate. . . . The influence of the industry was felt within the agency in many ways. . . .[7]

The relations between the LCB and the beer and liquor industries are probably not representative of agency-clientele relations; in most instances the elements of corruption probably do not exist, and industry domination is neither as obvious nor as complete. But the organized clienteles are the prime elements of the environment to which the agencies respond. The Department of Health is very responsive to the policy preferences of the medical profession; the insurance board has close relations with the insurance industry; and the Highway Department is very responsive to the wishes of highway contractors and the trucking industry.

Barbers Versus Cosmetologists

The Board of Barber Examiners was created in 1929 supposedly to protect the health and safety of the public. The board, which consists of two working barbers, two barbershop owners, and two barber school owners appointed by the governor, examines, licenses, and inspects barbers, barbershops, and barber colleges. It also restrains competition; on occasion the restraint is practiced within the profession, for often the enemy of barbers is the barber colleges, who graduate too many "undertrained" barbers. Cosmetologists are the primary outside competitors.

In 1935 the forerunner of the Texas Cosmetology Commission was created to do for beauticians, hardressers, and cosmetologists what the Board of Barber Examiners did for barbers. The commission is composed of six gubernatorially appointed members—a beauty salon operator, a beauty salon owner, a representative of the wig industry, and two public members—and the Associate Commissioner for Occupational Education of the Texas Education Agency.

The exact demarcation between barbers and cosmetologists is not clear, but until recently only barbers could legally give haircuts and cosmetologists could cut hair only if it was incidental to styling. In practice, barbers worked on men and cosmetologists on women. In 1971 legislation was enacted allowing cosmetologists to cut women's hair, but the provision limiting that privilege only to women was declared unconstitutional and until 1975 they apparently could cut anyone's hair.

The timing of the change was unfortunate for barbers, for longer male hairstyles, for which many of the barbers were unskilled, were becoming popular. Men were hesitant to patronize beauty salons; the result was "unisex" shops staffed by barbers and cosmetologists. This was not satisfactory to the barbers, whose job of cutting hair was being taken by the more numerous cosmetologists. The barbers had legislation introduced in 1975 requiring a physical separation within shops of barbers and cosmetologists, but the legislation was approved only after the cosmetologists had a provision added explicitly legitimizing their haircutting activities. Details of the separation were left up to the two agencies.

The cosmetologists adopted rules requiring a four-foot partition, but the barbers required an eight-foot wall, plus the display of a barber pole and separate entrances for barber customers. The new unisex shops in urban areas became illegal, as did many rural shops operated in the homes of husband/barbers and wife/cosmetologists.

Occasionally, conflicts occur between segments of an agency's clientele. For example, there is a long-standing conflict between "chain" optometry companies and individual optometrists, with the individual optometrists supporting the adoption of rules by the Optometry Board that make the operation of chains difficult. When such conflict occurs, either a winner or truce based on a comprise may emerge. Occasionally, the conflicts within an agency's clientiel reflect more general factional conflict: for example, a conflict between labor and management over policies of the Employment Commission or the Industrial Accident Board, or liberal environmentalists and industrial groups over the policies of the water pollution and air control agencies. In such instances the business and industrial groups tend to prevail over labor and liberal interests. This is a reflection of their overall political success, which translates into favorable legislation and appointments to key administrative positions.

Agencies and clientele groups ordinarily work closely together in formulating, adopting, and administering policy. The policy process largely operates in an insulated context in which such matters as party platforms or the program of the chief executive do not impinge. The pressure groups are also the most influential segment of the community in the selection of the legislature and its presiding officers. Thus, the legislature is not inclined to look with disfavor on the close relationships between the administrative agencies and their clienteles. This is not unusual; there is a tendency in the United States for policy to be made within specialized subsystems of the overall political system, which are composed of the administrative agency, organized clientele, and interested portions of the legislative body.[8] In Texas that tendency is aggravated by the absence of meaningful party programs and a strong chief executive; the political strength of business, commercial, and industrial interests; and the weakness of organized labor and spokesmen for consumer, environmental, and minority groups. The consequence is that the organized segments of the agencies' clienteles dominate policymaking. This situation reaches an extreme with a few of the licensing-examining boards. With some, board members are required to be members of the profession, and the boards' chief administrative officers, who serve on a part-time basis, traditionally double as executive directors of the professional associations.

POWER AND RESPONSIBILITY

The Texas administrative structure is characterized by fragmentation of authority and influence, and the politics of the administrative process contributes to the fragmentation. Although the governor's influence in the administrative process is relatively weak, his office has the appearance of power. The Texas Constitution seems to place broad responsibility for overseeing state administration on the governor, and the public often holds the governor responsible for almost everything that happens in the executive branch of government—if not in all of state government. But the governor's legal powers and political position do not endow him with authority adequate to meet his broad responsibility; in reality, his position is one of responsibility without formal power.

Conditions in Texas are not unlike those that exist or have existed in many states. A reform movement supported by a variety of citizen groups and social scientists has urged state governments to reform their executive branches by adopting an integrated administrative structure with the governor at its head, and reforms have been instituted in many states. Texas has not been completely immune to proposals for reform; discussions of reform occur regularly, especially among social scientists and the League of Women Voters. Reorganizations have occurred in a number of areas; agencies have been abolished, combined, and created; and activities have been transferred from agency to agency. Nothing, however, has been accomplished in the way of drastically reducing the number of administrative units; grouping them into a small number of departments; and giving the governor power to appoint, remove, and direct single heads of such departments. These are the activities that would be necessary to create an integrated executive branch.

Even the legislature occasionally conducts studies and makes recommendations. In 1975 it created a study group chaired by Lt. Gov. Bill Hobby that made several recommendations which, while not creating an integrated system, did make proposals which would have revised the structure in several policy areas. Not much came of the recommendations.

In 1977 a step was taken toward review of the administrative system with the enaction of a "sunset" law providing for the review on a revolving basis of all state agencies (except higher education institutions) over a 12-year period. If legislation continuing an agency is not enacted, it will cease to exist. A Sunset Review Commission, composed of four senators appointed by the lieutenant governor and four house members appointed by the speaker, advises the legislature as to action to be taken. During the first biennial review period 26 agencies, largely licensing and examining boards, are scheduled for review. Early indications are that a few inactive, or nearly inactive, agencies may be eliminated. While the "sunset" process may eliminate some statutory deadwood that does little but lengthen the list of state agencies, it is unlikely otherwise to have much impact on the structure of the executive branch.

Why has Texas persisted in the use of the weak-executive system when "good government" groups and social scientists have so widely favored the integrated executive model? The answer lies in the nature of the reorganization task and the balance of power among the political forces favoring and opposing reorganization. The legal and constitutional tasks confronting reorganizers are quite formidable. In addition to a monumental amount of statutory revision, the constitution would have to be revised to give the governor power to appoint, direct, and remove lesser administrative officials and to eliminate numerous references to elective officials and independent boards and commissions.

The balance of power now existing between the proponents and opponents of administrative reorganization constitute an even more formidable obstacle than does the technical problem of statutory and constitutional revision. Other than participants in and supporters of the reform movement, who tend to lack political influence and skill, about the only support for reorganization comes from occasional governors. Groups that enjoy more favorable access to the governor than to the legislature or administrative agencies might also be expected to support the creation of an integrated executive structure, but any such group is difficult to identify. Groups in the liberal/labor coalition that have not enjoyed favorable access to the legislature more often than not have not been favorites of the governor and have not favored strengthening the governorship.

The opposition to administrative reorganization comes from three sources: (1) the administrative agencies, which prefer autonomy from interference by the chief executive, who they fear might make use of agency positions for patronage or might disrupt existing practices and policies with which they have become comfortable; (2) the organized interest groups that enjoy favorable access and fear any disruption of the existing distribution of influence, especially a governor who appeals or responds to the unorganized and potentially conflicting interests of the general electorate; and (3) the legislators, who are distrustful of anything they perceive as threatening the strength of the legislature vis-à-vis the governor and thus oppose all changes that would restrict their ability to deal directly with agency administrators.

Changes in governmental machinery of the magnitude necessary to establish an integrated executive branch are difficult to achieve under any circumstances, for those resisting change in effect have the force of inertia as an ally. Given the political strength of the opponents of reorganization, attempts at administrative restructuring have been easily defeated. The abortive effort in 1974 to rewrite the constitution illustrates the weakness of the proponents of reorganization. At the same time the proposed constitution bestowed limited removal power on the governor, limited the life of state agencies to ten years unless renewed through legislative action, and required the governor to submit periodic reorganization plans for legislative consideration, it also increased the number of officials whose election was mandated in the constitution, guaranteed the continued existence of most agencies established in the Constitution of 1876, and defeated efforts to restrict to a stated figure the number of administrative agencies that could be created by the legislature. Almost certainly the provisions would have perpetuated the existing weak-executive system.

NOTES

[1]Joseph A. Schlesinger, "The Politics of the Executive," in Herbert Jacob and Kenneth Vines, eds., *Politics in the American States,* 2nd ed. (Boston: Little, Brown, 1971), pp. 210–211.

[2]For information on a particular agency, the best single source is usually its annual report. Good summary sources are *Guide to Texas State Agencies,* 5th ed. (Austin: University of Texas, Bureau of Government Research, Lyndon B. Johnson School of

Public Affairs, 1978); and *Fiscal Size-up of Texas State Services* (Austin, Legislative Budget Board, 1975).

[3]*Quality Texas Government* (Austin, Office of the Governor, Division of Planning Coordination, 1972), p. 21.

[4]Ibid., pp. 49–54.

[5]Ibid., p. 6.

[6]Ibid., p. 4.

[7]*Attorney General's Report Concerning Investigation of Texas Liquor Control Board* (Austin: Attorney General of Texas, 1968), pp. 15–16.

[8]J. Leiper Freeman, *The Political Process: Executive Bureau—Legislative Committee Relations* (New York: Random House, 1955).

The Judicial
System

The English philosopher John Locke, writing three centuries ago, concluded that man is forced into political society because he perceives the need for a common superior to judge disputes between himself and his fellows.[1] Present-day government has created an elaborate set of structures and practices for judging the many conflicts that cannot be resolved privately among the members of a community. The nature of this judgmental process has been disputed. One tradition emphasizes the impartiality of the judges themselves, who are pictured as dispassionate appliers of general rules to particular cases. The judge does not create law, he simply draws out the details implicit in the constitutional or legislative edicts in question.

A tradition of legal realism has challenged this Olympian view of law and judgeship with considerable success in recent years. This realistic view holds that when a man becomes a judge he is not suddenly cleansed of all prejudices or immunized against social pressures. His actions, like those of other human beings, will depend on his personality, background, attitudes and beliefs, likes and dislikes. A judge is not merely an automaton consistently applying rules in particular cases. Rather, a judge creates law as he dispenses it because he is constantly called on to decide cases where laws or precedents are unclear, contradictory, or ambiguous. The realists have further attacked the contention that the judicial process is equally open to all, and they have called attention to the varying patterns of compliance that characterize the enforcement of court decisions.

The legal realists affirm that the judicial system is very much concerned with politics, or with what David Easton calls the "authoritative allocation of values and resources for a society."[2] These allocations are in the form of policy outputs and are authoritative in the sense that they are made by government and are backed by the coercive power of the state. Judges, like legislators and executive officials, make decisions that benefit some citizens at the expense of others.

Judicial outputs affect a broad range of interests. Consider a case recently decided by the Texas Court of Criminal Appeals. In 1973 changes in the state's dangerous-drug laws revised the criminal penalties for possession and sale of drugs classified as "dangerous." Among the major changes was a reduction in the penalties for first-offense possession of small amounts of marijuana; included in the law was a provision allowing persons sentenced under the more stringent statute to be resentenced under the provisions of the new law. The lessening of penalties for possession of marijuana was especially popular among younger voters, particularly college students, and had been widely supported by a broad spectrum of candidates during the 1972 campaigns. The resentencing provision was popular with the same voters because the long sentences given some offenders were regarded as unjust.

Many prosecutors, however, opposed the resentencing provision because they thought it a bad precedent in that it might encourage violations of other unpopular laws in the hope that future legislative actions would negate or reduce convictions. Additionally, the handling of numerous resentencing cases threatened sharp increases in the work load of the staffs of some district attorneys. The district attorney of Travis County brought suit asking that the resentencing provision be invalidated because it granted the power to commute sentences to the judicial branch of government, whereas the Texas Constitution gave that power to the executive branch. The case thus had consequences involving moral, electoral, and administrative considerations, even though the decision invalidating the resentencing provision was couched in constitutional terms. The judges engaged in an act of policymaking, whatever the grounds of their decision.

Nevertheless, there are differences between the judicial process and other segments of the Texas political system. The courts and those who man them operate in a highly formalized, structured manner. Decision-making roles are more clearly spelled out, as in the procedural process, than is the case in other policymaking areas. While values, biases, and prejudices undoubtedly affect judicial decisions, Texas political leaders rarely if ever try to dictate court rulings and direct partisan involvement in the judicial process is usually minimal.

These general considerations aside, the following sections discuss the staffing and structure of the court system and the nature of the judicial process in Texas. Additionally, attention is directed to several problems associated with the Texas judicial system and the prospects for remedying these shortcomings.

STAFFING THE JUDICIAL SYSTEM

THE TEXAS BAR

The Texas bar includes all persons admitted to practice law in the state—probably about 30,000 lawyers. The composition of the bar is important not just because it includes the attorneys representing contesting parties in the courts but also because the judiciary is recruited from within the ranks. In contrast to the practice in most European countries, the office of judge in the United States is not treated as a distinct profession separate from that of lawyer. Most lawyers are eligible for service on the bench at any time.

In regard to socioeconomic characteristics, Texas lawyers differ substantially from the state's population as a whole. Members of the legal profession are disproportionately drawn from high-status and high-income groups, with few coming from blue-collar backgrounds. In fact, lawyers tend to come from families with a tradition of legal-professional experience or other public service. Ethnically, the legal profession is far more homogeneous than is the state's population. Black and Mexican-American lawyers number only in the hundreds, and there are comparatively few women practicing law in the state.[3]

Most Texas lawyers are educated within the state; over a third are graduates of the University of Texas Law School. Numerically, the legal profession has grown very fast in recent years. The 1960 census identifies 10,363 lawyers in Texas, but a 1967 survey showed an increase to 15,252. In 1950 there was one lawyer for each 953 persons in Texas, and in 1960 the ratio was one for every 924 persons; by 1967 there was one for every 450 residents,[4] but since then has declined to only one for every 425 persons. Although lawyers are a good deal better off financially than are most occupational groups, there are indications that their income is below national standards for the profession.[5] Although Texas does not suffer from a shortage of legal practitioners, over 6000 students are enrolled in law schools within the state. The number might be larger but for the successful opposition of the bar association and the higher education coordinating board to the creation of additional state-supported law schools.

Considered as a whole, lawyers represent one of the most important subgroups of the population. Not only are judges and prosecuting officers drawn from their number, but a substantial segment of other public officials are members of the bar. If there is a ruling elite in Texas, a goodly segment of it comes from the legal profession. The members constitute a rather uniform group: They come from well-to-do segments of society, often have relatives who have been lawyers, are educated at a handful of law schools, and are almost entirely Anglo males.

JUDICIAL SELECTION

The Texas Constitution, faithful to the principles of Jacksonian Democracy, provides for the popular election of judges. Trial judges are elected for four-year terms, appellate judges for six-year tenures. Most judges, however, first reach the bench by appointment. T. C. Sinclair and Bancroft Henderson found that of the state judges serving during the 1940–1962 period, 66 percent first came to their office by appointment.[6] The governor fills vacancies in district and appellate judgeships. County commissioners courts, the nonjudicial governing body of county government, make appointments when vacancies occur at lower levels, except for the municipal courts, where appointment practices vary. The appointee's term expires at the next general election, but he usually has little trouble holding the position. Incumbent judges, whether appointed or elected, are seldom challenged and almost never defeated.

The Texas Constitution requires that district and appellate judges be citizens of the United States and Texas and that they have practiced law, or have been a lawyer and a judge of a court of record, within the state for at least 4 and 10 years respectively. Legal training and experience are usually not required to hold posts below the district-judge level. In general, those making appointments have a free hand in filling vacancies. Governors may seek advice and counsel on judicial appointments from a wide range of friends, political allies, and representatives of the bar, but they retain the decisional power. The Texas Senate, though possessing the power to block gubernatorial appointments, rarely disapproves a nominee. In a state not noted for its competitive politics or strong party organizations, the governor can resist almost any political pressure in selecting his choice. Of course, he is likely to seek someone who he thinks will not discredit his administration and can be reelected. So while governors select individuals on the basis of friendship and partisan support, they usually insist that nominees be competent and qualified. Generalization about the 254 commissioners courts' appointive patterns is difficult, but friendship and political support appear to be crucial, with competency stressed less.

A number of Texas judges do reach the bench by election. Sinclair and Henderson found that in the 1952–1962 period about one-quarter of those judges elected to the bench defeated an incumbent, two-fifths won in a race than did not involve an incumbent, and one-third won without opposition. In contrast to state courts in general, members of the Texas Supreme Court usually attain the bench via election.[7] From 1950 through 1974 only three men were appointed and eight were elected in open races. Supreme Court justices usually resign at the conclusion of an elected term, thus denying the governor an opportunity to fill vacancies. Recent Supreme Court winners have—with three exceptions—won preprimary bar poll, which is conducted by mail ballot in contested races. In contests not involving an incumbent, winners have tended to come from large cities where there are substantial numbers of lawyers as well as voters. Once on the bench, Texas judges are reasonably secure because incumbents are usually unopposed and those with opposition survive three-fourths of the challenges that do occur. Nevertheless, judges lament that when contests do occur, they must neglect their courts while tending political fences in the months prior to the election.

The state operates a judicial retirement system, and district and appellate judges must retire at age 75; they qualify for increased pensions if they leave office upon or before reaching the age óf 70. In an effort to provide a mechanism for removing the unethical or incompetent, a 1965 constitutional amendment established a Commission on Judicial Conduct. It is composed of two civil appeals court justices and two district court judges appointed by the Supreme Court, two lawyers appointed by the directors of the state bar, four laymen appointed by the governor, and one justice of the peace. The commission can issue private reprimands, public censures, or even recommendations for removal of judicial officials ranging from officials of the highest appellate court to local courts of limited jurisdiction; recommendations for removal are submitted to the Texas Supreme Court for action. Its impact is difficult to assess, since the most serious cases are apparently disposed of by resignation before commission action is completed. The commission was created to provide an alternative to the cumbersome traditional methods of removal—by impeachment, with charges brought by the House and conviction by two-thirds of the Senate, and by the governor upon address of two-thirds of each house. In the two most famous situations occurring since its creation (the impeachment and conviction of District Judge Oscar Carillo of Duval county and the resignation at the beginning of address proceedings of Supreme Court Judge Don Yarbrough) the legislature began action before the commission.

Texas judges are almost always Democrats. Appointees are

selected in most cases by elected Democrats, who favor members of their party. Electoral decisions are in effect made in the Democratic primary since the Republican party rarely nominates judicial candidates. In factional terms, it helps if the judicial aspirant is aligned with the conservative wing of the Democratic party. Democratic governors have come from this faction, and this is reflected in their appointments. Additionally, conservative Democrats fare better in elections than do liberals. No identified liberal has been elected to the Texas Supreme Court in modern times, although several have made the race. Lawyers apparently perceive the realities of selection: Sinclair and Henderson found that most lawyers feel that being known as a Republican or liberal disqualifies more "otherwise competent" persons from judicial service than being known as a conservative Democrat.[8]

The family backgrounds of judges in Texas are even less representative in occupational terms than are lawyers' backgrounds. Judges are more likely to come from prominent families, to have had relatives on the bench, and to have attended the University of Texas Law School than are other lawyers.[9] The number of women and Mexican-Americans on district or appellate courts is small.

In summary, the state judiciary is more homogeneous than is the state bar, which is considerably more homogeneous than is the adult population of the state.

JURIES

The jury system provides a means for involving the ordinary citizen in the judicial process. Two types of juries are used in Texas: grand juries, which indict persons alleged to have committed crimes if the evidence warrants, and petit or trial juries, which decide cases. The grand jury is composed of 12 persons, 9 of whom must concur in an indictment. District judges have considerable control over the composition of grand juries, since they appoint the commissioners who select a group of 20 county residents from which the judge selects 20 for jury service. Critics of the process have complained that grand juries are usually made up of individuals from the more affluent segments of society. That this occurs is probably due as much to the fact that most salaried employees cannot afford the time for service during the typical three-month grand-jury term as to the biases of the judges. Grand juries are usually dependent on the office of the district attorney for legal advice, and indictments often represent the sentiments of that office as much as that of the grand jury.

Texas makes extensive use of juries for deciding cases. All serious crimes must be tried by a jury, and jury trial is available on request for all other cases, civil and criminal. Trial jurors are randomly selected from among those eligible for service, that is, registered voters or adult property owners who reside in the county. Over the years statutes were enacted allowing numerous categories of persons to claim exemption from jury service. This was presumably because of the overriding importance of their activities to the community, but in actuality, it was because group spokesmen had enough legislative influence to have their group added to the exemption list. Most of the exemptions have been repealed, with mothers of small children and students constituting important exceptions.

Judges may excuse people from service, and many are excused for business and occupational reasons. Others are excused from particular trials because the opposing attorneys and the judge believe they are disqualified for some reason (e.g., a prospective juror might have preexisting opinions or biases). Additionally, each attorney is allowed a limited number of preemptory challenges by which he can disqualify a potential juror at his discretion. This form of negative selection undoubtedly prevents juries from accurately representing a cross section of the population. Not enough is known about the process to indicate just what social groups are underrepresented or overrepresented, although the poor and ethnic minorities probably constitute a smaller portion of jury membership than they do of the general population.

CONCLUSION

Quite clearly the judicial system is staffed by a relatively select segment of the population. The legal profession itself is of course unique in that lawyers have undergone special training and possess skills not common to the populace as a whole. But beyond this, the bar and the state judiciary are atypical socioeconomically and politically. The question can legitimately be raised as to what difference all this makes. Can lawyers and judges and grand juries objectively apply the law, irrespective of their partisan, sexual, ethnic, or social characteristics? National studies support the view that at least in certain types of cases, judicial background correlates with judicial decisional patterns.[10]

Unfortunately, the relationships between judicial characteristics and judicial decision making in Texas have not been tested. Although personal background may not lead to conscious prejudice on the part of judges, it may well provide a general social and political orientation or evaluative framework that is reflected in judicial rulings. If this is the case, the narrow base from which Texas judges are recruited may be of substantial import to the operation of the state's judicial system.

Partisan unrepresentativeness may decline over the next few

years. If the conservative Democratic hegemony declines, one consequence will be the opening up of the judicial ranks to groups previously
excluded. For example, if a Republican or liberal Democrat is elected
governor he will assuredly reward his friends and deny his enemies just
as his conservative Democratic predecessors have done over the years.

Other changes will not be so easy. Before the composition of
judicial personnel can be substantially altered, the base from which
judges are recruited—the state bar—will have to diversify its membership. But for blacks, Mexican-Americans, women, and people from
poor or low-status backgrounds to become lawyers, great changes will
be required. Children from these groups will have to be socialized to
higher occupational expectations, and better educational training will
have to be provided if they are to qualify for admission to law schools.
Additional space in law schools must be provided, along with financial
support, to accommodate individuals from these groups. Tentative
efforts are being made by some of the state's law schools, and efforts to
close the predominantly black law school at Texas Southern University
on grounds of inefficiency have subsided. Supporters of the law school
pointed out that most of the state's black lawyers had studied law at
Texas Southern and that the practical consequences of closure would
be a reduction in the number of blacks entering the legal profession.

THE STRUCTURE OF THE COURT SYSTEM

The Texas court system is complicated, diffused, and at times confus-
ing, with series of layers and special courts within layers (see Table
8.1). The Texas Constitution provides for a supreme court, a court of
criminal appeals, courts of civil appeals, district courts, county courts,
and justice of the peace courts. In addition, the legislature has created a
number of other courts. Courts may be classified into three types: local
trial courts of limited jurisdiction, trial courts of general jurisdiction,
and appellate courts.[11] Generally, trial courts are responsible for
making the basic decisions in cases, and appellate courts review their
findings. Emphasis in review is placed on legal questions, and on
factual questions appellate courts defer to the findings of trial courts. In
Texas, however, there is considerable overlapping between layers,
with courts sharing jurisdictions and exercising original jurisdiction
over some cases and appellate jurisdiction over others.

TRIAL COURTS OF LIMITED JURISDICTION

Probably the greatest variety in the names, kinds, and jurisdictions of
Texas courts occur among the trial courts of limited jurisdiction, most
of which are structurally part of county or municipal governments. The

TABLE 8.1 • TEXAS JUDICIAL STRUCTURE*

Type of court	Name of court	Jurisdiction			
		Criminal: original	Civil: original	Criminal: appellate	Civil: appellate
Local trial courts of limited jurisdiction	Justice of the Peace	Misdemeanors with no confinement and fines not exceeding $200	Cases where amount does not exceed $200; decisions are final for amounts of $20 or less	None	None
	County Court	All misdemeanors involving confinement and/or fines of over $200; cases not exceeding $100 are final	All cases $200–$500; concurrent with district court $500–$1000; cases $20–$100 are final	All cases from JP court (trial *de novo*)	All cases from JP court over $20 (trial *de novo*)
Trial court of general jurisdiction	District Court	All felonies	All cases over $1000; concurrent with county court for $500–$1000; certain specified classes of cases	None	None

Appellate courts				
Court of Criminal Appeals	None	None	None	All cases involving confinement and/or fines exceeding $100 from county and district courts
Court of Civil Appeals	None	None	None	All cases over $100 from county and district courts; decisions involving divorce litigation are final
Supreme Court	None	Writs against judicial, state government, and political party officials	None	From trial courts: validity of state statutes and/or administrative actions. From civil appeals courts: dissents, conflicts, invalidity of statutes, revenues of the state, Railroad Commission, substantive error

*Corporation courts, courts of domestic relations, juvenile courts, and probate proceedings are not included.

constitution established two such courts (justice of the peace and county courts), with limitations based on the importance of the cases they handle, and the legislature has established several courts to handle cases based on specialized subject matter.

The court at the bottom of the judicial hierarchy is the justice of the peace, or JP, court. The Texas Constitution provides that each commissioners court shall divide its county into not less than four or more than eight justice precincts, with a court in each. In precincts where there is a city of 8,000 or more inhabitants, the constitution provides for two JP courts. JPs are elected by the voters of the precinct for four-year terms; the only qualification is that the holder must be a qualified voter of the state.

JP courts have jurisdiction over criminal cases involving misdemeanors (minor criminal offenses) not punishable by confinement and/or fines of over $200 and in civil cases where the amount involved is less than $200 (a constitutional amendment approved in 1978 extended that jurisdiction to $1000, with the new jurisdiction concurrent with that of county and district courts). The JP courts handle a tremendous variety of minor cases, most notably traffic and hunting and fishing violations and small claims. A person charged with a misdemeanor is entitled to a jury trial if he requests it, and either party in a civil case may request a jury trial, although the requesting party must pay a small jury fee. Juries in JP courts are composed of six persons; there is a right of appeal to county court, where the cases are tried anew, in all criminal cases and in civil cases involving more than $20.

The JP performs several other roles. If the county has not created a position of coroner (and most have not), he acts as coroner. He also acts as magistrate at arraignment proceedings, at which he makes a preliminary determination of whether an accused person should be discharged, have bond fixed, or be remanded to jail. Additionally, he has authority to issue warrants for the apprehension of persons charged with crimes. As a magistrate, the JP may perform weddings; since tradition demands remuneration and fees are not provided by law, the practice of tipping makes the position quite profitable in many urban areas.

In each incorporate municipality there is a municipal court, commonly known as traffic court. Municipal courts have jurisdiction over all criminal cases arising under municipal ordinances, and they have concurrent jurisdiction with JP courts over criminal cases falling under JP jurisdiction. They have no civil jurisdiction. In the larger cities the municipal court judge is a full-time official, but in smaller cities and towns the mayor, city clerk, or other municipal official serves as judge. Appeals from municipal court go to the county court.

In each county there is a county court presided over by the county judge, who is elected by the voters of the county for a four-year term and who must be "well versed in the law." County courts have original jurisdiction over all misdemeanors not under the jurisdiction of the JP courts (those punishable by confinement or fines of over $200) and all civil cases in which the amount involved is $200–$500. In civil cases involving from $500 to $1000, the county court has concurrent jurisdiction with state district courts. It also has jurisdiction over the commitment of mentally ill persons to mental hospitals. In civil cases involving less than $100 and in criminal cases not involving imprisonment or fines of less than $100, county court decisions are final. Otherwise, appeals are taken from the county court to the Court of Criminal Appeals or the courts of civil appeals. The county court serves as an appellate court for appeals from decisions of the JP courts.

In the larger urban areas the judicial functions of the county judge conflict with his other duties as an official of county government by making demands on his time, and the docket may include more cases than even a full-time judge could handle. In a number of such counties the legislature has established courts called county courts at law, presided over by elected judges, who assume much of the judicial responsibilities of the county judge. In some cases these courts are specialized, with county civil and criminal courts at law.

Over the years a variety of special courts were created in the urban counties to handle specialized problems at the trial court level. Students of judicial administration prefer courts of general jurisdiction, and the legislature apparently is adopting that preference by concentrating on creating new district courts. The 1977 legislature, for example, converted 31 courts of domestic relations and juvenile courts into state district courts. Appeals from the special courts generally go to the Court of Criminal Appeals or the courts of civil appeals.

TRIAL COURTS OF GENERAL JURISDICTION

The chief trial courts are the district courts, which handle both civil and criminal matters. The state is divided into judicial districts; a district judge, elected by the voters of the district for a four-year term, presides over each district court. In rural areas districts often include several counties, and in the larger urban counties there are several judicial districts, each encompassing the entire county. Some of the latter are statutorily established to handle criminal or civil cases only. District judges must be residents of the district for two years immediately preceding their election, be at least 25 years old, and have four years of experience as a lawyer or judge. In 1978 there were 326 district courts, and new ones are created by almost every legislature.

District courts have original jurisdiction over all criminal cases involving felonies (offenses punishable by lengthy confinement) and all civil cases involving over $1000; they share original jurisdiction with county courts for amounts from $500 to $1000. Additionally, they have original jurisdiction over misdemeanors involving officials misconduct, suits for damages and slander, controversies over land titles, contested elections, and suits in behalf of the state to recover penalties, forfeitures, and escheats. Any party to a suit may require that trial be before a 12-person jury; but in civil cases the request must be made by one party to the suit, who is required to pay a small jury fee.

APPELLATE COURTS

The procedures used by appellate courts differ considerably from those of trial courts. In trial courts the plaintiff presents evidence designed to prove his case; if he succeeds in presenting enough evidence to demonstrate that he has a legitimate case, the defendant must then present evidence in rebuttal. Witnesses are examined and cross-examined, and attorneys summarize the case; the jury then decides. During this process lawyers may object to the introduction of evidence, challenge the interpretation of the law by the judge, and undertake other legal maneuvers designed to call attention to errors by the judge. If they lose the case, they can appeal to a higher court to reverse the decision because of an error.

Appellate courts ordinarily do not retry cases (an exception in Texas is appeal from JP courts, when a complete new trial is held). Instead, they review the record of the original trial to determine if errors that justify the reversal of the decision were committed by the trial court. Ordinarily appellate courts accept the findings of fact of trial courts and concern themselves with questions of law, although they may insist that the record reveal substantial evidence to support the findings of fact of the trial court. In reviewing the record of the trial court, appellate judges may consider the written record of the trial, the allegations of error contained in the appeal, and the briefs on the law and the oral arguments presented by opposing attorneys. If the court discovers a reversible error it may send the case back for retrial, dismissal, or other appropriate action; if not, the original decision must be executed.

An unusual feature of the Texas court system is that above the level of district court the system divides into two branches, with separate civil and criminal appellate courts. All appeals in criminal cases go directly to the Court of Criminal Appeals, but there are two layers of civil appellate courts: an intermediate group of courts of civil appeals and the Supreme Court.

The Court of Criminal Appeals has appellate jurisdiction over all criminal cases except those over which the county court's decisions are final (i.e., those involving fines of $100 or less). The court consists of nine elected judges; they must be at least 35 years of age, be citizens of the United States and residents of the state, and must have been practicing lawyers or judges of a court of record for a total of 10 years. (The Texas Constitution establishes these qualifications for members of the Supreme Court and provides that the members of the other appellate courts must meet the same qualifications.) Judges of the Court of Criminal Appeals serve overlapping terms, and one position on the court is designated presiding judge. Five judges constitute a quorum, but all decisions must be concurred in by five judges.

The Court of Criminal Appeals handles about 1600 cases and writs annually, a monstrous workload since opinions must be written in all cases. Various efforts have been made to cope with this burden and remove a serious backlog of cases. First, two commissioners, who essentially functioned as judges but whose opinions had to be approved by the judges before being handed down as decisions, were statutorily added to the court; a constitutional amendment was adopted making them members of the court in 1966; two permanent and then two "rotating" commissioners were created; and finally in 1977 a constitutional amendment was adopted increasing the size of the court to nine members, with the permanent commissioners becoming members and the governor appointing two members.

The state is divided into 14 intermediate courts of civil appeals, which have appellate jurisdiction over civil cases. Each of these courts consists of a chief justice and two associate justices who are elected for overlapping six-year terms. The jurisdiction of the civil appeals courts extends to cases from the district courts, county courts, and the various special courts, excepting those cases decided by county courts involving amounts of $100 or less. Civil appeals court decisions are final in divorce matters, cases of slander and contested elections other than for state offices or when the validity of a statute is questioned, and appeals from interlocutory orders; otherwise, cases may be appealed to the Texas Supreme Court.

The highest civil court in the state is the Supreme Court, which is composed of nine members, one of whom is designated chief justice. Members are elected for six years and serve overlapping terms.

As Thornton Sinclair notes, the Supreme Court is easily the most important and prestigious court in the state:

> The Texas Supreme Court stands at the head of the civil judicial system of the State. Since civil law is so overwhelmingly important to lawyers, and the court of criminal appeals is pushed into the background, the Texas

Supreme Court emerges in bar circles as the unrivaled head of the Texas judicial system. In this capacity, the court performs in fact or in theory many functions. First of all, it is the last resort in the State for deciding civil cases, and thus for developing the case law in this area. The court makes the rules of civil procedure, which bind civil courts and the lawyers who work in them. It is the supreme court which prescribes and administers the rules and examinations for admission to the bar, and in so doing, states the minimum requirements for legal education. . . . The court draws up rules of ethics which serve as the basis for disciplining and expelling bar members. The supreme court is the instrument for removal of judges (including judges of the theoretically coordinate court of criminal appeals). Insofar as there is any centralized administration of courts in Texas (and there is very little), the supreme court or the chief justice is in charge.[12]

Framers of the amendment to the Constitution of 1876 creating the framework within which the Texas Supreme Court still operates hoped that the existence of a two-layer appellate system for civil cases would allow the courts of civil appeals to handle the correction of errors by trial courts. The Supreme Court could then devote its attention to achieving unity of decision making among the courts of civil appeals and to developing case law by handling only the difficult legal problems facing the state courts.[13] Three developments have frustrated these intentions.

First, there is a small but potentially important group of cases in which the Supreme Court has original jurisdiction. The statutes provide that the Court or any justice thereof may issue various writs against district and appellate court judges, officers of state government, and political party officials. Party officials were included so that persons ruled off the ballot might obtain quick relief.

Second, the legislature has provided that appeals may be taken directly from trial courts to the Supreme Court from any order granting or denying an injunction on the ground of the constitutionality or unconstitutionality of any state statute or on the ground of the validity or invalidity of any administrative order issued by any state board or commission under any state statute. This in effect provides for the direct appeal from trial courts of cases in which state administration might be frustrated over a long period of time by fully deliberative judicial processes.

Third, and most important, the legislature has expanded the scope of Supreme Court review of court of civil appeals decisions beyond earlier intentions. Six categories of cases may be appealed to the Texas Supreme Court: (1) cases in which judges of a court of civil appeals disagreed, (2) cases in which two or more courts of civil appeals disagreed, (3) cases in which a statute was held void, (4) cases involving the revenue of the state, (5) cases in which the Railroad Commission is a party, and (6) cases in which it appears that an error of substantive law which affects the judgment in the case has been committed by a court of civil appeals. The first three categories are essential to the purpose of securing a Court whose objectives are unity of decision making and development of difficult case law through the handling of cases presenting difficult legal problems. The last three categories add to the case load of the Supreme Court even though the cases may not be of great public importance; this is especially true of the "substantive error" category, which obligates the court to review a case if the judgment of the civil appeals court appears erroneous and which, in effect, merely gives litigants a second chance in the appellate process.

THE JUDICIARY AND THE POLICYMAKING PROCESS

The courts intervene in the policymaking process through the settlement of disputes. Controversies in the courts may concern almost any form of political activity, and judicial participation may occur at almost any point in the policymaking process; however, policymaking in the courts differs from that in other governmental institutions because special legal factors influence the judicial process and legal conceptions limit the scope of court decisions. Courts may only decide cases and controversies. They cannot levy taxes or appropriate funds, although decisions on particular cases may influence the distribution of power or wealth in the community. This is especially the case when courts possess the authority to rule on the consistency of statutes with the constitution.

The highest appellate courts have by far the greatest political significance; through a process of elimination they get the most controversial cases with the most at stake, since these are the cases most likely to be appealed to the end of the judicial process. The courts of last resort are the ultimate decision makers in the judicial process and, occasionally, in the political process. As Kenneth Vines emphasizes, in stressing the importance of appellate courts the policymaking functions of trial courts should not be neglected. Their interpretation of statutes and application of law necessarily involve them in the making of important policy decisions. They make the initial decisions and may shape the manner in which the case is approached by appellate courts. Furthermore, for most litigants the trial courts are also the courts of last resort, for only a small portion of cases are appealed. Nevertheless, most of the highly controversial cases of major political significance are appealed to higher courts.[14]

The political role of Texas courts has not been thoroughly examined by social scientists, and little is known of the political significance of Texas court decisions. Sinclair's exploration of the Supreme Court, however, points to certain factors of political significance about that most important of Texas courts. In general political terms, all the Supreme Court justices since 1949 have been identified with the conservative faction of the Democratic party. But analysis of the voting behavior from 1965 to 1967 on cases that were considered as presenting a choice between liberalism and conservatism did not indicate that a majority of the justices consistently voted for conservative positions; if anything, the reverse was true.[15]

In Sinclair's analysis of the Supreme Court's interrelationships with the rest of the Texas political system, he identifies six elements with which the Court has had continuing important interaction: other courts, the legislature, the governor, the attorney general, law schools, and the state bar. The in-state law schools and the state bar were found to have the most persistent and pervasive relations with the Court (interactions range from the selection and use of briefing clerks to judicial membership in the bar); but the policy and political significance of these relationships are not clear. Overall, the Supreme Court was found to be hardworking and competent but, since its work load is large and it is unable to select cases for their importance, it has been only mildly innovative in its policymaking.[16]

One particular aspect of the Supreme Court's responsibility deserves further consideration. As do many other American courts, Texas courts exercise the power to rule on the consistency of statutes with the state and national constitution; ultimately, judicial review in civil cases is exercised by the state supreme court. The nature of the Texas Constitution—especially its inclination toward great detail and its tendency to limit the power of the legislature—makes for many challenges to statutory enactments, and many of them are successful. The Texas Supreme Court probably has less discretion than its national counterpart in allowing or disallowing statutes, for its decisional process on constitutional questions resembles a comparison of two narrowly drawn statutes more than the interpretation of the consistency of a statute with broad constitutional provisions. In terms of constitutional interpretation, the Texas Supreme Court has been neither a force for modernization through giving the constitution a broad and flexible interpretation nor a reactionary force inclined to unduly restrictive interpretation. The nature of the constitution prevents it from taking either route.

JUDICIAL PROBLEMS

STRUCTURE AND ADMINISTRATION

Students of judicial administration believe that justice is best served by a unified and simplified court system, a belief that has led to considerable criticism of the Texas system. At the top of the Texas system are two branches of appellate courts, a division found in only one other state. There is even more duplication at the trial-court level, where district courts, county courts, justice of the peace courts, and municipal courts all operate.

Other problems arise from the nature of judicial districts in Texas. State district and civil appeals courts vary greatly in the populations and case loads they serve. Courts in metropolitan centers, like Dallas and Houston, frequently have case loads that are many times larger than those of their rural counterparts. The Supreme Court can shift cases about at the civil appeals level, and metropolitan areas can hire underemployed district judges from outside the area to assist with their dockets. The state is divided into nine administrative judicial districts, with each district presided over by one of the district judges designated by the governor with concurrence of the Senate. The presiding judge may assign judges in his district to hold court in any county in the district in order to dispose of accumulated business or when the regular judge of a district court is absent, disabled, or disqualified. These measures have not solved the problems resulting from unequal judicial districts because the aid received by overburdened urban courts has not been extensive.

The absence of equitable districts has contributed to a most serious problem in the Texas judicial system—the delay in bringing

"Justice delayed is Justice denied." All courts in urban areas have crowded dockets.

cases to trial. Dockets in metropolitan areas are often 18–24 months behind schedule. This delay in the administration of justice produces all sorts of consequences. In civil cases, one of the parties may be forced to accept a less favorable settlement than would otherwise be necessary; for example, a worker injured in an industrial accident may settle for a smaller sum than he otherwise would receive because he cannot afford to wait two years for a judgment. If anything, the consequences for criminal cases are even more serious, as the report of the Chief Justice's Task Force for Court Improvement makes clear:

> The criminal dockets of the courts are clogged to the point of crisis in most cities. Such overcrowding operates at the same time to the advantage of the habitual criminal and the disadvantage of the first-time offender or the innocent person. Crowded dockets mean that the time of the courts and the prosecution is at a premium. Since trials take time, it is a physical impossibility for every case actually to proceed to trial. Most cases are disposed of through a bargaining process between defense lawyers and prosecuting attorneys, usually culminating in a plea of guilty in exchange for a lighter sentence.[17]

The experienced criminal understands the system and its delays, while the first offender or the innocent may be willing to accept a "deal" rather than risk a long sentence.

SELECTION OF JUDGES

There has been continuing debate in the United States on the desirability of electing judges. The formal Texas system of election, which usually results in appointment, has drawn fire from both sides. Critics contend that the appointment system makes politicians into judges and the election requirement makes judges into politicians. They maintain that governors and commissioners courts use their virtually unrestrained appointive powers to elevate friends, cronies, and political supporters to the bench and that considerations of competency and ability are only secondary. At the same time objection is raised to the necessity for judges to stand for election or reelection every four or six years. Electioneering takes judges from their benches for considerable periods and raises the possibility that in their search for popular support they may incur political obligations that will affect their independence and impartiality. Additionally, there is likely to be little relation between a candidate's vote-getting abilities and his qualifications for judicial service.

A number of legal scholars and practitioners have urged that a modified system of appointment-election, sometimes called the Missouri Plan because it was first adopted in that state, be used instead of a

The Rise and Fall of a Judge

The most meteoric career in the Texas judiciary was experienced by former Supreme Court Judge Don Yarbrough. Prior to his successful race for a position on the court, he was little noticed. After law school he worked for two state water agencies and the Campus Crusade for Christ, and then established a law practice in Houston and became involved in several business and banking enterprises. In 1974 he made an almost unnoticed race for state treasurer.

In 1976 Chief Justice Charles Barron of the San Antonio Court of Civil Appeals won the support of leaders of the bar association and apparently had an easy race for an "open" seat on the Texas Supreme Court, for Yarbrough, his only opponent, apparently was not a serious contender. During the campaign Barron emphasized his judicial background, won the bar association poll, and outspent his opponent; Yarbrough's only visible support derived from his evangelical religious activity. Yarbrough received 831,621 and Barrow 537,394 votes; political analysts attributed the victory to the resemblance of Yarbrough's name to that of Don Yarbrough, a popular liberal Democratic candidate for governor.

The state's lawyers were surprised, but surprise shortly became shock. Yarbrough held a press conference and indicated that God put him in the race and won him the nomination. He added that his decisions would be interpreted in harmony with God's word. Shortly thereafter, the media discovered several civil suits that were pending against Yarbrough, as well as complaints to the bar association dating back to August 1975. In June a jury found him guilty of civil fraud, and throughout the summer of 1976 additional suits and bar grievances were filed.

Efforts were begun to prevent Yarbrough's election. He did not have a Republican opponent, and the most likely write-in candidate, former dean of the Texas law school Page Keeton, decided a campaign was impractical. Two would-be candidates undertook write-in campaigns, but Yarbrough won overwhelmingly.

Yarbrough's troubles mounted as indictments for forging an automobile title and perjury in testimony before a grand jury were added to the charges against him. At the conclusion of a special summer session in 1977, the legislature began proceedings to address him out of office, but he announced his resignation from the court.

---

pure appointive or elective system. Under this plan the governor fills vacancies on the bench from a list submitted to him by a nonpartisan nominating commission. After the newly appointed judge has served for a specified period, his name is placed on the ballot for voters of the area to determine whether he shall be retained in office. A similar referendum is held periodically so the electoral nexus is not broken.

Sinclair and Henderson found (see Table 8.2) that while Texas lawyers and judges are far from agreement on the best method of selecting judges, the Missouri Plan enjoys a substantial margin of support over the present system and the purely appointive and elective

TABLE 8.2 • FIRST PREFERENCES OF BENCH AND BAR FOR VARIOUS SYSTEMS OF JUDICIAL SELECTION

	Ranked first by	
Preference	Lawyers (*n* = 177)	Judges (*n* = 155
Present system	30.0%	20.0%
Missouri Plan	44.5	49.6
Gubernatorial appointment	8.5	1.9
Election—but for a longer period	17.0	28.5
Totals	100.0%	100.0%

SOURCE: T. C. Sinclair and Bancroft Henderson, *The Selection of Judges in Texas* (Houston: Public Affairs Research Center, University of Houston, 1965), p. 104.

alternatives. Various bar association groups, under the leadership of former Texas Supreme Court Chief Justice Robert Calvert, have endorsed the Missouri system. If fundamental change occurs, it probably will be in the direction of some variant of the Missouri Plan, but the experience of the abortive effort at constitutional revision indicates that partisan nomination and election is firmly entrenched. The convention repeatedly defeated other alternatives.

THE POOR AND THE LAW

The concept of equal treatment before the law is a principle widely acclaimed and deeply cherished as an integral part of our political system. But is this principle realized in fact? Evidence points to the contrary. The legal system in the United States, including Texas, is highly complex, and legal practitioners have knowledge, skills, and techniques relevant to this sytem not possessed by the general public. Their specialized knowledge is available to the public, but usually on a laissez-faire fee basis. This fee system tends to restrict legal advice and assistance to those who can afford it. From the onset, then, Texans of low income are at a disadvantage in their dealings with the law.

There is irony in this, for the poor are often the economic groups most in need of legal service. To begin with the poor, because of patterns of education and socialization associated with poverty, are generally unfamiliar with the law and their rights under it. Two observers conclude: "Urban poor, in particular, often are abused by the legal process because they are ignorant of even the most elementary of its principles. They frequently submit to illegal acts and baseless legal claims."[18]

Though ignorant of the law, the poor cannot escape involvement with it. Most individuals charged with criminal offenses are from low-income groups. Additionally, the national and state governments have created new classes of entitlements—social security, job benefits, retirement benefits, and welfare—that are available to the poor. They have a right to these programs, but fulfillment of their right often depends on legal efforts on their behalf. The poor also have ordinary legal needs with respect to housing, wages, civil rights, consumer transactions, and domestic relations; these legal needs are perhaps more pressing than those of other segments of society because of their economic marginality. However, few lawyers are interested in the problems of the poor because little money can be made in handling their cases.

An increased awareness of the needs of the poor in legal matters has developed in recent years. The federal courts, recognizing this need in a series of decisions, have prodded the states toward insuring greater legal equality in criminal cases. Texas adopted a revised code of criminal procedure in 1965 that provides procedural guarantees for persons suspected of criminal offenses. Police are required to inform individuals they arrest of their basic legal rights, and the state must see that legal counsel is provided in cases where individuals cannot themselves afford it. In many areas of the state, the organized bar has assisted in providing competent counsel for indigents.

Although progress has been made in reducing the impact of poverty in Texas's sytem of criminal justice, similar steps in civil law have lagged behind. Traditionally, most services available to the poor in civil matters have been provided by legal aid offices financed largely from private funds, but the assistance provided has proved wholly inadequate to the needs of the economically underpriviliged.[19] The War on Poverty, launched in the mid-1960s, recognized this deficiency and sought—through grants—to improve services for the poor in the area of civil law. A number of Texas cities now use various federal grants to support such services, but much remains to be done.

PROSPECTS FOR REFORM

The possibilities for extensive judicial reform in Texas are reduced by the basic inertia of the governmental system. As with most reform efforts, the public is not very interested in the issue and their disinterest is shared by many political leaders. Past attempts at substantive reform of the judicial system have produced little in the way of results.

There is some movement for change. An entire new code of criminal procedure (the procedural rules followed in criminal cases) was enacted in 1965, and a new criminal code (the entire set of criminal statutes) was adopted in 1973. Piecemeal reforms that provided for mandatory judicial retirement and some administrative direction of the court system were enacted in 1965. The chief justice of the Supreme Court can shift cases from one civil appeals court to another, and district judges from one court to another. The presiding judge of each of the administrative judicial districts into which district courts are grouped can transfer judges within the administrative district. In 1977 the legislature converted the staff of the Judicial Council, a long-standing but not very active body charged with making continuous studies of the operations of the judicial system, into the Office of Court Administration. The duties of the office are limited: It is to assist the chief justice in discharging his administrative responsibilities and prepare and submit budget requests for the judicial system.

In 1972 former Chief Justice Robert Calvert's Task Force for Court Improvement recommended a thoroughgoing reform with only four types of courts: (1) county courts (trial courts of limited jurisdiction), (2) district courts (trial courts of general jurisdiction), (3) courts of appeals (regional intermediate appellate courts), and (4) a supreme court. The county courts were to replace the various courts of limited jurisdiction, with county courts at law judges becoming judges in the county courts and the current county judges becoming either judges in the county courts or continuing as presiding officers of commissioners courts. Justices of the peace and constables were to become magistrates of the county courts, handling nonjudicial administrative functions and uncontested cases. Judges of the criminal district courts, juvenile courts, and domestic relations courts were to become regular district judges. The courts of appeals were to have authority over criminal and civil cases, as was the Supreme Court. The chief justice of the Supreme Court would have authority to transfer cases between courts at the same level. Judges of the Court of Criminal Appeals were to become members of the Supreme Court, with the size of that court temporarily increased until death or departure reduced the membership to nine. The recommendation also provided that the method of selecting district attorneys, district judges, county attorneys, county clerks, and sheriffs, all currently elective officials, would be left to the legislature. A separate constitutional amendment was suggested to provide for selection of judges through a version of the Missouri Plan, with its use optional with the legislature for district judges but compulsory for appellate judges.[20]

After preliminary action by the 1973 legislature, supporters of judicial reform decided not to attempt passage, opting instead for an attempt to include the plan in the new constitution to be written in 1974. A modified version failed along with the rest of the proposed constitution. The adoption of the constitutional amendment in 1977 increasing the size of the Court of Criminal Appeals is an indication that judicial reformers have, at least temporarily, abandoned efforts at comprehensive change.

Dealing with the legal problems of the poor is even more difficult than reforming the court structure. Basically, what is needed is some means-of acquainting disadvantaged individuals with the legal services available and providing financial support so they can utilize these services, irrespective of the ability to pay. Assuming there are sufficient numbers of lawyers available and ready to provide such services, substantial subsidization will be required in support of their efforts. Some private monies and public grants have been used and substantial progress has been made, but an adequate program will require a considerably larger infusion of public funds. Even the existing programs occasionally come under attack and find their funding threatened because of involvement in politically sensitive cases.

The continuing failure to provide for equality under the law in Texas, as in other states, is not without consequence. So long as legal services and protections are available only to those who have money or the "right connections," the disadvantaged person is likely to view the law and the courts as his enemies. Until there is more nearly equal justice under law, the poor are not likely to develop a feeling of trust and confidence in our system of justice and those who administer it—or in the institutions of society in general.

NOTES

[1]John Locke, "An Essay Concerning the True Original, Extent and End of Civil Government," in *Social Contract* (New York: Oxford Univ. Press, 1962), pp. 51–52.

[2]David Easton, *The Political System* (New York: Knopf, 1953).

[3]T. C. Sinclair and Bancroft Henderson. *The Selection of Judges in Texas* (Houston: Public Affairs Research Center, University of Houston, 1965), pp. 51–68.

[4]"Facts v. Fancy: The Economic Survey of Texas Lawyers. 1967," *Texas Bar Journal* 9 (January 1968): 5–80.

[5]Ibid.

[6]Sinclair and Henderson, op. cit., p. 21.

[7]T. C. Sinclair, "The Supreme Court of Texas," *Houston Law Review* 7 (September 1969): 23–24.

[8]Sinclair and Henderson, op. cit., pp. 86–88.

[9]Ibid., pp. 51–68.

[10]See John R. Schmidhauser, "The Justices of the Supreme Court: A Collective Portrait," *Midwest Journal of Political Science* 3 (February 1959): 2–37, 40–49; Stuart S. Nagel, "Testing Relations between Judicial Characteristics and Judicial Decision-Making," *Western Political Quarterly* 15 (Sept. 1962), 425–437; and S. Sidney Ulmer,

"The Political Party Variable in the Michigan Supreme Court," *Journal of Public Law* 11 (Fall 1962): 352–362.

[11]Herbert Jacob and Kenneth Vines, "State Courts and Public Policy," in Herbert Jacob and Kenneth Vines, eds., *Politics in the American States,* 3rd ed. (Boston: Little, Brown, 1971), p. 246–247.

[12]Sinclair, op. cit., p. 41.

[13]Ibid., p. 42. The discussion of the jurisdiction of the Supreme Court draws heavily on pp. 41–45.

[14]Kenneth Vines, "Courts as Political and Governmental Agencies," in Jacob and Vines, eds., *Politics in the American States* (Boston: Little, Brown, 1965), pp. 241–243.

[15]Sinclair, op. cit., p. 59.

[16]Ibid., pp. 63–69.

[17]Chief Justice's Task Force for Court Improvement, *Justice at the Crossroads* (Austin: 1972), pp. 1–2.

[18]Norman L. Miller and James C. Daggatt, "The Urban Law Program of the University of Detroit School of Law," *California Law Review* 54 (May 1960): 1009.

[19]Henry J. Schmandt, *Courts in the American Political System* (Belmont, Calif.: Dickenson, 1968), p. 103.

[20]Chief Justice's Task Force, op. cit.

Local Government

Although in geographical terms local governments are closest to the people (or the "grass roots"), they are frequently less salient and "visible" than the state and national governments. Popular attention is attracted by the important events and large controversies that occur at the state capital and in Washington. Issues involving such matters as foreign policy, income tax reform, or energy shortages are more likely to stir the citizen's interest than the construction of a new sewage disposal plant or the budget for the sheriff's office. Moreover, the happenings at the state capital and in Washington are likely to be better reported by the news media, and the distance at which they transpire probably serves to enhance their glamour.

Yet, local governments have a direct, immediate, and large impact on the day-to-day lives of most citizens—their convenience, comfort, safety, and happiness. It is local governments that bear primary responsibility for operating public schools; supplying water, garbage collection, and sewerage services; providing police and fire protection; keeping public records; maintaining parks and recreation facilities; administering public health and welfare programs; controlling traffic and maintaining streets; and regulating land use by planning, zoning, and other means. Many of these activities are taken for granted, notwithstanding their vital nature, especially by the urban dweller, and their substantial cost. (See Table 9.1.)

Paradoxically, while the average citizen may be little informed on local government matters (and little interested, as indicated by the low

TABLE 9.1 • DIRECT EXPENDITURES BY GOVERNMENTS IN TEXAS, 1972 (IN THOUSANDS OF DOLLARS)

State government		3,102,741
Local governments		5,055,024
Counties	445,878	
Cities	1,576,975	
Special districts	540,006	
School districts	2,492,164	
Total Expenditures		8,157,765

SOURCE: Bureau of the Census, *Census of Governments*, 1972, Vol. 4, No. 5, pp. 119, 180.

turnout in local elections), the value of local government, often referred to as local *self*-government, is a traditional theme in American politics. The supporters of local government argue that it is "closer to the people" than the national and state governments and is therefore more representative and responsible in operation. Related to this is the contention that local control and decentralization are desirable goals in themselves. Politicians have much to say concerning the virtues of grass-roots democracy and the need to return government closer to the hands of the people. This was one of the professed objectives of the Nixon administration's "New Federalism." Another argument on behalf of local government is that it provides an opportunity for many citizens to participate and obtain experience in governmental affairs at a readily accessible level. Certainly the existence of a variety of local governments increases greatly the opportunities for holding elective offices. In Texas in 1978 there were over 22,000 elected local government officials. Many thousands more served on appointed boards, commissions, and committees. Still another argument is that local government permits experimentation and flexibility in the development and implementation of public programs. Local governments can take into more particular account the varying needs and circumstances of their constituents.

The existing pattern of local government is not without its critics, however. A common contention is that there are too many local governments and that they are characterized by overlapping activities and inefficiency, with substantial inequalities existing in the number and quality of services provided by various units. Moreover, the critics assert, local officials are often shortsighted and parochial. Further, the existence of the long ballot and many elected officials is said to confuse the voter and hamper rather than promote popular control of local government. Finally, doubt is expressed whether decentralization is a desirable goal, at least when it leads to an excessive fragmentation of power among too many local governments.

In this chapter we will not attempt to resolve the controversy over local government. The reader should, however, remember the various arguments and form some tentative conclusions concerning their relative merits, keeping in mind also that an argument is not necessarily a description of reality.

Whatever their motivations, there is no denying the fact that Americans have created a multitude of local governments and that they take a variety of forms. In 1977, the U.S. Bureau of the Census reported the existence of 80,120 local governments in the United States (in addition to the national and state governments). This figure included 3,042 counties, 18,856 municipalities (cities, towns, and villages), 16,882 townships, 15,260 school districts, and 26,140 special districts. Texas, with its total of 3,883, ranked fifth among the states in number of local governments. The leader was Illinois, with 6,386 units, Hawaii, with 20 units, had the least. The average number of units per state was 1,565.

At this point we need to raise the question of what is a local government. What characteristics must a governmental entity possess to be considered a unit of local government and not simply an agency of another government? A widely accepted definition is that used by the U.S. Bureau of the Census in its surveys: "A government is an organized entity which, in addition to having governmental character, has sufficient discretion in the management of its own affairs to

"Is local government equipped to meet today's problems?"

distinguish it as separate from the administrative structure of any other governmental unit." Analysis of this definition yields three criteria for a "government." First, an "organized entity" is one that has specified powers and is organized to carry them out, having its own officers, administrative structure, and so on. Second, "governmental character" means that the entity performs activities which are regarded as governmental in nature; may possess the power to levy taxes; and is characterized (at least formally) by public accountability, as by the election of its officials or public reporting of its activities. Third, the entity must have substantial financial and administrative autonomy, as when it can impose taxes or adopt a budget without the approval of other local governments and when it is not really controlled by another government. In Texas, for instance, mosquito-control districts are governed by the county commissioners court and do not possess the autonomy needed to classify them as units of local government. Rather, they are administrative appendages of county governments. Under the definition, a wide and disparate variety of governmental units are classified as local governments, ranging from New York City with its several million inhabitants to a Texas water district with its half dozen constituents.

Numerical changes and trends in local governments in Texas in recent decades are illustrated by Table 9.2. Texas has no townships, which is a form of rural local government especially prevalent in the Northeast and Midwest. The number of Texas counties has remained constant at 254 since 1924, when the last county was organized. Three trends are especially noticeable:
(1) The number of municipal or city governments has been constantly growing, which reflects the increasing urbanization of the state's population. Most of these new city governments are located adjacent to existing urban areas. (2) School districts have been decreasing in number as districts with small enrollments are consolidated to provide

TABLE 9.2 • LOCAL GOVERNMENTS IN TEXAS, 1952–1977

	1952	1957	1962	1967	1972	1977
Counties	254	254	254	254	254	254
Municipalities	738	793	866	884	981	1066
Special districts	550	645	733	1001	1215	1425
School districts	2479	1794	1474	1308	1174	1138
Total	4021	3484	3327	3447	3624	3883

SOURCE: U.S. Bureau of the Census, *Census of Governments for 1952, 1957, 1962, 1967, 1972, and 1977.*

more adequate educational programs and as dormant districts (those that have not operated a school for two consecutive years) are merged with adjoining districts in compliance with the Gilmer-Aiken Law (Texas) of 1949. (3) Special districts have greatly increased in number because of various factors, which are discussed later in this chapter.

Local governments are dispersed throughout the state, although the number differs very much from one county to another. Four thinly populated rural counties (Borden, Glasscock, Kennedy, and King) have only two local governments each, whereas three highly populated counties (Dallas, Harris, and Tarrant) have 59, 308, and 62, respectively. Generally, local governments are especially numerous in the urban and metropolitian areas.

The various types of local government, some of their political aspects, and the problems of metropolitan areas will be treated in this chapter. The different categories of local government will be taken up separately for ease of discussion. However, this should not be taken to mean that they exist and act independently of one another. The various local governments in an area often serve the same public, and they frequently cooperate in their operations. For example, they often raise revenue from the same sources (e.g., taxes on property) and collect it for one another. Even when they do not cooperate, they will be affected by what others do, whether it involves law enforcement, road and street maintenance, the annexation of territory, or the operations of territory. There is no way, for example, that the many local governments in the Dallas-Fort Worth area can simply ignore each other, whatever their inclinations. Also, open conflict between local governments is not a rare occurrence, as in "annexation wars" or disputes over the location of garbage disposal facilities.

COUNTY GOVERNMENT

Among the American States only Alaska, Connecticut, and Rhode Island do not have county governments. Traditionally, and particularly in the South and West, the county has been the principal unit of local government. This is still the case in rural areas. The 1970 population census revealed that approximately 175 Texas counties have populations of less than 20,000 each and thus can be fairly classified as rural counties.

COUNTY-STATE RELATIONSHIPS

According to legal doctrine, the county is established by and exists for the convenience of the state government to enforce and administer state laws and programs. Unless the state constitution provides other-wise, the state government formally has complete legal control over the structure, legal authority, and very existence of the county govern-ment. The county can undertake only those programs and activities that are authorized by the state constitution and legislation. This is a fairly accurate statement of one facet of the state-county relationship today in Texas. On the other hand, in practice there is very little supervision by state officials of the everyday operations of county governments. Once a given activity is authorized or delegated to the counties or their officials, they are left largely on their own. For example, the county sheriff enforces state criminal laws, but there is little if any state control over how he does this or over the prosectuion of offenders by the district attorney. Moreover, since county officials are elected locally and hence accountable to a local constituency, localism influences their actions. As has been observed:

> . . . although counties are created to carry out a common policy of the state and not mainly to advance the interests of a particular locality, the fact that a county is a local area, and that county officials are elected by a local rather than a state-wide electorate, brings about an anomalous situation in which county officials tend, in most instances, to apply state laws and regulations in the light of local conditions rather than with reference to conditions in the state as a whole.[1]

Thus, some counties collect personal taxes on automobiles, while many others do not; all are supposed to on the basis of existing law.

Harris County Decides to Build a Jail

The administration of jails in Texas is primarily a task for county governments, who have often been quite indifferent to jail conditions. Consequently, county jails have frequently been understaffed, over-crowded, and inhumane institutions. Until recently, lack of concern for the rights of prisoners permitted such conditions to go largely unchallenged. This has changed, and now in many states, including Texas, jails have come under judicial scrutiny.

In Harris County, a suit by the American Civil Liberties Union brought the overcrowded conditions of the county jail (2300 prisoners were confined in space intended for 1600) under the preview of a federal district judge. In 1975 the Judge held the county must act to alleviate the overcrowded, physically depressing, sometimes brutal conditions of the county jail.

What to do? Essentially, Harris County officials had two choices. One was systemic reform to reduce the number of prisoners, of whom about 70 percent are pretrial detainees. This could be done by developing a better pretrial release program and by speeding the movement of cases to trial, among other things. The second alternative was to build a new, larger jail.

County officials opted for the second alternative in 1975 and began planning for a new jail. This appeared to be a quicker, easier solution than systemic reform, which would require the cooperation of several dozen elected and appointed administrative and judicial officials. It was also in line with the notion that "the people in jail wouldn't be there if they didn't belong there." The new jail, to hold 2000 prisoners, is scheduled for completion in the mid-1980s at an estimated cost of $40 million. In all likelihood, it will be filled to capacity the day it opens, barring action to reduce the jail population.

Direct confrontations between the state government and county or other local governments are rare. Bargaining, cooperation, and accommodation rather than coercion are more likely to characterize state-local relationships. State legislators are usually quick to accede to the requests of local officials for special legislation. Also, associations of local officials have sufficient political power to secure desired legislation and to ward off or modify what is unwanted. Opposition to the Texas Tort Claims Act of 1969, which curtailed somewhat the immunity of local governments from damage suits, came from such organizations as the Texas Municipal League, the City Attorneys Association, and the County Judges and Commissioners Association. Although they failed to prevent its adoption, they did succeed in restricting its scope.[2] (The doctrine of immunity of governments from suit is archaic, stemming from the old notion that "the king can do no wrong.")

Since the early twentieth century, proponents of reform in county government have advocated home rule for counties, under which counties could do whatever they wanted in organizational and policy matters so long as they did not contravene the state constitution and laws. Home rule for cities has been long established and accepted.

Home rule would provide counties with greater flexibility and operating discretion and permit them to deal with problems more expeditiously and effectively. The experience with city home rule seems, on the whole, to have been quite satisfactory. Nonetheless, there continues to be strong opposition to county home rule, and the balance of political power appears to rest with the opposition. Many county officials, especially elected ones, have strongly resisted home rule. Thus a county attorney has indicated a belief that home rule could lead to "managerial-type government" in which a county manager might appoint various officials now elected. Such opposition is based partly on the belief that such officials should properly be elected. (On the other hand, a frequent criticism of county government is that too many officials are elected.) There is also in this opposition, though usually denied, a strong element of job protectionism. Some see home rule as a step toward "metro government," in which the governmental units in a metropolitan area are consolidated into a single unit. This they find highly disturbing.[3] Some basic opposition to change as such also blends in. Also, it should be noted that county government is not very visible or salient to much of the population; nor has it attracted the attention of reformers, as have city governments. While county home rule may seem like a good idea to many people, there has not been strong pressure in its support. In contrast, the intensity of the opposition enhances its power.

As the situation now stands, counties must ask the state legislature for permission to do many things that home-rule cities do as a matter of course, such as adjusting speed limits on county roads, concluding contracts with other governments, and removing fire hazards on private property. Some authorizations are general in nature, such as a 1954 law which permits all counties to adopt rabies control measures. More commonly, however, the laws granting regulatory power to counties deal with specific local circumstances. Thus, in 1975 the legislature enacted laws authorizing: (1) certain west Texas counties to regulate lighting installations near the McDonald Observatory and (2) counties of over 235,000 population to regulate parking in lots adjacent to a county courthouse. Such laws illustrate the dependence of county governments on legislation to enable them to deal with problems in their local communities.

Moreover, counties generally lack legislative, or rule-making, authority, whereas home-rule cities have broad legislature power. To illustrate, compare the positions of city and county health officers. Both are expected to follow the rules and regulations of the State Board of Health. However, the city can also adopt ordinances relating to health and sanitation and have these enforced by the health officer, whereas the county has no such authority.[4] The lack of rule-making power handicaps counties as units of general local government. In 1975 and 1977 proposals in the state legislature to grant general rule-making authority to counties were defeated, largely because of the opposition of organized real estate groups. They feared counties would use such authority to regulate land use and development adversely to their interests.

COUNTY GOVERNMENTAL ORGANIZATION

The structure of county government is set forth in much detail in the state constitution and laws. Although all counties have certain officials and bodies, there are variations among counties in their structure of offices, depending on the size of their populations; in special laws pertaining to them; and in accepting local practices, such as simply not filling some positions whether elective or appointive. Predictably, the more populous counties have considerably larger, more elaborate administrative systems than do rural counties. We will not attempt to describe the structure of county government in detail. Some categorizations are possible.

1. Each county has a governing body called the county commissioners court, whose members are elected for four-year terms.

2. Each county has a number of other officials, elected for four-year terms in partisan elections. They may include the following: sheriff, treasurer, county clerk, county attorney, tax assessor-collector, district clerk, county surveyor, county superintendent of schools, one or more justices of the peace, one or more constables, county board of school trustees, and inspector of hides and animals. (This last position is still open to counties on an optional basis. A person was elected to this position in Harris County in 1976. He apparently has no duties.) The familiar generalization that the structure of all county governments is essentially the same lacks complete accuracy, as there are many variations from one county to another.

According to law, in counties with fewer than 10,000 residents, the sheriff also serves as tax assessor-collector. However, in 1973 some 63 counties with populations below that figure still filled the office separately. Some had dropped below 10,000 at the time of the 1970 census; most, however, had either never had 10,000 residents or had long been below that figure.

The jurisdiction of the county attorney is given to the district attorney in some small counties (as is also the case in populous Bexar County), while others simply leave the office vacant. The offices of county surveyor is filled mostly in the larger, urban counties, where the occupant may develop close ties with real estate developers and promoters.

All counties elect at least one justice of the peace, with the number varying from 1 each in 40 counties to 11 each in Cameron and Hidalgo counties in the Rio Grande Valley. Duval County (population 11,700) elected 8 justices of the peace, while Harris County (population 1,741,000) elected 9. The number of constables varied from none in 63 counties to 8 each (the maximum possible) in Dallas, Duval, and Galveston counties. By law, each county is to elect at least 4 justices and 4 constables. Some counties may not hold elections for some positions, while in others low or nonexistent salaries discourage candidates. Some counties (e.g., Duval) prefer large numbers of elected officeholders for patronage or other purposes.

3. There are a number of appointed officials and boards or commissions. Each county is required to have a health officer (a "competent, licensed physician") who is appointed by the commis-

sioners court. In counties with over 35,000 population or $15 million in tax evaluation, there is an auditor, who exercises oversight of county financial practices. In counties with over 225,000 people, he becomes the chief budget officer. The auditor is appointed by the district judge or judges having jurisdiction in the county. Most counties participate in the agricultural extension and home demonstration programs and have appointed county agents in charge. Some counties, especially larger ones, have a variety of appointed officials or boards to head programs authorized but not required by law. Examples include the medical examiner, county librarian or library board, fire marshal, probation officer, and juvenile board.

4. Each county may have a number of administrative departments, such as the health department, welfare department, county library, or county clerk's office, presided over by an elected or appointed official. These administrative departments, especially those headed by elected officials, operate with substantial independence because of the belief on the part of other officials that "you can't tell an elected official what to do" and the absence of any coordinating power.

The county commissioners court is the principal governing body in the county (it is not a judicial body despite the word *court* in its title). It consists of four commissioners, one elected from each of the four commissioner's precincts into which the county is divided, and the county judge, who is elected from the county at large. The county judge serves as presiding officer of the commissioners court and has a vote but no veto power over decisions.

The boundaries of the precincts from which the commissioners are elected are established by the commissioners court itslef. In many counties these precincts have been or are highly unequal in population size, either as a consequence of deliberate action or as a result of population changes without realignment of precincts. A study published in 1965 found that approximately 60 counties had not redrawn their commissioners precincts since 1900.[5] As with legislative malapportionment at the state level, urban areas within counties received the short end of this situation.

Legal action challenging the constitutionality of inequality in commissioners precincts was started in Midland County, where one precinct containing the city of Midland had 97 percent of the county's population and the other three precincts had the remainder. In 1968, in *Avery* v. *Midland County,* the U.S. Supreme Court held that commissioners precincts had to be set up on the basis of the one man-one vote criterion used in legislative reapportionment cases and be of substantially equal population size.[6] Some counties subsequently took action in accordance with this decision. In recent years Chicano groups have been exerting pressure for reapportionment to give them a better opportunity to elect county commissioners.

County reapportionment may result in the commissioners court giving more attention to the municipal areas within a county, especially when there is a single large city containing most of the population. The Supreme Court indicated in the Avery case that it believed this was necessary. Concerning the condition that had existed in Midland County, the Court remarked: "Indeed, it may not be more coincidence that a body apportioned with three of its four members chosen by residents of the rural area surrounding the city devoted most of its attention to the problems of that area, while paying for its expenditures with a tax imposed equally on city residents and those who live outside the city."[7]

Some, however, have expressed reservations concerning the impact of reapportionment on county politics and policy. One observer doubts that reapportionment to give greater weight to urban voters will bring about either "a major reform of county administration or a pronounced expansion of services to urban residents."[8] Such changes, particularly the latter, cannot occur without legislative actions to remove constitutional and statutory limitations on counties, and the prospects for such legislation do not seem very good. Furthermore, available evidence on county redistricting in other state shows that most incumbents are reelected following reapportionment. However, realignment of commissioner's precincts may improve the opportunities of Republicans and ethnic minorities to gain direct representation on commissioners courts. In Travis County (Austin), it contributed to the election in 1972 of a Mexican-American for the first time as a commissioner.

A principal basis for the importance of the commissioners court in county government is its control of county finances. Although the taxes that can be collected and the maximum rates which can be levied are specified in the state constitution and laws, the commissioners determine which taxes will be used and to what extent to raise revenue for the county. The county's annual budget is prepared by the county judge (or the county auditor in large counties) and adopted by the commissioners court, which usually displays much interest in budgetary details and can raise or lower budget requests from various officials and departments. The entire county budgetary process attracts little public attention, and little effort is made to inform the public. In all, the commissioners court has much discretion in budgeting, and it can use its power to attempt to influence or control county officials and agencies over whom it has no formal authority. Also, the commissioners themselves directly handle the expenditure of a large portion of appropriated funds, particularly for roads and parks.

The commissioners court also decides whether the county will undertake programs or activities that are authorized but not made mandatory by legislation. In some cases these authorizations apply to one or a few counties (e.g., authority to prevent littering on public beaches); in other cases they are open to all counties. Thus, whether a given county has such programs as food stamp distribution, county parks, pollution control, or county hospitals depends on action by the commissioners court. The trend in recent years has been continual expansion of such authorizations, which has served to increase the discretionary power of the commissioners court. The officials who direct the administration of such programs are usually appointed by the court unless the programs come under the jurisdiction of regular county officials. The court also fills vacancies when they develop in many elective county and precinct offices; their appointees hold office until the next general election.

In most counties each of the four commissioners is in charge of the county road and bridge program in his precinct, with the available money usually being allocated equally among the precincts. Each commissioner has his own road crews, equipment, and sheds; contracts for the purchase of construction materials; and determines what will be done and where. So important is road construction and maintenance that in many counties the commissioners are called "road commissioners." One-third of total county expenditures go for roads, with some rural counties spending as much as half their funds for this purpose. In planning his road program, each commissioner usually goes his own way, making little if any effort to coordinate his activities with those of the other commissioners. In 1947 the legislature enacted the Optional Road Law, which permits the voters in a county to adopt a unified road system that would be under the supervision of a professional county highway engineer. Basic road policy would still be made by the commissioners court. Although a unified road system probably would eliminate waste and duplication, among other things, only around twenty counties (including Bexar, Brazoria, Galveston, and Potter) currently operate on this basis. Most commissioners prefer the existing individualized arrangement because of the power it gives them, while most voters are too satisfied, uninformed, or uninterested to demand change.

The county judge has a variety of legislative, administrative, and judicial duties. As presiding officer of the commissioners court, he participates in the exercise of its power and in most cases prepares the county budget. Along with the sheriff and county clerk, he is a member of the County Election Board and has numerous duties relating to the administration of elections. In some counties he may also serve in such capacities as ex officio county school superintendent or as a member of the Juvenile Board (which is concerned with the treatment of juvenile lawbreakers). And, as his title indicates, he is judge of the county court, which is part of the state judicial system and should not be confused with the county commissioners court.

There is no formally designated chief executive in a county, although in some counties the county judge may appear to act in this fashion. If he does, it will be primarily because of his personality, leadership abilities, political standing, or tenure in office rather than official authority. This lack of a chief executive, frequently cited by reformers as a major defect in county government, often leads to fragmentation and particularism in the operation of county government. Other factors also contribute. Commissioners tend to resist "outside" control or interference in their precincts. A controversy in Tarrant County over the county's role in maintaining dump grounds caused a reporter to state that "each commissioner feels that his precinct is his sole domain, that the other three commissioners should keep their hands and, in this case, their noses out of his affairs."[9] As county services expand in urban counties, there is a tendency to assign primary responsibility for certain departments (e.g., welfare) or certain programs (e.g., parking facilities) to each of the commissioners. The election of a number of administrative officials also serves to hinder the development of common policies and coordinated action in the implementation of policy. Just as there is a reluctance to tell elected officials what to do, so too are they reluctant to take outside direction. A proposal to set up a central computer system in Harris County was opposed by the county clerk because, he said, "no one is going to tell me how to run my office."[10] Executive leadership, which is a preferred value in the literature of public administration, is a scare item in Texas county government.

It is not possible to present a neat, comprehensive review of the functions counties are authorized to perform or the functions they actually do undertake. A multitude of general and special laws and constitutional provisions variously authorize, prescribe, or limit what some or all counties can or must do. Generally, though, county functions fall into two groupings. First there are things they are required to do as administrative arms of the state government. Included are such functions as administering and collecting some taxes; enforcing criminal laws; servicing the state courts by, for example, providing clerks and prosecuting attorneys; keeping records of births, deaths, deeds, and other matters; registering voters and administering elections; and enforcing health laws. Second, there are functions they perform as units of general local government, especially for people outside of municipalities. Examples are road construction and maintenance; provision of parks and recreation facilities; operation of county hospitals, libraries, and airports; administration of local welfare services; and control of environmental pollution. Generally, urban counties operate a more extensive variety of programs than do rural areas.

MUNICIPAL GOVERNMENT

About 82 percent of Texans now live in urban areas, and as a consequence municipal governments have become the most significant form of general government. Municipal or city governments perform a variety of protective and welfare activities (e.g., police and fire protection, public housing and health programs) and provide many services (e.g., water and sewerage systems, parks and recreation programs) that are of great importance for the safety, convenience, and well-being of city dwellers. The tendency is for the demand for municipal services to increase as urban population continues to grow. Necessity more than ideology shapes the response to such demands.

Legally, cities are regarded as "municipal corporations" that have received operating charters from the state government. A city charter, which is akin to a constitution, sets forth a city's boundaries, governmental structure, legal authority, sources of revenue, and methods for selection of officials. It is intended to grant the power of local self-government to a community at its own request. The legal authority of city governments is not unlimited, however, because they have only that authority permissible under the state constitution and laws. Cities must also conform to the relevant provisions of the U.S. Constitution and laws (which restrain but do not empower cities), such as those pertaining to civil rights and minimum wages; cities are also subject to some supervision by state administrative agencies. City governments, in short, operate within the context of an extensive network of legal guidelines.

American courts traditionally followed the practice of narrowly interpreting the powers granted to cities by their charters and state laws. This standard of interpretation is known as Dillon's Rule, after its nineteenth-century formulator, Judge John F. Dillon.

> It is a general and undisputed proposition of law that a muncipal corporation possesses and can exercise the following powers and no others: First, those granted in express words; second, those necessarily or fairly implied in or incident to the powers expressly granted; third, those essential to the declared objects and purposes of the corporation not simply convenient, but indispensable. Any fair, reasonable substantial doubt concerning the existence of power is resolved by the courts against the corporation and the power is denied.[11]

Although in recent years it appears that the courts have been more lenient in their interpretation of municipal powers, considerations of legal power are still quite important in the operation of city govern-ments. The city attorney is often a pivotal figure in the decision-making process, and judicial review of municipal activity is rather extensive.

The goal of municipal reformers and others seeking greater self-government for cities has long been to free cities of excessive dependence on the legislature for legal authority, with the attendant possibility of legislative "interferences" in city affairs. Until the middle of the nineteenth century, Texas cities were governed only under special charters issued directly on an individual basis by the legislature. In 1858 the legislature enacted a general law under which cities could be incorporated by meeting stated requirements, but little is known concerning experience with this legislation. A major change in the state-city relationship came with the Constitution of 1876. It provided that cities and towns with populations of 10,000 or less (the figure was reduced to 5,000 or less by a 1909 amendment) could be incorporated only under general laws, whereas only cities over 10,000 (later 5,000) could have charters issued and amended by special acts of the legislature. The movement toward more local self-government culminated in the adoption of a constitutional amendment in 1912 permitting home rule for cities with more than 5,000 residents.

Under the home-rule amendment, eligible cities are able to draft their own charters and put them into effect with the approval of a majority vote in a referendum. Home rule, which is intended to allow cities to set up their governmental structure and undertake programs with a minimum of state control, permits a city to do anything not prohibited by the state constitution and laws. In other words, a city operating under a home-rule charter is not limited to doing only what is clearly authorized by existing law. The practical effect of this is to substantially overturn Dillon's Rule as a guiding principle for home-rule, but not for general-law, cities. Home-rule cities are still subject to legislative policies, such as those defining the workweek of firemen, authorizing cities to levy sales taxes with voter approval, and reducing the immunity of cities from tort liability. Home rule does relieve cities of the necessity of seeking legislative authoritzation every time they want to engage in a new activity.

For charter purposes, Texas cities presently can be classified as general-law and home-rule cities. Cities with fewer than 5,000 inhabit-ants are governed in accordance with general statutes. Those over the 5,000 mark have a choice between general-rule and home-rule status; almost all (214) have opted for home rule. Home-rule cities have more discretion in the adoption of governmental structure, as well as broader powers of taxation and annexation. Beyond these matters, there does not appear to be great differences in the operating authority available to each.

FORMS OF MUNICIPAL GOVERNMENT

Municipal governments in the United States, including Texas, display considerable variation in their organization and policies as a consequence of their adaption to local interests and conditions. It is possible, however, to group them under three general forms on the basis of their structural characteristics: the mayor-council, council-manager, and commission forms.[12] Most general-law (small) cities use the mayor-council form, while the council-manager form is most popular among the larger home-rule cities. (Like home rule, the council-manager form is associated with the municipal reform movement.) Some, mostly general-law, cities still cling to the commission form.

The *mayor-council* form is both the traditional and the most numerous form of city government in use. Indeed, in the nineteenth century it was the only form of municipal government. It features an elected mayor and an elected council chosen at large or by wards, or by some combination of the two. In the strong-mayor variations, the mayor is vested with strong administrative and legislative authority, including the appointment (subject to council approval) and removal of most department heads, the preparation of a budget for the council's consideration, and (usually) veto power over council actions. The council acts primarily as a legislative body. The strong-mayor form thus concentrates much power in the mayor and requires him to be both an administrator and a political leader. Some express a preference for this type on the ground that it concentrates responsibility and provides for, or at least facilitates, strong executive leadership in city government. These are seen as requisites for effective municipal government.

A second variation, the weak-mayor council type, has a mayor with quite limited administrative power, although he may have substantial power in policymaking, including the veto. Most of the administrative departments are headed by persons who are either elected or appointed by other officials, which results in a dispersion of power. Responsibility is likewise diffused, and the voter may find the whole system rather confused. Dissatisfaction with its operation has caused most cities to abandon this form.

The *commission* form of city government developed early in the twentieth century, with Galveston often being cited as its place of origin. Problems created there by a hurricane in 1900 led to dissatisfaction with the existing city government. As a consequence and to deal with the emergency, a charter was secured from the legislature providing for a five-man commission that was to govern the city. All legislative and administrative powers were to be centered in this commission. The commission form gained rapid popularity, and by

1920 some 500 cities in the nation were using it. This experience suggests two things: Governmental structures are sometimes more a product of chance than deliberate design, and the adoption of governmental structures and practices is sometimes a form of imitative behavior.

Under the commssion form as it now exists, there are from three to nine commissioners, with five being the most common number. Collectively, this group is the city council and exercises legislative powers. Individually, the commissioners serve as the heads of the various administrative departments. The mayor is selected from among the commissioners, and his duties are mainly symbolic in nature. Under this form, there is often a lack of leadership, a dispersal of administrative power, and a tendency for each commissioner to be concerned especially with the protection and promotion of "his" department. This form has lost popularity and is clearly on the decline. It can be observed in action in such cities as Palestine, DeLeon, and Texas City. A number of cities combine the commission form with a city manager.

The *council-manager* is the most recent major innovation in municipal government forms and has enjoyed much popularity in recent decades. This form has a small part-time council, usually elected at large in nonpartisan elections, which possesses all legislative power. The mayor, who is either elected by the voters or chosen by the council from among its members, presides over council meetings and serves as the political and honorific head of the city government. Control of the city administrative system, however, is vested in a professionally-trained city manager, who is appointed by the council and is accountable to it. The city manager has the power to appoint and remove department heads, prepare the city budget, and implement policies made by the council. Municipal reformers and many others have found this form attractive because of such attributed virtues as strong administrative leadership by a professional manager, the separation of policymaking and administrative activities, its efficient operation, and nonpartisanship. Among large Texas cities, Dallas, Fort Worth, San Antonio, Corpus Christi, and Austin use it; Houston and El Paso use the strong-mayor–council form.

In actuality, the council-manager form often does not provide a separation of administration from politics and policymaking. Although managers usually avoid partisan politics, they often become deeply involved in the politics of policymaking, both making (especially if they seek to be innovative) and being expected to make policy recommendations. Certainly it is accurate to regard as political in nature such actions as recommendations for tax increases or bond issues, the refusal to recommend a salary increase for public employees, or the proposal of a new housing or street improvement program. Not only do managers make such recommendations, but they also usually seek to develop support for them within permissible limits. Some managers work primarily through official channels, while others look for support in the general community. On matters which are strongly controversial, however, such as electoral law changes and the handling of minority grievances, managers are less active in policy formulation.

General-law cities may choose any of these forms of government, although what the statutes designate as the "commission" form appears more like the mayor-council form. In comparison, home-rule cities are free to adopt a charter providing whatever organizational structure for their governments they desire. However, once a charter is adopted the form of government so provided cannot be changed by charter revision or amendment at less than two-year intervals. Voter approval is required for all changes in home-rule charters, and sometimes sharp political conflicts may arise over proposed changes. But apathy often prevails. A charter revision election in Dallas in 1973 attracted less than 5 percent of the registered voters, while in El Paso in 1977 less than 13 percent turned out for a charter revision election in which single-member districts were adopted for the city council.

No particular form of city government will automatically provide "good" government, not withstanding the large amounts of time and argument devoted to the question of what is the best form of city government. While formal governmental structure may indeed affect the character or style of government in a community, it is by no means necessarily *the* crucial variable, as some apparently assume. Formal authorizations are certainly one basis for the possession and exercise of power. However, whether a mayor is "strong" or "weak" in fact, for instance, will depend not simply upon the formal powers he possesses but also upon how he uses those powers, the amount of political support he has in the community, the kinds of problems confronting him, and the like. Whether the mayor has the veto power is a significant fact, and from the perspective of mayoral power it is better to have it than to lack it, but it should not be assumed that without this power he is automatically less able to block council action than is a mayor with such power. He may be able to persuade or otherwise cause the council not to pass unwanted ordinances while a mayor with veto power may find himself sufficiently hemmed in by political pressures so that he may be unable to use the power he formally possesses. In short, formal structure should be viewed as the starting point for the analysis of the governmental process in cities. A comprehension of formal structure is a necessary but insufficient condition for understanding how government operates.

ASPECTS OF CITY POLITICS

Prior to 1958, all elected and appointed city official in Texas served two-year terms. In 1958, a constitutional amendment provided that, with the approval of their voters, cities could specify either two-, three-, or four-year terms for their officials. If a city were to select four-year terms for its council members, election would have to be by majority rather than plurality vote (where whoever gets the most votes wins, whether the amount is half of the total number or not), thereby sometimes necessitating run-off elections. Some home rule cities do utilize plurality elections.

In an effort to insulate municipal politics from state and national politics, city elections are usually held in "off-years" (i.e., odd-numbered years), when state and national elections are not held. They are also usually nonpartisan with no political party designation for candidates appearing on the ballot. A few cities, however, such as Beaumont, do permit partisan elections. Reformers have contended that nonpartisanship would help take "politics" out of city govern-ment, raise the quality of candidates seeking public office, focus campaigns on local rather than national and state issues, and contribute to efficiency in municipal government. It is not really possible to determine conclusively the effect of nonpartisanship on city politics. It probably has lessened the impact of political parties on local politics and, at the same time, caused greater emphasis on personal popularity and relationships in local elections and less stress on policy issues and differences.

Local political organizations have arisen in some cities and have shown considerable continuity. Such organizations may screen and "nominate" slates of candidates, finance and manage their campaigns, and influence those elected once they are in office. Examples are the Citizens Organized for Public Service (COPS) in San Antonio, the Citizens Committee for Good Government in Wichita Falls, and the Amarillo Citizens Association. The Good Government League[13] and the Citizen's Charter Association, which long dominated politics in San Antonio and Dallas, respectively, have faded from power in recent years. The Good Government League, which was a conservative, business-oriented group, was displaced by COPS, which draws its strength from liberal and Mexican-American elements in San Antonio. This marks a distinct change in the nature of politics in San Antonio. In Dallas, no group has yet developed to replace the Citizen's Charter Association. In Crystal City, La Raza Unida has dominated city politics in recent years. (It also controls Zavala County.)

Notwithstanding organizations of this sort, it is more common for local candidates either to run as individuals, as in Austin or Houston, or to join together and run as an informal slate, as in El Paso.

Nonpartisan politics of this sort, unstructured by political parties, works to increase the influence that pressure groups, downtown associations, or the press can have on elections. Without party labels to aid them in identifying and sorting out candidates, voters must rely on such other means as newspaper or pressure-group endorsements or personal contacts. Those seeking office, especially in larger cities, have to develop campaign organizations and secure financial support on their own without the aid of a party organization. (Contractors and others hoping to do business with the city are often a fertile source of campaign contributions.) Personal relationships appear to be especially important in smaller cities and towns.

Several election systems are used by cities for selecting council members.[14] One is the at-large system, whereby the voters in the entire city select all the members of the council; each voter is entitled to cast votes for as many candidates as there are positions to be filled. In the absence of slates, each candidate in effect runs against all other candidates. Another is the ward (or district) system, whereby council candidates must reside in the ward or district they seek to represent and are elected by the voters of that ward alone. A third is the place system. This provides for the election of all council members on a citywide basis; but each candidate runs for a particular seat, or place, on the council—as place one, place two, and so on. Candidates file for a particular place and run only against the other candidates seeking that place. Finally, cities can use some combination of these three systems. For example, in Houston five members of the council must live in particular districts of the city while three others run for places; all are elected by the voters in the entire city. Many cities, such as Abilene, Beaumont, and Texarkana, use the combination of residence in wards and election by the entire city. In home-rule cities, the place system or some variation thereof is the most frequently used electoral device. (General-law cities do not have legal authority to use the place system.) Only three home-rule cities use the ward system, which was the traditional form of municipal election and is often associated with such bad things as machine politics and boss rule.

What difference does it make whether one or another of these systems is used? What are the consequences? Those who prefer at-large elections (including the place system) contend that such elections cause council members to consider the needs of the city as a whole, whereas under the ward system council members are said to become "nothing but local errand boys" looking after the interests of their constituents and being amenable to log-rolling.[15] Whether this is really the case is open to question and empirical analysis. Under the place and at-large systems, it is quite possible for most council members to come from one area of the city and to identify the interests of their area and friends with those of the whole city. Certainly one can find many examples in Texas where some sections of a city receive more or better services than other sections. At-large elections, with or without the place system, have been adopted in some cities to prevent racial minorities from electing council members, as they well might under a ward or district system.[16] Whatever their actual effects, election systems are not regarded by many as neutral in impact, and those in dominance will usually select a system that seems best geared to serve their interests.

In the 1970s considerable pressure has developed in support of election of city council members from single-member wards or districts. Cities such as San Antonio, El Paso, Waco, and Paris have converted to single-member districts, either through voter-approved city charter revisions or as a consequence of court-ordered changes. In other cities, such as Dallas, Houston, and Austin, citywide elections are under judicial attack as discriminating against minority groups by reducing their electoral chance. Liberal and minority groups have been the primary supporters of these efforts. In 1977, in the first election in San Antonio held under the single-member district scheme, those winning election to the city council were five Anglos (including the mayor), five Mexican-Americans, and one black. Until then, the Council had been dominated by Anglos. Also in 1977 single-member districts contributed to the election of the first Mexican-American to the Waco City Council in its history.

Voter participation is usually quite low in city elections; probably less than 25 percent of the potential electorate turns out for most elections. In Austin during the 1954–1964 period, according to one study, the turnout in city elections ranged from around 20 percent to about 6 percent.[17] A hotly contested mayoral election in Houston in 1973 brought out 40 percent of the registered voters. The usual low turnout in city elections is the result of such factors as the low salience of local politics for many voters, holding city elections in "off years" when state and national elections do not help attract voters to the polls, nonpartisanship, and the frequency of local elections.[18] Most Texas city elections are nonpartisan, and available evidence indicates that turnout is typically lower in nonpartisan than in partisan elections. In the latter, the parties help to generate interest, define issues, and get voters to go to the polls.[19] Low voting turnout likely has a conservative impact on city government because it means low participation by lower socioeconomic groups. Officials are thus most likely to be concerned with the attitudes and interests of the middle-class voters who go to the polls and tend to be more conservative.

Another facet of municipal politics, and of local politics generally, is the widespread use of the voter referendum, which provides for direct popular participation in the decision-making process. Cities and other local governments usually must secure the approval of the voters to issue bonds and, occasionally, to change tax rates. We have already noted that city charter revisions require voter approval. Other matters may be submitted to the voters in order to get a "sense of the community," as on a proposed zoning ordinance or housing code. In 1967 the legislature authorized cities to levy a 1 percent sales tax after approval in a local referendum. Winning approval in most instances, the local sales tax was instituted in 846 cities as of January 1978. Another notable illustration of the referendum involves "liquor by the drink." As a result of a 1970 constitutional amendment and subsequent legislation, when approved in local option elections in "wet" precincts of counties, liquor may be sold by the drink. By the end of 1977, the sale of mixed drinks had been voted in in all or part of 73 counties.

The percentage of voters who participate in referenda is usually low, and the amount of information available to them on the issue at hand is likely to be minimal. (Voters in liquor-by-the-drink referenda are unlikely to feel the need for much information, being either "for or agin' it." It tends to be an emotional issue to which voters often have a "gut reaction.") It has also been said that "Widening the scope of the decision-making arena inevitably means the inclusion of a high percentage of people to whom the proposal will mean little or nothing."[20] As a form of "participatory democracy," experience with the referendum has not been particularly encouraging. As much as anything, continued use of the referendum in many instances reflects the notion that local officials cannot be fully trusted, especially on financial matters. In some other instances, as liquor by the drink it becomes a way for elected officials to avoid having to make decisions alone on controversial matters.

SPECIAL DISTRICTS

Special districts, although little known and even less loved, except perhaps by real estate developers, are the fastest growing form of local government in Texas. The 1977 *Census of Governments* reported the existence of 1425 special districts in the state. Included in this total were water control, improvement, and supply districts; housing authorities; conservation and reclamation districts; soil and water conservation districts; hospital districts; levee improvement districts; drainage districts; navigation districts; rural fire prevention districts; airport authorities, noxious weed control districts; and miscellaneous districts. Although school districts are also a form of special district, because of their number and importance they are treated separately in this chapter.

The number of special districts grows apace. While some become inactive or are abolished (as when water districts are absorbed by cities), more are created, either on the basis of general laws or by special legislative enactments. The legislature authorized 84 special districts in 1967, 108 in 1969, and an apparent record 139 in 1971. (One Houston legislator alone batted in over 50 water districts in 1971.) In 1973 the number authorized declined to 11, probably because of the unfavorable publicity the creation of districts had received and the reformist atmosphere in the legislature.[21] Few inhabitants of Texas do not come under the jurisdiction of and help support at least one special district, whether they are cognizant of it or not.

In contrast to county and municipal governments, which possess general governmental powers, special districts are usually created to provide one or a few services for the inhabitants of a defined area. Few are authorized to regulate or control the behavior of people. The diverse characteristics of special districts are well pointed up in the following statement.

> Special districts are the most varied of all governmental units. . . . Thus some districts may tax, but others may not. Some may incur debt, but others may not. Many are governed by elected officials, many by appointed officials. A number possess police powers, but some do not. Most districts are intrastate, but a few are interstate. Many are more or less affiliates of another government, but a large number are virtually autonomous. A handful are highly responsive to public opinion, yet most operate in the shadows. Many are staffed by unpaid, part-time amateurs, many by highly paid professionals. A majority are informal, personal, and intimate; a minority are formal, impersonal, and autocratic. Some are "grass-roots" in the extreme, others are multi-purpose million-dollar operations. Most are well established governments; however, a considerable number are sheer speculations.[22]

THE CREATION OF SPECIAL DISTRICTS

As with other units of local government, special districts trace their legal origin to general or specific state laws and constitutional provisions. A number of hospital districts have been authorized by constitutional amendments. In most instances the general laws permitting the establishment of special districts require that they be approved by a majority vote (of those actually voting) of the district's resident property owners. This is usually done in perfunctory fashion, and often only a few dozen voters or less cast votes. A notable exception was the controversy in Harris County over the establishment of a hospital district. It was twice rejected by the voters before winning approval in 1965, following an extensive campaign for it by city and county officials and community leaders.

Still, the general-law route to special district creation can be tedious and time consuming. Public notice, hearing, and election requirements may take several months. Consequently, special legislation creating special districts, especially water districts, is often sought. Such bills are handled on the local and consent calendars and receive little legislative consideration. Earlier comment was made on the volume of such bills in recent legislative sessions. Advocates say special acts permit greater adaptability of districts to local conditions, while critics contend they permit avoidance of procedural safeguards and controls in existing laws. (In actuality, many of the bills passed by the legislature have been identical except for the name and description of the water district.)

A number of factors have contributed to the establishment and proliferation of special districts. First, regular local governments may have defects or inadequacies that special districts are intended to overcome. In some instances, it appears easier to set up a new governmental unit to handle an activity than to try to alter existing units. The area boundaries of existing governments are inflexible, and their geographical jurisdiction may be larger or smaller than necessary to carry on a desired activity. For example, the residents of a river-basin area may want a flood-control program; but the area that should be covered may exceed the jurisdiction of existing local governments. Financial restrictions on city and county governments, as on tax rates and debt limits, may be avoided by resort to special districts for particular programs, such as hospital districts or airport authorities. Or the officials of a general local government may simply want to shift a costly activity elsewhere. Administrative deficiencies, especially in county governments, may also encourage resort to special districts.

A second general cause cited for the creation of special districts is political expediency. Special districts usually can be set up with comparative ease to handle new activities. To reorganize or alter an existing government may bring much opposition from local officials and interests who perceive a threat to their positions and relationships. Special districts do not appear to disrupt the status quo and offer quick solutions to given problems.

Third, special districts may be viewed as a means for taking an activity "out of politics." By virtue of the special-district device, the activity is taken away from the politicians who dominate the city hall and county courthouse and is put into the hands, perhaps, of non-salaried, public-spirited businessmen or local people who will operate it in an efficient manner. The desire to take activities out of politics is a tradition of long standing in American politics. Whether it really can be done and whether it should be done are quite different matters.

Fourth, considerations of personal gain may motivate those seeking to have special districts established. Water districts in particular can be easily created, have in the past been subject to little or no supervision, and operate in semisecret style. Special districts may be established to create business opportunities, turn a quick profit, or provide jobs for friends and relatives. In urban areas, most notably Harris County, they have been used for promotional purposes by real estate developers. Districts have been established and millions of dollars in bond issues voted by a half dozen or less voters to provide water supply and sewer systems to new developments. These would have to be paid for by the developer in the absence of the special (water) district. When the territory covered by such promotional districts is annexed by the nearby city, as often happens, the city assumes liability for payment of the bond issues.

GOVERNMENTAL STRUCTURE AND ADMINISTRATION

In their formal organization, special districts encompass a plethora of forms.[23] Approximately three-fourths of them are governed by boards of elected officials usually commissioners or directors, with 5 members being common. (The appointed boards of river authorities may have as many as 24 members.) The rest are controlled by appointed officials. In most instances the governing officials are selected for two-year terms, although some may serve longer. Generally, they are part-time officials and receive only expenses or a small per diem allowance.

All soil conservation districts and many of the water districts have elected officials. For water districts with appointed officials, the appointing is usually done by the Texas Water Rights Commission or other creating agencies. Directors of river authorities are usually appointed by the governor. The governing bodies of housing authorities are customarily appointed by the mayors of the cities in which they are located, whereas city councils do the appointing to urban renewal authorities. The county commissioners normally make selections for hospital, noxious weed, and rural fire-prevention districts. For some special districts, the selection process can become quite involved. To illustrate, control of the Reagan County Water Supply District is lodged in a five-man board of directors appointed by a three-member citizens committee. One member of this citizens committee is chosen by the Reagan County commissioners, one member by the Big Lake city council, and the third member by the first two. What becomes of democratic accountability or popular control in a situation such as this?

The primary sources of revenue for special districts are property taxes and user charges for their services. All, except soil conservation districts, have authority to issue revenue bonds to finance their activities, using their reserve sources as backing; but in some cases this requires voter approval.

While a few special districts are large operations employing hundreds of people, many of them have no full-time staff whatsoever. Woodworth G. Thrombley concludes that with the exceptions of housing and urban renewal authorities, hospital districts, and a few water districts, the administrative operations of special districts are "decidedly amateur" in style:

> Few of these districts make use of the tools of professional management. Such things as merit and budget systems, machine operations, double-entry accounting, and competitive purchasing are unknown to these little governments. Most of them do little or nothing in the way of reporting their activities. And many do not even maintain offices. (Their addresses may be the offices of a local attorney or the county clerk.) District employees are almost always employed on a part-time basis, and often such functions as property assessment and tax collection, annual audits, legal actions, and the conduct of elections are "farmed out" to other local governments. A number of districts, namely soil conservation districts, have no paid employees.[24]

Special districts, in short, usually do not fit the image of a "government" that most of us have.

CRITICISM AND REFORM

Many persons have been critical of the extensive use of special districts, alleging that they are undemocratic because they are obscure in operation and resistant to effective popular control; that by their vast number they fragment, confuse, and complicate the local government scene; and that their small scale of activities often renders them uneconomical in operation. Clearly, the proliferation of special districts does contribute to the decentralization of governmental authority. In some counties, for example, the control and development of water resources are dispersed among a considerable number of special districts and other governmental units. This dispersion of authority makes comprehensive and integrated handling of local problems difficult and hampers popular control of goverment at the grass-roots level. Operating costs are often higher. For instance, the operating costs of sewage treatment plants operated by two small special districts in Dallas County are more than twice those of a nearby, larger city of Dallas plant. Interest rates on special-district bonds tend to run high because of their poor credit ratings.

In 1973 complaints about the operation of water districts led to legislative adoption of a package of 13 statutes intended to reform their operation. Under them, districts are required to maintain offices in their districts and keep their records open to the public. Annual audits by certified public accountants must be filed with the Texas Water Rights Commission, which was given increased power of supervison. Petitions to create districts must be sent to cities within whose extraterritorial jurisidicion they lie. Relatives and employees of developers cannot serve as directors, tax assessors, or collectors in districts in which the developers own property. Those who buy property within a water district must be informed of its existence. Whether this legislation will prevent the abuses often associated with the use of water districts remains to be seen. Much will depend on how the legislation is administered, especially by the Water Rights Commission.

SCHOOL DISTRICTS

In 1977 there were 1123 school districts in Texas, including independent school districts (which accounted for about 90 percent of the total), common school districts and rural high school districts. Our focus will be on independent school districts because they enroll almost all of the state's public school students. Common school districts number less than 125 and come under the control of the county superintendent of schools and school-board trustees. Most of them are quite small, having few students and fewer teachers. In most counties the school superintendent and board of trustees have relatively little to do because of the scarcity of common school districts. In many counties (over 150) these offices have been abolished or are unfilled.

The independent school district is a regular unit of local government, having its own governing body (the board of trustees), defined territorial jurisdiction, and the power to levy taxes. In most districts the school board is comprised of seven part-time, unsalaried members who are elected for three-year terms by the district voters in nonpartisan, at-large elections, with the candidates receiving the largest number of votes being elected. Because of special laws that apply to some districts, there are various exceptions to these generalizations. In some districts terms are longer, the place system is used, a majority of the votes cast are needed to win election, and so on. The school board acts as the legislative body of the districts, making decisions on tax rates and bond issues, adopting the budget, approving the appointment of teachers and other personnel, making disciplinary rules, and formulating other school policies. The board also selects the superintendent of schools, who is the chief administrative officer of the district and is in charge of the day-to-day operation of the school system.

Although conventional wisdom holds that education should be kept out of politics or vice versa, in practice the operation of local school systems is often highly political in the sense that this means conflict and struggle over policy. School-board elections are often hotly contested; liberal and conservative groups put up slates of candidates in some districts, while urban-rural cleavages appear in others. Conflicts in districts may develop over the location of new school buildings; the level of tax rates; the performance of the superintendent; the nature of the instructional program (with many assertions concerning "frills," the three Rs, and the like); the desegregation of schools; disciplinary and dress codes; and even whether teachers with too much hair, wherever located on their head, should be hired or retained. Since the mid-1950s public school desegregation has been a volatile and acrimonious issue in many districts, and various positions have been taken on what should be done (or not done) to conform to the law of the land. Not a little procrastinatory and evasive action has been taken. Potent symbols in this controversy include "freedom of choice," "busing," "neighborhood schools," and "affirmative action." As with many symbols, they serve to confuse and oversimplify as well as clarify political discussion.

The independent school districts receive their operating funds from a combination of national, state, and local sources. (Construction of facilities is customarily financed by local bond issues.) The state and local method of financing education is complicated; only its general outline will be presented here. The Available School Fund provides flat grants to school districts, without regard to wealth, on the basis of average daily attendance in their schools. The Minimum Foundation School Program, established in 1949, provides financial support intended to insure that districts maintain specified minimum standards in regard to such matters as teachers salaries (the 1977 minimum teacher's salary was $8460), teacher-student ratios, nurses and counselors, and transportation. The state contributes 80 percent of the funds for this program, with the school districts—as a unit—being responsible for the remaining 20 percent. The exact percentage paid by each district depends on a complex economic index for the county in which it is located that purports to measure the tax-paying ability of the county. On this basis some districts pay more and some pay less than 20 percent of the program's costs. The minimum foundation program provides no money for school construction, which remains the sole responsibility of the district, as do any expenditures for operations above the minimum standards (as for higher teachers' salaries). Every school district does provide funds beyond the minimum required in order to enrich their educational programs.

For the 1970-1971 school year, 41.1 percent of the funds expended on Texas public schools came from local sources, 48 percent from the state, and 10.9 percent from the national government. The trend in recent years has been toward increasing national and state contributions. Local districts depend heavily on property (ad valoreum) taxes for their own funds and encounter much resistance to increases in property-tax rates, which in some cases require voter approval. It is often easier to look elsewhere for needed funds, which, whether intentional or not, becomes a way of shifting the financial burden of local schools beyond the district.

The idea of using local funds to raise educational programs above the standards of the minimum foundation program rests on the assumption that districts have roughly equal capability to raise such funds. This in fact is not the case. The school districts vary in taxable property per student from $1000 to $1 million. Some tax cars, other do not; some tax improvements on rural areas, other do not; some levy taxes on 20 percent of the property's marketable value, others on 40 percent; and so on.

In December 1971 a three-judge federal district court held that the use of property taxes to provide local school funds caused such disparities in levels of support among Texas school districts, because of disparities in the value of taxable property, as to violate the Fourteenth Amendment's guarantee of equal protection of the laws.[25] In the words of the court: "the current system of financing public education in Texas discriminates on the basis of wealth by permitting citizens of affluent districts to provide a higher quality of education for their children while paying lower taxes. . . ."[26] In the Edgewood school district in San Antonio, where the case originated, there was $5,900 of taxable property per student; in the nearby wealthy' Alamo Heights district, there was $49,000 in taxable property per student. The Edgewood district, which was composed largely of Mexican-Americans, taxed its residents at a higher rate but raised only $26 per student compared to $333 per student for Alamo Heights. When added to the minimum-foundation program funds, these local funds produced substantial differences in the total funds spent in the various districts.

The district court gave the state two years in which to come up with an alternative financing system. The state appealed the case to the U.S. Supreme Court. While the appeal was pending, something of a crisis atmosphere existed. Many groups, officials and private, began to study the problem of school finance and make recommendations.[27] School finance was regarded as a primary problem on the legislative agenda in 1973. Then, in March 1973, the Supreme Court overturned the district court ruling by a vote of five to four.[28] Justice Lewis F. Powell, Jr., who spoke for the majority, held that the right to an education was not of such fundamental character, nor was there sufficient evidence of discrimination against a "suspect class," as to uphold a finding of unconstitutional discrimination because of differences in educational expenditures among districts. On the other hand, he did not endorse the status quo, as the following passage indicates:

> The need is apparent for reform in tax systems which may well have relied too long and too heavily on the local property tax. And certainly innovative new thinking as to public education, its methods and its funding, is necessary to assure both a higher level of quality and greater uniformity of opportunity. These matters merit the continued attention of the scholars who already have contributed much by their challenges. But the ultimate solution must come from the lawmakers and from the democratic pressures of those who elect them.[29]

The Supreme Court's decision took the pressure off of the legislature. In 1975 and 1977 the legislature did pass legislation making some funds available ($100 million in 1975 and $148 million in 1977) for the equalization of expenditures in the districts. This legislation, however, made no basic or major changes in school expenditure patterns. Equalization of public school financing is not an easy problem to solve.

Mention should be made here of the state's free textbook program, which was authorized by a constitutional amendment adopted in 1918. A 15-member textbook committee is appointed annually by the State Board of Education to evaluate textbooks and develop a list of recommended titles for use in the public schools. Public hearings are held by the committee, at which persons may appear and express support or opposition for particular textbooks. Spokesmen for fundamentalist groups can usually be counted on to appear and oppose the approval of biology textbooks that present evolution as "a fact rather than a theory." Whether history books give proper treatment to American heroes is another common concern. In 1973 Women's rights group protested the stereotyped treatment of women in various textbooks. Another critic protested a sixth-grade health book because it told students "a pesticide should not be used when a flyswatter will do": this was a "hysterical reaction" caused by the "pollution bugaboo."[30] Books that make it onto the approved list are provided free to the districts. A district can use textbooks not on the approved list, but it must pay for them itself. This obviously serves as an incentive to draw on the state's approved list and injects an element of both uniformity and central control into textbook usage.

METROPOLITAN AREAS

In 1972 the Killeen-Temple area became the twenty-fourth standard metropolitan statistical area (SMSA) in Texas. The U.S. Bureau of the Census defines an SMSA as one that includes a central city of at least 50,000 population and its adjacent urban areas. So defined, metropolitan areas contain more than two-thirds of the state's population. The cities of Houston, Dallas, Fort Worth, and San Antonio account for around 30 percent of the state's population. This represents a marked contrast with 1900, when Texas was a predominantly rural state with only one city (San Antonio) of more than 50,000 residents. Although the popular image of the Texan is often that of a taciturn, weather-beaten resident of the wide open spaces with, perhaps, a Marlboro tattoo or a can of Lone Star, there are no longer many of that kind around. Today the typical Texan is an urban dweller (albeit, perhaps, with a pickup truck), and in the future even more Texans will be urban dwellers as the movement away from small towns and rural areas into the cities continues.

METROPOLITAN PROBLEMS

A great many of the domestic problems confronting all Americans are essentially metropolitan problems. Typically, when a person thinks of urban or metropolitan problems, such things as police and fire protection, water supply, garbage and sewage disposal, traffic congestion, parks and playgrounds, and land-use planning come to mind. And, indeed, these often are problems with which the urban dweller becomes well acquainted when the water pressure decreases or disappears in the summer, when he sits in his car on a clogged freeway, or when he searches for open recreational space only to find people and clutter. These traditional urban problems have been compounded by the rapid metropolitanization of the population.

Many other problems that have a place on the public agenda and are often regarded as national problems because of their scope and the attention they attract from national policymakers are also essentially metropolitan problems. Poverty and welfare, racial conflict and civil rights, environmental pollution, mass transportation, slum housing and center-city decay, crime and juvenile delinquency, even unemployment: These are problems of the city and not of the countryside. "Crime in the streets" is of little immediate concern to Dime Box while air pollution is not much of an issue in Marathon. How these problems are dealt with has much importance for the safety, comfort, and quality of life in the metropolitan areas. Increasingly, policymakers are expected to come to grips with these problems and provide "solutions" for them, preferably at low financial cost.

A number of factors that handicap and complicate the efforts of metropolitan-area governments in dealing with their problems are frequently cited. These include the lack of financial resources; restrictive provisions in state constitutions and laws; public and official indifference; diversity and conflict among social, ethnic, and economic groups; the fragmentation of governmental authority; and lack of knowledge concerning the causes of some problems. The fragmentation of governmental authority has especially attracted attention, perhaps because Americans seem intrigued with the effort to solve public problems by tinkering with governmental structure. The failure to treat adequately such problems as slum housing, however, is undoubtedly often more due to lack of will and concentrated effort than governmental structure.

Still, there is no denying the fact that, in Texas, metropolitan areas contain local governments in abundance. The 1972 Census of Government reported that the state's four most populous SMSAs contained a total of 956 units of local government; Houston had 488; Dallas—Fort Worth, 368; San Antonio, 80; and El Paso, 20. If many metropolitan problems require policy unity and areawide action for effective treatment at the local level, then this proliferation of governments and fragmentation of authority must have a negative impact. Reorganization and reduction in the number of local governments is often recommended.

One should, however, make the distinction that Edward Banfield and Morton Grodzins do between problems that "exist in metropolitan areas" and problems which "exist by virtue of the inadequacies of governmental structures in metropolitan areas."[31] Thus, such problems as a lack of parks and recreational areas, inadequate garbage collection, discrimination in public employment and services, unpaved and rutted streets, billboard blight, and abusive behavior by the police can probably be handled without any reorganization of local government. Ask yourself why such problems persist. If you think "who cares?" you have come up with part of the answer. If your response attributes them to a "sick society" or the local "establishment," or something else equally unimaginative and unhelpful, try again, and strive to be more precise.

Other problems, such as air and water pollution, mass transportation, urban sprawl, and inadequate water supply are not respectors of governmental boundaries, and areawide handling appears required. But a government with metropolitanwide jurisdiction will not automatically generate workable or adequate solutions for such problems if it lacks political leadership, financial resources, or public support.

Moreover, there is likely to be conflict as to what should be done among those favoring action. There is, after all, more than one way to provide for clean air or mass transportation facilities. With these considerations in mind, we can briefly survey some of the policies that have been proposed or tried for ameliorating, if not solving, metropolitan problems.

POSSIBLE SOLUTIONS

Annexation. This involves the absorption and incorporation of new territory into existing cities as a means of preventing urban sprawl and the development of many small, independent municipalities ringing the central city and choking off its growth and jurisdiction. Generally, Texas cities have stronger powers of annexation than do cities in most other states. Under the Municipal Annexation Act (1963), cities may annex up to 10 percent of their land area each year; unused allocations are usable in the future up to a limit of 30 percent in any one year. Annexation is accomplished unilaterally by the use of city-ordinance power and does not require the approval of residents of the area being annexed. In states where their approval is required, it often results in rejection of the proposed annexation. The Texas annexation law also gives cities extraterritorial jurisdiction ranging from one-half to five miles (for cities of over 100,000) beyond their corporate limits, depending on their size. Although a city cannot levy taxes within its extraterritorial area, it can exercise control over the development of subdivisions in it, and the residents therein are restricted in their ability to incorporate as separate cities or towns. Once an area is annexed, it must be provided with city services within three years or it can be disannexed by court order upon petition by residents and property owners.

One observable consequence of the use of Texas annexation laws is that they have helped prevent central cities in the state's metropolitan areas from being surrounded and hemmed in by suburban cities to the extent that they are in most states. Most of the population in SMSAs in Texas is located in the central city. Whether this has resulted in the more effective handling of urban needs and problems is not self-evident.

Special districts. The special district having authority to undertake some activity on an areawide basis is another approach to metropolitan problems. Perhaps the best known illustrations are the Port of New York Authority and the Bay Area Rapid Transit Authority in the San Francisco area. Although the special district is widely utilized in Texas, only limited effort has been made to adapt it to metropolitan problems. Some countywide hospital districts have been created in populous counties. The Gulf Coast Waste Disposal Authority was established in 1969 to abate pollution in three heavily industrialized gulf-coast counties (Harris, Galveston, and Brazoria), and an airport authority controls the new Dallas-Fort Worth Regional Airport. Special districts can provide services or facilities that exceed the authority or capabilities of existing city and county governments. Some believe, however, that extensive use of special districts could further divide authority and compound the problem of governmental coordination in metropolitan areas.

Governmental consolidation. Some students of urban government have been much interested in various forms of governmental consolidation in metropolitan areas. They point to the federated government adopted by Toronto (Canada) and its suburbs, the Nashville-Davidson County (Tennessee) consolidation, and the metro government of Dade County-Miami (Florida) as examples of the possibilities. Texans, however, have manifested little interest or enthusiasm for such innovations, which are difficult to effect under existing laws. Some consolidations, mostly of smaller cities, have occurred, such as that of Freeport and Velasco in the gulf-coast area. Although there has been considerable interest and support for consolidation of the El Paso city and county governments, this has not yet happened.[32]

More significant, perhaps, has been the movement toward greater use of county governments, with their broader jurisdiction, for handling programs and services in large urban areas.[33] Thus, Ector County (Odessa) almost completely supports the public parks system; Tom Green (San Angelo) and Ector counties support all library facilities; Jefferson County (Beaumont) operates a commercial airport; Tarrant County (Fort Worth) handles all purchasing for state highway rights-of-way; and Harris County has its domed stadium. Since most of the population of most Texas SMSAs resides within a single county, the county is a logical unit for providing areawide services. Legal authority for such developments is provided by a 1970 constitutional amendment that authorizes consolidation of governmental functions within counties and by the Interlocal Cooperation Act of 1971, which permits local governments to contract with one another for the provision of services.

Councils of Government (COGs). These are "multi-jurisdictional organizations of local governments created in an effort to provide forums for the consideration of common urban and regional problems."[34] Beginning with the North Central Texas Council of Governments in 1966, 24 of these organizations have been created in Texas. Twenty of them include within their areas the state's 24 SMSAs. COGs are voluntary organizations and are controlled by councils composed largely or entirely of representatives of member local governments. They are supported by financial contributions from their member governments and by state and federal grants; each has a permanent staff and an executive director.

COGs perform two basic functions for their member governments.[35] One is regional planning on such matters as transportation, land use, water and sewerage facilities, and health services. There are many federal grant-in-aid programs for which evaluation and comment by a regional planning body is required, although favorable comment by that body is not always required before a grant application is approved. However, the sanction of negative review and the possible withholding of federal funds does encourage local governments to negotiate changes in their proposals so as to bring them into closer accord with regional plans. Second, COGs also provide a variety of services for their members, including technical assistance in seeking federal grants-in-aid, the development of information systems, the operation of a police academy (in the Dallas-Fort Worth Area), and help in developing modern personnel systems. Many of the councils run in-service training programs and engage in research and planning activities for their member governments.

Member governments of each COG remain independent and have full control over their own policies and finances. There is no effective way by which a COG can compel them to do something they consider adverse to their interests. The COGs must depend for their effectiveness on the value of their services and recommendations and their skill in persuasion. They can move no faster in bringing about governmental and policy changes to provide regional coordination than their member governments are willing to move. In actuality, they have had to be fairly deferential to the central cities in their areas as part of the cost of organizational survival.

Revenue-sharing. Two familiar complaints from urban spokesmen have been that (1) cities have inadequate financial resources to meet their many needs and problems and (2) federal grant-in-aid programs (over 500 existed in the early 1970s), while providing needed funds, are often too narrow, restrictive, and complicated and are focused on national objectives. Many have said that general revenue-sharing, under which the national government would make funds available on an unrestricted basis to state and local governments, is needed. State and local officials have often argued that they are in the best position to develop solutions to local problems, including metropolitan problems.

In October 1972 Congress, with the urging of the Nixon administration, adopted the State and Local Assistance Act, which authorized the provision of $30.2 billion to state and general local governments over a five-year period; within broad limits, the money can be used as they see fit. In late 1972 the first checks, totaling $5.7 billion, were mailed to some 38,000 general-purpose governmental units. The state of Texas received $81.5 million, and its city and county governments received $163 million. They received slightly larger amounts in subsequent years. Practically all Texas cities and towns, whether Houston or Cotulla, Dallas or Impact, received funds based on such criteria as their population and tax effort. In 1976, under strong pressure from state and local officials, Congress extended the revenue-sharing program for another four years.

Studies of the revenue-sharing program indicate that cities and other local governments generally have used most of the funds received for existing programs rather than for new or innovative programs.[36] Some governments did use their funds to reduce local taxes, as critics contended they would. A study of the use of revenue-sharing funds by the 16 most populated Texas counties found that about two-thirds of their funds were used for five purposes: courthouse and jail construction and repairs; roads and bridges; voting machines; data processing; and law enforcement.[37] Local governments have found revenue-sharing to be a desirable source of funds, and they are coming to depend upon it. Whether general revenue-sharing really will contribute to the easing or solution of metropolitan problems is still an open question.

The various "solutions" to metropolitan problems discussed here can facilitate the easing of these problems. They are not, however, panaceas. Much depends, ultimately, on politics—on the will and desire of the people and their public officials to come to grips with their problems, devise policies to redress them, and follow through with their implementation.

NOTES

[1] A. J. Thomas, Jr., and Ann Van Wynen Thomas, *Vernon's Annotated Constitution of the State of Texas,* vol. 2 (Kansas City, Mo.: Vernon Law Book Company, 1955), p. 630.

[2] C. Ed Davis, "Waiver of an Ancient Doctrine: The Texas Tort Claims Act," *Public Affairs Comment* 15 (September 1969), pp. 1–4.

[3] *Houston Chronicle,* February 3, 1974, p. 1, sect. 1.

[4] Robert E. Norwood, *Texas County Government: Let the People Choose* (Austin: Texas Research League, 1970), pp. 21–22.

[5] Charldean Newell, *County Representation and Legislative Apportionment* (Austin: University of Texas, Institute of Public Affairs, 1965), pp. 13–14.

[6] Avery v. Midland County, 88 S.Ct. 1114 (1968).

[7] Ibid.

[8] Minor B. Crager, "County Reapportionment in Texas," *Proceedings of the*

Eleventh County Auditors' Institute (Austin: University of Texas, Institute of Public Affairs, 1969), p. 10. See also Minor B. Crager, "County Reapportionment in Texas," *Public Affairs Comment* 17 (March 1971), pp. 1–4.

[9]*Fort Worth Star-Telegram,* August 22, 1969. Quoted in Norwood, op. cit., p. 64.

[10]*Houston Chronicle,* September 22, 1968. Quoted in Norwood, op. cit., p. 67.

[11]Quoted in Duane Lockard, *The Politics of State and Local Government,* 2nd ed. (New York: Macmillan, 1969), p. 129.

[12]This discussion benefits from *Forms of City Government,* 7th ed. (Austin: University of Texas, Institute of Public Affairs, 1968).

[13]See Bill Crane, "San Antonio: Pluralistic City and Monolithic Government," and August O. Spain, "Fort Worth: Great Expectations—Cowtown Hares and Tortoises," in Leonard E. Goodall, ed., *Urban Politics in the Southwest* (Tempe: Arizona State University, Institution of Public Administration, 1967), chaps. 3, 7.

[14]Roy E. Young, *The Place System in Texas Elections* (Austin: University of Texas, Institute of Public Affairs, 1965); and Philip Barnes, "Alternative Methods of Electing City Councils in Texas Home·Rule Cities," *Public Affairs Comment* 14 (May 1970), pp. 1–4.

[15]Young, op. cit., p. 13.

[16]Ibid., p. 21.

[17]Harry Holloway and David Olsen, "Electoral Participation by White and Negro Voters in a Southern City," *Midwest Journal of Political Science* 10 (February 1966): 108–109.

[18]See, generally, Delbert A. Taebel, "The Municipal Reform Movement, Elections and Constitutional Revision, *Municipal Matrix* 5 (December 1973), (Denton: North Texas State University, Center for Community Services), pp. 1–4.

[19]Thomas R. Dye, *Politics in States and Communities* (Englewood Cliffs, N.J.: Prentice-Hall, 1969), pp. 224–226.

[20]Lockard, op. cit., p. 251.

[21]Harvey Katz, *Shadow Over the Alamo* (New York: Doubleday, 1972), chap. 9, presents an exposé on the legislative creation of water districts.

[22]Woodworth G. Thombley, *Special Districts and Authorities in Texas* (Austin: University of Texas, Institute of Public Affairs, 1959), p. 6. The discussion of special districts relies heavily on this study, which remains a leading work on its topic. Also of much value has been David W. Tees, "A Fresh Look at Special Districts in Texas," *Governmental Authority and Organization in Metropolitan Areas* (Arlington: University of Texas at Arlington, Institute of Urban Studies, 1971).

[23]See Tees, ibid., p. 47, for a tabular summary.

[24]Thombley, op. cit., p. 11.

[25]Rodriguez v. San Antonio Independent School District, 37 OF. Supp. 280 (WD Tex 1971). A similar California case was Serrano v. Priest, 5 Cal. 3rd 584 (1971).

[26]Ibid., p. 291.

[27]See the discussion in *The Texas Observer,* December 15, 1971, pp. 1–6.

[28]San Antonio School District v. Rodriguez, 36 L Ed 2d 16 (1973).

[29]Ibid., pp. 57–58.

[30]*Houston Post,* September 22, 1973, Section A, p. 9; also *Houston Chronicle,* September 16, 1973, p. 24, sec. 1.

[31]Edward Banfield and Morton Grodzins, *Government and Housing in Metropolitan Areas* (New York: McGraw-Hill, 1958), p. 32.

[32]See *Unite El Paso* (Austin: Texas Research League, 1970).

[33]Norwood, op. cit., chap. 3; and James W. McGrew, "The Texas Urban County in 1968: Problems and Issues," *Public Affairs Comment* 14 (March 1968), pp. 1–4.

[34]Philip W. Barnes, "Councils of Government in Texas: Changing Federal-Local Relations," *Public Affairs Comment* 14 (July 1958), p. 1.

[35]Ibid., pp. 2–3. See also Philip W. Barnes, *Metropolitan Coalitions: A Study of Councils of Government in Texas* (Austin: University of Texas, Institute of Public Affairs, 1969); "The COG in Texas: Policy Needs and Alternatives," in Tees, op cit., pp. 15–35; and *Directory 73: Regional Councils in Texas* (Austin: Office of the Governor, 1973).

[36]See, for example, Richard P. Nathan, Allen D. Manuel, and Susannah E. Calkins, *Monitoring Revenue Sharing* (Wahsington: Brookings Institution, 1975).

[37]Richard L. Raycraft, *Metropolitics and County Government in Texas* (Unpublished doctoral dissertation, University of Houston, 1976), ch. 5.

Government and Money

The preceding chapters have been concerned with the structure of Texas government and the process by which demands are expressed and decisions made in the state political system. This chapter focuses on the substance of governmental activity—on outcomes of the political process. The analysis of policy outcomes may be approached by describing and analyzing policy in various substantive areas. An alternative approach to the analysis of policy is to ask where the government gets it money and what it spends it on. That is the approach used in this chapter; concern is for the sources of state revenue, the process by which the state government decides to spend this money, and the general pattern of state expenditures.

Admittedly, analysis of government and money does not provide a description of all governmental policy, but much policy does involve either securing or spending money. Certainly, decisions on taxes and expenditures constitute some of the most basic and important political decisions that governments make. Their outcome plays an important part in the determination of who will be benefited by government activity and who will pay the financial costs of government. Consequently, taxation-expenditure decisions are often productive of conflict and controversy. Such conflict provides a convenient area in which the influence on policy outcomes of the factors analyzed in previous chapters may be examined. Of special interest will be the influence of party and factional divisions and relations between, and relative strength of, the governor and the legislature.

GETTING THE MONEY

Taxes and expenditures are often viewed as two sides of the same coin, but such a view is somewhat misleading. Taxes finance governmental programs, but they also allocate the material costs or burdens of government among its citizens. The politics of taxation often appears fairly distinct from the politics of expenditure, and politicians find that their constituents respond more favorably to increased spending than to increased taxes. Economists may argue that decisions on taxation and expenditure should be part of a total process in which the marginal utility of additional expenditure for one objective should be weighed against the utility derivable from its expenditure for another objective and/or against the utility derivable from leaving funds in the private sector of the economy. But such calculations are for all practical purposes impossible.

Nevertheless, taxation and expenditure decisions of necessity are interrelated in the American states. Lacking the flexibility that national governments derive from the operation of a central treasury, states of necessity must closely relate the intake and outgo of funds. Lacking such resources and power, the state's expenditure-taxation decision makers are not direct participants in macroeconomic policymaking. Manipulation of taxes and expenditures to hold down inflation or check depressions occurs largely at the national level.

The order of decisions on taxation and expenditure varies. When decision makers are more interested in programs than how to finance them, expenditure decisions are made first; but on other occasions taxes may be given first priority. Regardless, the decision on the amount of money to be raised, from whom it will be raised, and how it will be raised are of major political import, and substantial variation occurs among the states because of their different political and economic situations.[1]

In Texas the normal procedure is to develop an estimate (usually provided in the process of preparing the budget submitted by the Legislative Budget Board) of the cost of continuing existing programs at roughly the current level of operation, and then to compare that figure with the revenue that will be provided by existing law. Estimates are then made of the costs of the program changes for which the greatest need or support exists, and speculation begins as to tax needs. The governor presents his spending recommendations and, if the revenue system is not adequate to finance them, a plan for raising the needed revenue. His revenue plan becomes a first approximation of an expenditure ceiling; but through a complex process of opinion formation and negotiation among legislative leaders and the governor, an appropriations bill is prepared that may require adjustments in that ceiling. After final spending totals are determined, legislation to raise the necessary revenue is enacted. It is possible, of course, for the existing system to produce adequate revenue. But from 1949 through 1971 revenue-raising legislation was enacted by every legislature. The 1973, 1975, and 1977 sessions, which enjoyed first the availability of federal revenue-sharing funds and then the unprecedented increases in receipts from oil and gas severance taxes attributable to sharp increases in oil and gas prices, did not have to enact such legislation.

LEGAL, IDEOLOGICAL, AND ECONOMIC CONSIDERATIONS

The U.S. Constitution does very little to limit the power of the states to tax. They may not tax imports or exports without the consent of the U.S. Congress; use the taxing power to deny persons equal protection and due process of law; or levy taxes that burden (i.e., interfere with) interstate commerce, a provision which has frustrated some attempts by the legislature to levy natural-gas-gathering taxes.

Typically, state constitutions contain a variety of limitations on the legislature's taxing power. Limits are placed on some taxes; others, such as income taxes, may be entirely prohibited; and exemptions of various sorts are granted. Texas is less restrictive than most states, few limitations being built into the constitution. Among those that do exist are the requirements that taxation be equal and uniform; the exemption of $3000 of assessed value of homestead residences from state taxation; and the exemption of farm products in the hands of the producer and family supplies for home and farm use from all taxation, except by vote of two-thirds of the membership of both houses of the legislature. On the other hand, taxation of incomes is explicitly authorized although some authorities contend that it could not be graduated because of the equal and uniform requirement. Suggestions are occasionally heard, usually during political campaigns and most often originating with Republicans, that the constitution be amended to prohibit the taxation of incomes. But when such amendments have been proposed in the legislature, they have received little support.

Thus, tax issues in Texas are essentially political issues to be resolved in the legislature through the political process rather than by recourse to the courts and the constitution. There are a variety of factors that may affect the outcome of tax controversies.

Major innovations in a state's tax system are usually stimulated by some type of crisis: for example, a decline in the yield of existing taxes or sharp increases in expenditure, which necessitate a large increase in revenue. A major revenue shortage, as measured against spending needs, led to the Texas legislature's enactment in 1961 of the first broadbased tax in the state's history—the general sales tax.

The timing of decisions on major taxes also appears to influence tax choices.[2] The states having major income taxes adopted them in the early 1930s or before. Since World War II, the sales tax has usually been resorted to when additional taxes are needed. The high level of national income taxes and the general level of affluence seem to have lessened the appeal of progressive state taxation on incomes. The current "climate of opinion" in Texas appears to be in favor of sales taxes.

Notions as to the proper theory of taxation also affect tax decisions. The theory of progressive taxation holds that taxation should be based on the principle of "ability to pay" and favors higher rates of taxation as a person's income increases. Those who accept this theory show a preference for graduated income taxes. Another theory holds that those who benefit from governmental programs should pay for them. This theory is manifested in the earmarking of motor-fuel taxes for highway construction and maintenance. Another notion is that all citizens should make some contribution to the support of their government, a notion that is satisfied by the sales tax.

Beliefs are motives for action, but people are influenced in tax decisions by more than notions of what is correct or proper; they are influenced by considerations of material advantage. Very few people enjoy paying taxes, and most (no matter what their income bracket) show a marked preference to let someone else do it. Consequently, the balance of political forces (which often reflects the strength of economic interests in a state) helps determine who pays. Texas secures significant revenue from the petroleum industry, but not at any major disadvantage to the industry. Business groups have been able to stave off a corporate income tax; they strongly supported the sales tax in 1961. Agricultural groups have been able to secure exemptions from the sales tax and other levies. But organized labor has not been able to prevent the heavy reliance on sales taxes, nor have liberals and labor been able to secure the enactment of a corporate income tax.

Taxes that are selective in their impact are often easier to enact than those of general effect. The selective tax is less visible and, as fewer are affected, the opposition may be weaker; selective taxes are often levied on persons or groups whose ability to resist is particularly weak. Some selective taxes, such as those on hotel and motel rooms, are directed against tourists; others are placed on items regarded as "evil," such as liquor and cigarettes. The demand for these last items is rather inelastic, and consequently higher taxes yield higher revenues rather than discourage their use. The knowledge that taxes on liquor and cigarettes produces substantial revenue has resulted in high tax rates on them in most states, including Texas.

Interstate competition also affects taxation. That one state has a particular tax will often serve as an argument for its adoption in neighboring states. Conversely—and despite a substantial volume of evidence indicating that such factors as availability of natural resources, skilled labor, and transportation facilities are decisive—the argument is still made that higher taxes will keep out new industry or drive away existing businesses. Occasionally, reductions are justified in order to allow competition with similar industries in other states, as in 1963 when the state tax on sulfur was reduced to enable Texas sulfur to better compete with sulfur from Louisiana and Mexico. One liberal senator was quoted as saying that the Texas sulfur companies "had a legitimate, reasonable argument."[3]

THE CURRENT REVENUE SYSTEM

The present Texas revenue system represents the culmination of a century of development and is comprised of a variety of taxes, fees, interest and sales receipts, and miscellaneous items, plus a substantial amount of federal grant-in-aid money.[4] Tax decisions tend to be cumulative and, once adopted, a tax that is a good source of revenue is not likely to be abandoned (although modification or tinkering with it is quite possible). As state spending has increased and existing taxes have proven inadequate, new taxes have been added or existing taxes increased in piecemeal fashion and nontax revenues have been sought.

Rather than discuss in detail the many tax and revenue sources, their rates, exemptions, yield, and impact, the following discussion simply outlines the patterns of revenue. Major categories are noted, along with some illustrations of each. Table 10.1 illustrates the yield of various taxes since 1940, and Figure 10.1 indicates the relative importance of various sources of revenue in fiscal 1973.

General sales tax. After an intense political struggle whose outcome was to determine the direction of tax policy for at least a decade, the legislature adopted a 2-percent general sales tax in 1961. Subsequent legislatures enacted increases, with the most recent in 1971 resulting in a 4-percent state tax. Most Texans now pay a 5-percent sales tax, however, for many cities levy a 1-percent tax covering the same items as the state tax; the state collects the tax for the cities. The sales tax is levied on most sales of personal property and merchandise and is to be collected by the seller from the purchaser. Various items are exempted from the tax, some for the purpose of preventing "double taxation" (cigarettes and motor vehicles, but not liquor and beer); others are exempted to reduce political opposition (food, prescription medicines, farm machinery, and fertilizer). The exemption of food and medicine

TABLE 10.1 • DEVELOPMENT OF TEXAS TAX
REVENUES, 1940–1976 (IN MILLIONS)

Tax	1940	1950	1960	1970	1977
Retail sales tax	—	—	—	$ 550	$1689
Selective sales taxes					
Motor fuel	$ 46	$ 87	$185	312	444
Motor vehicles	—	14	27	97	328
Tobacco	7	30	86	187	288
Alcoholic beverages	7	17	35	58	105
Other	—	1	—	—	—
Severance taxes					
Oil	15	81	123	172	428
Natural gas	1	10	52	96	474
Sulfur	1	5	4	4	4
Other	3	5	4	—	—
Business taxes					
Corporation franchise	2	9	60	110	237
Insurance companies	4	13	31	55	120
Gross receipts	2	5	19	41	177
Motor-vehicle registration	9	31	76	148	234
Property tax	22	30	38	64	43
Inheritance tax	1	5	13	23	67
Other	3	7	17	12	17
Totals	$123	$350	$770	$1316	$4655

SOURCE: Annual Reports of the Comptroller of Public Accounts.

made the sales tax more acceptable (or at least less unacceptable) to moderates and liberals and, some economists argue, makes the tax regressive only when moderately high income levels are reached.

Selective sales taxes. These are taxes, sometimes called excise taxes, that are levied on particular goods or services. As with general sales taxes, they are assumed to fall on the consumer. A partial listing of items subject to selective sales taxes include gasoline and diesel fuel (when used for highway travel); cigarettes, cigars, and chewing tobacco; alcoholic beverages; and motor vehicles. To illustrate further, the levies on alcoholic beverages are $2.00 a gallon for distilled spirits, $5.00 a barrel for beer, and 13–33 cents a gallon for wine.

Severance taxes. Rather than try to determine the value of natural resources for property taxation, taxes are imposed on the market price of such resources at the time of production. Severance, or production, taxes currently apply to crude oil, natural gas, sulfur, and cement.

Major business taxes. Significant among these are the corporation franchise tax, paid by corporations for the privilege of doing business in the state and based on their financial structure; the gross-receipts tax, charged against a variety of public utilities and other businesses as a percentage of their gross receipts; and a tax on insurance companies determined by the total premiums received inside the state.

Motor-vehicle registration fees. All motor vehicles—cars, trucks, buses, motorcycles—must have a license to operate on the public highways. The amount of the tax, or fee, is based on the vehicle's

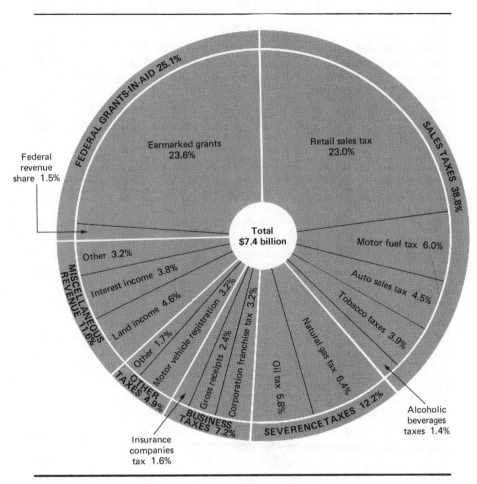

Figure 10.1 • Texas state revenue sources, fiscal year 1976.

SOURCE: *1977 Annual Financial Report of the State of Texas* (Austin: Comptroller of Public Accounts, 1977), p. 11.

weight and is graduated upward as weight, but not necessarily value, increases. This tax is collected by the counties, and part of the funds received are retained by them.

Miscellaneous taxes. Several other taxes levied by the state include those on inheritances, chain stores, property, and hotel and motel rooms. The chain-store tax, enacted in the 1930s, was an attempt to use the taxing power for regulatory purposes. The tax, which is graduated from $5 for the first store to $826 for each store in excess of 50, was designed to limit the operations of multiunit businesses for the benefit of small retailers; but it has had little restrictive effect and raises only a few million dollars.

Nontax revenue. In 1977 about 40 percent of the state's income came from nontax sources, primarily federal grants-in-aid for highways, welfare, and education. Earmarked federal grants totaled $1.7 billion, and the unearmarked revenue share added another $103 million. Other nontax revenues include college tuition and fees, mineral leases, oil and gas royalties, dividends and interest, game and fish licenses, and pay patient collections.

TAXATION
AND POLITICS

The Texas tax system relies on sales taxes, with a secondary emphasis on business and severance taxes. Over the past two decades the reliance on business and severance taxes has decreased, as a review of major tax legislation enacted since 1960 indicates. In 1961 a 2-percent general sales tax was enacted, and in 1963 several exemptions from that tax were removed. In 1965 the cigarette tax was increased from 8 to 11 cents a package, and in 1968 the motor-vehicle and general sales taxes were increased to 3 percent. In 1969 the general sales tax was increased to 3.25 percent, and the cigarette tax to 15.5 cents. However, the production tax on natural gas was increased from 7 percent to 7.5 percent, and the corporation franchise tax from $2.75 to $3.25 per $1000 of taxable capital and surplus. The franchise tax was also revised in the expectation that the changes would produce additional revenue. In 1971 the motor-vehicle and general sales taxes were increased to 4 percent, the cigarette tax to 18.5 cents, the per-barrel tax on beer from $4.35 to $5.00, and the per-gallon tax on liquor from $1.68 to $2.00. The corporation franchise tax was increased to $4.50 per $1000 of taxable capital and surplus.

A comparison of the percent of tax revenue derived from sales, business, and severance taxes in the years reported in Table 10.1 also indicates an increasing reliance on sales taxes. In 1977 general and selective sales taxes provided 61 percent of the state's tax take, as compared with 49 percent in 1940. Between 1940 and 1950 the percentage actually declined to 40, and the portion derived from severance taxes rose from 16 to 29 percent. In 1960 the sales tax percentage was still 43; but by 1970, sales taxes provided 62 percent of the tax take. The portion of tax revenue derived from severance taxes increased from 1940 to 1950 and then began a decline which lasted until 1973, when it began to rise sharply because of huge increases in the well-head price of oil and gas. Severance taxes constituted 16 percent of tax receipts in 1940, 14 percent in 1970, and 20 percent in 1977.

The portion of tax revenue derived from business taxes has not fluctuated as much as the take from sales and severance taxes, although the high of 14 percent in 1960 declined to 12 percent in 1977. Sales taxes fall directly on the consumer, and many business taxes are undoubtedly passed along to the consumer in the form of higher prices. The result is a tax system that is substantially regressive in that its burden tends to rest more heavily on low-income groups, for the proportion of income paid in sales and property taxes declines as income rises.[5]

The desirability of regressive or progressive systems of taxation depends on the values of the person passing judgment. The type of tax system in use does, however, reflect the balance of political forces in the state and the relative influence of economic groups with those forces. Upper-income and business groups have enjoyed favorable conditions of access to the conservative faction of the Texas Democratic party, whose members have controlled the important policy positions in both the executive and legislative branches of state government. In the clashes over taxation the liberal Democrats, who have supported social programs benefiting low-income or minority groups, have favored taxation of natural resources (especially those with potential for transference to out-of-state consumers); business taxes; and, increasingly in recent years, a corporate income tax. As indicated by the tax legislation enacted in the 1961-1971 period, they have not been very successful; however, the inclusion of increases in the severance and corporate franchise taxes in 1969 and the franchise tax in 1971 are largely attributable to a sharp upturn in liberal strength in the Texas Senate. A personal income tax has received little public support from Texas liberals, although this may be more a reflection of political realities than personal preferences.

Conservatism in Texas has generally been associated in the area of public finance with opposition to progressive forms of taxation, frugality in government expenditures, and encouragement of business and industrial development through a tax structure attractive to business. Conservative Democrats have shown a marked preference for sales taxes of one sort or another. The financial policies of the small contingent of Republicans in the legislature have emphasized reductions in expenditures rather than the use of any form of taxes. But indications are that, if forced to choose, Texas Republicans favor sales over income taxation.

A ranking of the "legislative climate" for the "business environment" reinforces the conclusion that the tax system of Texas has been predominantly shaped by conservative business forces. Fifteen criteria were used, and all but three which dealt with labor-management relations, were involved either directly (e.g., whether the state employs a corporate income tax) or indirectly (unemployment compensation rate) with taxation. Texas was considered to have the most favorable business environment in the country.[6]

THE BUDGET MACHINERY

There are several ways in which budgets may be described. First, a budget can be viewed as a financial document, a statement of estimated revenues and proposed expenditures to guide financial activities for the period covered. Second, budgets are also policy statements indicating priorities among policy areas, levels of activity within policy areas, and overall spending. In this sense budgets are "political" matters in that they entail choices among competing and conflicting interests, and there is never enough money to satisfy everyone. Third, a budget can be a means of administrative management, an instrument for directing the administrative system. In Texas, however, the budget has little of this last characteristic because of the absence of a system of budget execution.

A familiar way of classifying budgets is on the basis of who has major responsibility for their preparation. Such a classification yields three types: the executive budget, prepared by the chief executive; the legislative budget, prepared by an instrumentality of the legislature; and the commission budget, formulated by a board composed jointly of legislative and executive officals. Among students of public administration there is a marked preference for the executive budget, and indeed it is the most common type in American governmental systems. Its advocates contend that it permits the chief executive to lay a comprehensive, systematic program before the legislature; facilitates evaluation of both total spending and spending for particular programs in relation to one another; serves as a tool of executive management; helps increase citizen understanding of governmental activity; and contributes to strong and responsible executive leadership in government. Since one of the general consequences of the executive budget is to strengthen the chief executive, opponents of the extension of executive power occasionally oppose the pure executive budget; they argue that many of the alleged benefits are derivable from any comprehensive budget.

A budget of any type represents a change from nineteenth- and early twentieth-century practice, when there was typically neither a central budget agency nor a comprehensive budget and each administrative agency drew up its own budget and sent it directly to the legislature. The budget machinery of each state developed somewhat differently, since constitutional provisions and political traditions differed in each state. In Texas this development led to an unusual system in which there are two separate budget agencies, each of which develops and submits a budget for legislative consideration.

CONSTITUTIONAL FRAMEWORK
FOR BUDGET PROCEDURES

Three provisions of the Texas Constitution establish the framework within which budget procedures developed. First, the constitution provides that money shall not be withdrawn from the treasury except in persuance of specific appropriations and that appropriations shall not be made for a period longer than two years.[7] Since regular sessions of the legislature are held at two-year intervals, the state's budget is normally adopted for a two-year period, or biennium. Each biennium is composed of two fiscal years, with each fiscal year running from September 1 of one calendar year through August 31 of the next and taking its name from the calendar year in which it ends. Most authorities recommend annual budgets on the ground that they permit more careful and precise planning. But a minority contends that the process of preparing and adopting a budget is so complex and lengthy that a 12-month fiscal period is too short. Experience on the national level offers some support for the minority position: Budget requests and recommendations for a forthcoming year must be prepared before the appropriations for the current year are known, and appropriations bills for a fiscal year often are not enacted until after the fiscal year begins.

The second constitutional provision that affects budgeting requires the governor to present estimates of the amount of money required to be raised by taxation for all purposes at the commencement of each regular session of the legislature. This gives the governor a constitutional role in the process of financial planning. The governor's role is further specified in the budgetary process by the grant of the power to veto appropriations, including the veto of specific items of appropriations in general appropriations acts. His veto can be overridden by a two-thirds vote in each house of the legislature.[8]

The third provision of the constitution that importantly affects budgeting provides that the comptroller of public accounts shall submit to the governor and legislature an itemized estimate, based on the laws in effect, of the revenue that will be available for expenditure during the forthcoming biennium. Appropriations in excess of the anticipated revenue may not be made, and bills containing an appropriation cannot be considered as passed and sent to the governor until the comptroller certifies that the amount appropriated from a fund is within the amount estimated to be available. When the comptroller finds that an appropriation exceeds the estimated revenue, the bill containing the appropriation is returned to the legislature, where steps must be taken to bring it within the estimate. A four-fifths vote in each house can override his finding.[9]

The revenue estimate must contain such other information as required by law, a provision that allowed the legislature to establish an agency to review the estimates. In response to criticism of certain bookkeeping practices used in making the estimates, the legislature in 1959 specified certain procedures that were to be followed in preparing the estimates and established a Committee on State Revenue Estimates to review and report on them. The comptroller does submit his estimates to the committee members (the governor or his designated representative, state auditor, and staff director of the Legislative Budget Board), but the committee neither meets nor reports on the estimates.

The estimating process grew out of dissatisfaction with continuing deficits in the treasury in the 1930s and 1940s and was designed to eliminate deficit spending. The comptroller's estimates have a reasonably good record for accuracy, although there may be a tendency for them to be conservative, especially in the second year of the biennium.

A review of the general revenue estimates by the Texas Research League covering 1948 through 1967 indicates that during the first years of that period, when the staff was inexperienced, the estimates varied from actual receipts by as much as 29 percent. From 1954 onward, however, the record improved, with the largest margin by which receipts varied from estimates amounting to only 7.8 percent. Although receipts usually exceeded estimates, in 5 of the 20 years the revenue was overestimated; the largest overestimation amounted to 6.6 percent of receipts. Four of the 5 years were in the 1958-1961 period, when receipts from the oil production tax were badly overestimated. The closing of the Suez Canal in 1957 during an Arab-Israeli war resulted in sharp increases in receipts from that tax because of the increased demand for Texas oil. But in the following years the reopening of the canal and development of other transportation methods resulted in sharply increased production of Middle Eastern oil and a decline in the Texas position in petroleum extraction. Essentially, the comptroller uses extrapolative or mechanical estimating methods that project past performance into the future. When revenues dropped sharply with the reopening of the canal and remained at lower than anticipated levels, even judgmental modification of the estimates did not prevent receipts from being overestimated.[10]

Thus, the effort to put state spending on a pay-as-you-go basis can not entirely eliminate deficits, since inability to predict the future makes revenue-estimating an inexact process. Even when the overall estimates have not been in deficit, estimates of revenue from particular sources have occasionally been higher than actual proceeds. This usually occurred because changes in economic conditions affected receipts from sales taxes or adoption of a new tax or revision of existing tax laws required that estimates be almost entirely judgmental, since historical data were not available. Deficits thus are not impossible in Texas.

AGENCIES AND FUND STRUCTURE

Texas has developed budget machinery and procedures within the framework of these constitutional provisions. Prior to 1949 Texas did not have an effective system of budgeting, and financial procedures were criticized for being haphazard, fragmented, and arbitrary. The legislature in that year created a Legislative Budget Board and required all state agencies to submit their appropriations requests to it. The board consists of four members from each house, plus the lieutenant governor and speaker of the house, who in effect appoint the other members. The chairmen of the appropriations and revenue and taxation committees of the House and the finance and state affairs committees of the Senate must be included. Consequently, the Legislative Budget Board includes some of the most influential members of the legislature. The creation of a budget agency responsible to the legislative leadership was indicative of the legislature's desire for independence from and suspicion of gubernatorial power; the legislature had not been willing to grant the governor authority and adequate staff aid for preparing a state budget. The first budget board began the development of a professional staff, and later boards continued the emphasis on strong staffing; the combination of competent professional staff and the makeup of the board has meant that its recommendations carry much weight.

The creation of the Legislative Budget Board meant that Texas had two state budget agencies, for the Board of Control was also responsible for preparation of a budget. The Board of Control's budget division had never been adequately staffed, and its budget was not held in very high repute by the legislature. In 1951, following the recommendation of both the Legislative Budget Board and Gov. Allen Shivers, the legislature transferred responsibility for preparation of an executive budget to the governor. Preparation of the executive budget is handled by a special division in the governor's office.

The budget prepared by the Legislative Budget Board in 1951 included totals for all funds for the first time, and since then efforts have been exerted to prepare a budget that includes all expenditures. The state's fund structure makes this difficult, however; like many other states, Texas has followed a policy of segregating many of the taxes, fees, and other receipts and dedicating them to a particular purpose. These earmarked monies go into special funds, of which there are now over 200. Statutorily earmarked funds can be used for undesignated purposes only if legislation is enacted authorizing its use, and that occurs infrequently. Several of the more important funds are constitutionally dedicated and not even the legislature can authorize their use for other purposes. In addition to the special funds in the state treasury, there are more than 40 special state funds outside the treasury that are not subject to budgetary review and whose use does not require appropriation. About three-fourths of state expenditures are from funds other than general revenue, and about 60 percent of the state's tax revenue goes into earmarked funds.

The operation of the special-funds system can be illustrated by a short look at four major funds that collectively account for over two-thirds of all state revenue.[11] The Highway Fund is financed by the state's share of motor-vehicle registration fees and three-fourths of all motor-fuel taxes. The fund, which had net receipts of $872 million in fiscal 1977, can be expended only for construction, maintenance, and policing of the state highway system.

The Available School Fund receives one-fourth of motor-fuel taxes plus occupation, severance, gross receipts, and property taxes; it also receives the earnings of the Permanent School Fund, a trust of about a billion dollars supported by the proceeds from sales, leases, and royalties on public lands dedicated to educational purposes. These funds totaled $569 million in 1977.

The Omnibus Tax Clearance Fund was established to receive various severance, occupation, selective sales, and other taxes, and then to provide these funds to specified programs on a priority basis. Its net receipts in 1977 were $1.834 billion. In order of priority, the programs receiving support are farm-to-market roads, public assistance, teachers' retirement, and the foundation school program. The amounts of most allocations are determined by statute and not through the appropriations process.

Any funds left over go into the General Revenue Fund. The General Revenue Fund contains the nonearmarked tax revenues, which come mostly from the general sales and tobacco taxes and amounted to $2.62 billion in 1977. The general fund supports higher education, hospitals, youth correctional institutions, the judiciary, and many regulatory and service programs. A variety of agencies thus compete for general revenue, but even some of these legally unrestricted funds are politically untouchable because they are committed to programs enjoying strong support. The governor and legislature thus have substantial discretion over the use of only a small portion of available revenue. The practice of earmarking revenue has some undesirable consequences: for example, limitations on the flexibility of budget makers to allocate funds where needs are greatest and the tendency of those with dedicated funds to be better financed than those competing for general revenue. The beneficiaries of dedicated funds, however, strongly and usually successfully resist efforts to end earmarking.

There are some constitutional limits on state spending. Most notable is the limitation on welfare assistance payments, which provides that state contributions for assistance to individuals shall not exceed the amount provided by federal matching funds and, further,

"Some agencies are much better funded than others."

that they shall not exceed $80 million per year.[12] The ceiling, which does not include payments for medical assistance or administrative costs, was increased on three occasions in the 1960s, and an amendment to remove the ceiling was defeated in 1971. During the late 1960s, when the number of welfare recipients was increasing rapidly, the ceiling threatened to force sharp reductions in assistance payments; but a leveling-off in the number of recipients in the early 1970s made such reductions unnecessary. The assumption by the national government of responsibility for the aid to the needy aged, blind, and disabled means that the ceiling limits only the aid to families with dependent children program. At least temporarily, it no longer constitutes a meaningful limitation on the legislature.

THE BUDGETARY PROCESS

The budgetary process can best be understood as a continuous pattern of activity having several distinguishable but not entirely separate stages. The various people and agencies concerned with raising and spending money can be located in this process and their roles indicated, thereby providing information on both their particular activities and their relationships to the total process. In the budgetary process decision makers tend to develop particular perceptions and expectations; these are often associated with institutional patriotism. General revenue spending, rather than decisions affecting all expenditures, has been selected for analysis because the allocation of general revenue is competitive. Thus, an analysis of decisions on general revenue spending over a period of years should reveal the roles and policy predispositions of budgetary decision makers. The spending recommendations of various participants from fiscal 1954 through fiscal 1979 are summarized in Table 10.2.

The budgetary process consists of four basic stages: (1) preparation of the budget; (2) authorization of the budget (its enactment into law), which is a legislative task; (3) execution of the budget, or spending of the provided funds; and (4) the audit of expenditures. With such considerations in mind, the budgetary process is described for the biennium beginning September 1, 1977, and ending August 31, 1979.

PREPARATION OF THE BUDGET

June–December, 1975. Both the executive and legislative budget staffs begin initial planning. General policy problems are considered, and the two staffs, working independently, engage in research on various finance-related problems of state government.

TABLE 10.2 • EXPENDITURE DECISIONS ON THE
GENERAL REVENUE FUND (IN MILLIONS)

Fiscal biennium*	Agency requests	LBB budget	Governor's budget	Senate bill	House bill	Conference committee bill	Vetoed by governor
1954–1955	$ 220	$ 161	$ 173	$ 166	$ 161	$ 167	$0
1958–1957	263	199	196	205	212	222	0
1958–1959	343	255	264	292	281	282	4
1960–1961	387	286	330	302	331	316	1
1962–1963	429	356	392	354	379	394	0
1964–1965	555	435	475	456	437	474	8
1966–1967	739	563	595	617	605	618	2
1970–1971	1507	1087	1162	1199	1152	1227	0
1974–1975	2779	2289	2058	2233	2283	2315	2
1976–1977	4647	3794	3032	3893	3943	3479	9
1978–1979	7492	6030	4078	5760	5906	5624	0

*The 1968–1969 and 1972–1973 bienniums are not included. The legislature adopted annual appropriations acts for those years, thus making some of the information not comparable.

January–September, 1976. The next phase involves the preparation and analysis of agency requests for funds. Early in the year budget instructions developed jointly by the two budget offices are sent to the agencies. The instructions are largely technical, but in recent bienniums an important innovation was instituted when the instructions required that requests be zero-based. Zero-based budgeting supposedly requires that the entire request be justified, not just changes from the current budget as allegedly occurs under conventional budgeting. A notable feature of zero-based budgeting in Texas has been that it uses a programmatic format and requires alternative spending levels including, but not limited to, amounts that vary from current levels by specified percentages. Agency officials then begin to work up their budget requests, often consulting with officials of the two central budget offices along the way. The agencies, not unexpectedly, are advocates of increased spending. Their concern is that their programs operate at an optimum level; they are not concerned with the overall size of the budget or the necessary for new revenue sources. Table 10.2 indicates that the total of all general revenue requests increased sharply over current appropriations for every biennium represented, with the lowest total increase requested (1962–1963) representing a 36-percent increase over current appropriations and the highest (1978–1979), a 116-percent increase; the average of the requested increases was 61 percent.

After the agency requests are prepared, they are submitted to the two budget offices, where the examiners begin the analyses of the proposals. In the summer, hearings are conducted jointly by the governor's budget staff and the legislative budget staff; agency officials appear to explain their budget requests. Once these hearings are concluded, joint activity by the two budget agencies is ended and they go to work independently to develop budget recommendations for the governor and the Legislative Budget Board.

September–December, 1976. The next phase in the budget cycle involves the actual preparation of the overall budgets. Each staff continues its analysis of the requests and eventually prepares recommendations for those who are politically responsible for preparation of the budget.

Traditionally, budget offices tend to regard the operating agencies as spenders who are more interested in programmatic excellence than economy and efficiency and who have only a narrow agency-oriented perspective; they also perceive that they have a responsibility to protect the taxpayers from such attitudes by functioning as guardians of the treasury. Additionally, the Legislative Budget Board and its staff traditionally attempted to develop a budget whose expenditures do not exceed available revenue, a budget that would constitute an appropriation base from which the legislature can develop its own spending plan. The legislative budget staff consequently recommends large reductions in agency requests. The board tends to make marginal rather than major changes in the staff recommendations; it works through a consensual process that secures agreement, and votes are almost never taken. The budget developed by the board sharply reduces the requests of the agencies. During the 1954–1979 period (Table 10.2), the average reduction imposed was twenty-three percent of the amount requested; the largest reduction (1970–1971) was 28 percent, and the smallest (1962–1963) was 17 percent. The process of preparing the board's budget is completed by late December, and the budget is presented to the governor and the legislature for their consideration in early January.

Meanwhile, the governor's staff has been working on the executive budget. Acting on the basis of general guidelines as to what the governor wants to emphasize in the budget, the executive budget staffs works in a fashion similar to its legislative counterpart. The staff recommendations are usually presented to the governor in a summary fashion for his review; due to time limitations, he usually does not conduct an item-by-item detailed review of the budget (as does the Legislative Budget Board). The governor's budget also recommends large reductions in the budget requests (Table 10.2); from 1954 to 1979, the reductions for general revenue spending ranged from 9 percent (1962–1963) to 56 percent (1978–1979) and averaged 25 percent.

Nevertheless, the governor's budget traditionally was larger than the Legislative Budget Board's and is more likely to contain recommendations for new or significantly expanded programs. It was also more likely to exceed existing revenue. The governor thus acted more as advocate or innovator. His budget is presented to the legislators in December; early in the regular session in January, he presents his overall financial program (including proposals for raising, additional revenue if his spending proposals so necessitate) in an address to the legislature. Newly elected governors do not present their budgets until after their inauguration, but the outgoing governor is still responsible for presenting a budget in December. Thus, when there is a gubernatorial transition, the legislature has not two but three budgets presented to it. The recommendations of the outgoing governor are largely ignored.

Both the governor and the Legislative Budget Board recommend considerably smaller expenditures than the total amounts requested by the spending agencies. There is a definite incentive for both to reduce the spending requests; reductions in requests lessen the amount of revenue that must be raised, and raising revenue is almost always a painful process. According to the Texas Constitution, the governor must recommend where revenue should be obtained to meet expenditure requirements. The budget board is not required by the law to recommend sources of revenue if its expenditure recommendations exceed available funds, but the board members are likely to be leaders of the legislature that will be required to increase taxes. Total requests have always exceeded available funds; even by recommending sizable reductions, the governors since World War II have, until the three most recent bienniums, been faced with the necessity of recommending legislation to increase taxes. Spending apparently cannot be reduced beyond certain points. The recommendations of both the governor and the budget board have consistently been larger than total current appropriations (averaging 25 percent larger by the board and 20 percent larger by the governor). There is a point beyond which requests cannot be reduced without seriously impairing services, and neither the governor nor the Legislative Budget Board desires credit for such an accomplishment.

Significant changes occurred in the spending attitude of the governor and the Legislative Budget Board beginning in the mid-1960s. Changes in the position of staff director and membership of the board resulted in a less conservative, more aggressive board. The major changes involved Vernon McGhee, the staff director since the creation of the board, who was dismissed by a board majority led by Speaker

Ben Barnes, and the departure from the Senate and consequently the board in the early to mid-1960s of Wardlow Lane, Crawford Martin, and Dorsey Hardeman, all of whom had been members of the board since its inception. The board gradually abandoned the policy of presenting only a base (or "bare bones") budget and began developing a plan in line with what the board members wanted enacted. The influence of Barnes, who became lieutenant governor and thereby chairman of the board in 1969, and the implementation of a program format in 1976–1977, thereby focusing attention on overall program levels, appear crucial to the change of philosophy.

Changes in the governorship also contributed to the reversal of spending attitudes. Govs. Preston Smith and Dolph Briscoe are nonaggressive fiscal conservatives not inclined toward expansive budgets. Smith recommended slightly more than the board in his first budget (1970–1971), but less in his second, which does not appear in Table 10.2, and Briscoe has recommended less in all three of his budgets.

While the figures in Table 10.2 essentially present the correct picture, the differences, especially in the Briscoe years, are not as drastic as they appear. The board, while not adhering rigidly to the "bare bones" philosophy, has been hesitant to recommend broad statutory changes that affect spending, while Briscoe has made such recommendations, most notably in the areas of public school finance and highways. His plans diverted funds from general revenue and thereby are not included in Table 10.2. Even if such funds are included, however, the board's budget was higher than the governor's.

BUDGET AUTHORIZATION

Budgets are proposed plans of expenditure; the spending still must be authorized, and that is the task of the legislature. When the legislature meets in January, a bill enacting the recommendations of the budget board is introduced in each house and referred to committee.

January–March 1977. The appropriations process in the committees of the two houses is similar, but differs in one important respect. In the Senate, the bill is referred directly to the Finance Committee, and consideration is limited to that committee. In the House, the various substantive committees (i.e., Health and Welfare, Agriculture, etc.) consider the portion of the bill for which they have legislative responsibility and recommend amounts for those agencies. The recommended amounts may be reduced or increased by the Appropriations Committee, but increases require a two-thirds vote.

In effect, the substantive committees establish a ceiling that will be lifted only under extraordinary circumstances. The substantive committee recommendation process was first employed in 1975 and is so new that generalization about it is difficult. Nevertheless, it appears that the substantive committees naturally take a special interest in "their" agencies and, consequently, their recommendations are higher than the amount eventually approved by the Appropriations Committee, which must fit all the pieces into an overall budget. The key point of decision remains in the Appropriations Committee.

The House and Senate committees hold separate hearings, most of which are rather perfunctory. In their appearances before the committees and elsewhere, agencies are expected to be advocates of their original budget requests; this is unlike the situation at the national level, where agencies are expected to support the president's budget. If an agency is seeking to increase an item recommended by the board, it may utilize a higher recommendation in the governor's budget to support its position. But otherwise the agencies tend to explain why they need the amount requested, or at least more than was recommended by the board.

When the hearings are completed, the committees decide what to recommend for each agency on a program-by-program basis. Various influences are focused on the committees in the course of their deliberations. Agency officials lobby for their requests, pressure-group spokesmen attempt to influence decisions on selected items, and the governor seeks approval for this favorite proposals. Although attention is focused on committee members, especially the chairmen, interested parties may also seek to work through the lieutenant governor and the speaker, to whom the committee members are usually quite responsive.

The committees work from the budget and appropriations bill prepared by the budget board. Ordinarily, the board's recommendations are accepted as a base and changes involve additions. The bills are then reported to the two houses for floor consideration, which is usually rather perfunctory and seldom results in substantial changes. At no stage in the authorization process is there a thorough, general debate. Agreement with the pattern of expenditure, limitations of time and knowledge, lack of real alternatives given the statutory commitment of so much of the money and the political commitment of even more, and fear of antagonizing those in control of the bill and consequent loss of items important in one's district, and, at least in earlier years knowledge that the bill would be rewritten by the conference committee all contribute to the sparseness of debate.

Two recent developments indicate important changes from the usual patterns are occurring. First, criticism that the absence of restraints on members of the conference committee led to pork barreling and to pressure on members to support the leadership of the two houses or face the loss of appropriations for their districts led to the adoption of joint rules that limited the conference committee to resolving differences in the two bills. This presumably encourages a more serious attitude toward the bills approved by the two houses. Second, in the three most recent bienniums the house devoted significant amounts of its time to consideration of the appropriations bill. In 1977 the changes made on the floor were of considerable significance.

The amount approved in the House and Senate bills is usually larger than the amount recommended by the budget board. In the 11 bienniums included in Table 10.2, 8 bills appropriated more general revenue than was recommended by the board. The actions of the two houses differ in interesting respects. But their differences do not reveal a consistent pattern, such as that found on the national level, where the U.S. Senate is said to be the "upper" body because it usually increases the appropriations approved by the U.S. House.[13] In the bienniums included in Table 10.2, the Texas House bill was higher on six occasions and the Texas Senate bill on five.

A more consistent pattern is revealed when the higher of the two bills is compared with the liberal-conservative factional makeup of the two houses. Prior to 1963 (when the appropriations for the 1964–1965 biennium were approved) the Texas Senate was a more conservative body than was the Texas House, and for three of the five bienniums the house-approved bill was higher than the Senate bill. In the 1963–1971 period the Senate contained a larger portion of liberal and moderate members than did the House, and in the three bienniums from that period the appropriations approved in the Senate bill were higher than those approved in the House bill (Table 10.2). In 1973 the ideological complexion of the two houses shifted sharply, with the Senate becoming the more conservative of the two bodies; the House passed a appropriations bill that was higher than the Senate bill. In 1975 and 1977 both houses were predominantly conservative and the appropriating committees had conservative chairmen, but the house probably had a higher portion of liberal and moderate members. Thus, in 9 of the 11 bienniums the more liberal body approved higher spending. The exceptions were the appropriations for the 1954–1955 and 1958–1959 bienniums, when in fact the legislatures involved had strong conservative majorities in both houses. From 1959 onward, however, the body that approved the higher spending total had a majority or near-majority of liberal and moderate members. The inclination of liberals and moderates to be more oriented toward spending is apparently directly reflected in the appropriations bills approved in the two houses of the legislature.

April–May 1977. Because the bills passed by the two houses differ, the stage is set for the conference committee, since institutional patriotism is sufficiently strong to insure that neither house will accept the other's bill. Historically, the conference committee, composed of five members of the appropriating committees of each house, has actually written the appropriations bill. It was not limited to resolving the differences between the two bills, but could and did add entirely new items and struck out items already agreed to by both houses. The absence of restrictions on the conferees tends to increase the pressure from the same sources that attempted to influence the committee decisions.

Beginning with 1974–1975, the appropriations act has been prepared by conferees restricted to adjusting differences between the two bills; nevertheless, they have made numerous changes that were not strictly adjustments of differences. Statutory and other changes that occur between the preparation of the bill by each house and its final approval by the conferees make a strict adherence to the limitation difficult if not impossible. If for no other reason, the rapid changes having ramifications for appropriations that occur in basic statutes during a session that legislates in 140 days for a two-year period require some flexibility. Many of the conferees' changes involve matters that needed technical corrections not discovered until after the passage of the bills by the two houses, or provided additional money, or made other changes that were attributed to legislative action. Still other changes, however, involve new policies; the salaries of officials have been increased to put them on a level with similar positions in other state agencies, and some changes have been attributed simply to the availability of updated information. Under the joint rules adopted by the legislature, the changes that do not adjust differences in the two bills must be authorized by concurrent resolution.

When agreement is finally reached, the staff drafts a final appropriations bill. This is reported to the two houses, where it must be accepted in whole or rejected in whole; if rejected, a new conference committee would be appointed. The conference committee bill is invariably approved, usually with only perfunctory debate.

June–July 1977. Upon completion of action by the legislature, the appropriations bill goes to the comptroller for certification that the amounts appropriated will be available and then to the governor for his approval. The governor can veto the entire bill, as Gov. Preston Smith did in 1969 to a one-year bill, or veto specific line items while allowing the remainder to become law. The latter procedure is the standard pattern of gubernatorial action, with particular items regarded as wasteful, unnecessary, or of benefit to political opponents being eliminated. Since the bill ordinarily comes to the governor near the end of the legislative session, the vetoes in effect are absolute. The item veto gives the governor greater control over appropriations than does

the general veto, which gives him a choice between all or nothing—
with neither being a desired alternative in many cases.

THE FINAL PRODUCT

In addition to appropriations, the bill contains policy directives, or
riders, which the legislature includes as a means of exerting control
over the agencies. The appropriations act for 1978–1979 includes not
only the usual provisions for administration of the salary schedule, the
schedule of architectural fees, a prohibition on the use of appropriated
funds for the payment of salaries of employees who imbibe alcoholic
beverages while on duty, and a prohibition on the practice of discrimination based on race, creed, sex, or national origin; it also contains
provisions requiring the Board of Control to provide access to the fifth
floor of the state capitol and prohibiting the inclusion in the formula
used for preparing requests and making recommendations for appropriations for colleges and universities of semester credit hours earned in
undergraduate classes of less than ten students and graduate classes of
less than five students.

Riders are legitimate if they assert controls over the spending of
state funds, but they are invalid if they attempt to make basic changes
in state policy. Governors, however, may find them objectionable.
John Connally, Preston Smith, and Dolph Briscoe on occasion have
announced that they were vetoing riders, although the practice is of
doubtful legality. Many of the provisions are also legally questionable,
and the attorney general not infrequently rules them invalid. Article
III, Section 35 of the state constitution prohibits bills from containing
more than one subject, so an appropriations bill can contain only
appropriations and valid limitations on their expenditure. The distinction between a valid limitation and the enactment of policy is not
always clear, but the attorney general tends to be rather restrictive in
his interpretation, which usually is definitive. It is important to word
the riders properly if there is to be hope for their legality. Thus, the
rider that provides that none of the monies appropriated shall be used
to pay the salaries of any employee who uses alcoholic beverages while
on active duty would, if properly challenged, be more likely to be
upheld than the more generally worded prohibition against discrimination. The latter restriction provides that appropriated funds may not be
spent by agencies practicing discrimination; as such, it is not directly
tied to the expenditure of funds but instead prohibits funds from being
spent by agencies pursuing designated policies. Of course, such riders
may be of greater importance as statements of legislative intent than as
legal restrictions.[15]

The process of budget authorization appears to be of an incremental nature; the legislature works from (and adds to) the base prepared by the Legislative Budget Board. Each house tends to increase the board recommendations, and the conference committee makes further additions. In 9 of the 11 bienniums included in Table 10.2, the total approved by the conferees was larger than the amount recommended by the budget board; in 8 of 11 bienniums, it was larger than the governor's recommendation; in 7 of the 11, it was larger than both the House and Senate bills, and in 2 others it was larger than one bill and smaller than the other. The conference committee total was closer to the total recommended by the governor than that recommended by the board in 7 of 9 bienniums.

The Senate conferees, who as a group tend to be more influential politicians than their counterparts from the House, have usually been considered more influential in determining final outcomes. However, a comparison of general revenue totals does not reinforce this impression; the conference committee total was closer to the Senate bill in only 6 of the 11 bienniums. A more valid conclusion might be that the conference committee total is closer to the higher of the two bills, a situation that occurred in 8 of the 11 bienniums. Since the immediate pressures for spending are greater than the more diffused pressures not to make greater demands on the tax system, the tendency when the bills differ is to approve the higher figure or to compromise on an amount between that contained in the two bills. Thus, the compromise total is larger than either of the originals, even without additions not included in either bill.

The two most recent bienniums differ remarkably from preceding bienniums. Conference committee bills have been less than both the House and Senate bills, less than the budget board recommendation, and closer to the legislative than the executive budget. Three factors account for the deviation. First, the board was more liberal in its fiscal outlook than the governor and, since revenue-raising legislation was unnecessary, was not restrained any more than the governor by the necessity of staying within available revenue. Second, the fiscal process was shaped more than in previous years by consideration of substantive legislation that, while not directly spending general revenue, diverted money from that fund. For example, for the 1978–1979 biennium the legislative budget included funds from general revenue for highways; the executive budget diverted funds from general revenue; and separate legislation was enacted which provided general revenue for highways. Third, the roles of the participants have changed: Use of zero-based program budgets and less acceptance by the budget board of the attitude that is role is merely to provide a base upon which the legislature can build may portend permanent changes in the budget process. Whatever the relative influence of the participants in the process, final appropriations are considerably smaller than agency requests. The percent of requests appropriated ranged from 75 percent for fiscal 1954–1955 to 92 percent for 1964–1965 and averaged 82 percent. Even so, this represented sizable increases for each biennium over the previous biennium. The amounts approved by the conference committee represent an average increase in general revenue appropriations of 31 percent and range from an increase of 4 percent in 1954–1955 to 62 percent in 1974–1975.

Spending the Surplus

In mid-1976 it appeared that Texas would end the 1976–1977 biennium with $700 million in its general revenue fund, and that over $2.5 billion more than the $7.5 billion being spent from that and closely related funds would be available for the next biennium. Reference was made to a $2.6 billion "surplus," and Gov. Dolph Briscoe mentioned establishment of a $1-billion "nest egg."

Three important groups had other plans that would more than consume the "surplus." Highway interests were formulating plans to divert general revenue to the highway fund; plans were being drafted to "reform" the system for financing public schools; and public school teachers were pressing for a pay raise. Briscoe and the Legislative Budget Board ordered state officials to hold their requests to a minimum; they requested a 116% increase. Briscoe's budget gave first priority to highways, diverting $825 million from general revenue; he also recommended a school finance plan of $893 million and an 18% in general revenue spending. Overall, his budget allocated all but $59 million of available funds. The legislative budget increased general revenue spending by 89%, allocated $165 million from general revenue to highways, and left an unallocated balance of $1.2 billion for public schools and teachers.

The 1977 legislature began action on the gubernatorially designated "emergency" highway funding bill and then turned to general appropriations, school finance, and teacher pay. The House Appropriations Committee approved a general appropriations bill which, when combined with the highway bill and school finance and teacher pay plans, would have resulted in a $700 million deficit. The speaker and Appropriations Committee chairman successfully supported floor amendments which reduced the bill by $150—200 million.

The Senate-approved highway, general appropriations, school finance, and teacher pay bills spent somewhat more than the comptroller's January revenue estimate, but an updated estimate provided adequate funds for the Senate (but not the House) legislation. Conferees on the general appropriations bill decided to "save" more money for education and approved a conference report lower than either the House or Senate bills, leaving $1.1 billion, which was eventually spent in special session, for school finance and teacher pay. What was eventually a $3 billion "surplus" had been spent, without establishment of a "nest egg"; in the 1978 elections improvement in school finances and teacher pay were major issues.

The amounts approved by the conference committee are basically what the agencies receive to spend. Although the governor possesses the item veto, he has not used that power to significantly change general revenue spending totals. In 4 of the 11 bienniums in Table 10.2, no general revenue was vetoed, and the largest amount vetoed was only 1.7 percent of the total. John Connally was the perpetrator of those vetoes in 1963, when his reputation as the most prolific user of the item veto among recent Texas governors was born.

Expenditures and governmental activities. Decision making is incremental throughout the budgetary process. Despite the zero-based budgeting name applied to the system, the process remains diffused with comparisons of past with proposed appropriations. Most significantly, the alternative, supposedly zero-based, spending levels that agencies are required to submit were based on variations from current spending levels. For example, requests for the 1978–1979 biennium specified four alternatives—Level I at 10 percent below the current level, Level II at the current level, Level III at 10 percent above current level, and Level IV at 20 percent above current level. Additional alternatives were optional. The important change made in budgetary practice was not the naming of the process but the adoption of a program format and the requirement of alternative spending levels. Agencies still take their current budgets as a base from which to work and ask for increases. The budget board reduces those requests to a level much closer to their current budgets, and the legislature increases the board recommendations to a level quite close to that recommended by the governor. The result is that the agencies receive more than they currently have but less than they request. The similarity attained between the recommendations of the governor and the legislative appropriations is somewhat surprising. The conventional wisdom has held that the legislature favors the budget board's recommendations and largely neglects the governor's budget, except in cases when the governor's appeals gain legislative consideration for specific recommendations.

Three explanations for the similarity seem plausible. First, the conventional wisdom may be wrong and the governor may have more influence than is thought; his leadership may be instrumental in persuading the legislature to arrive at totals similar to his recommendations. Second, the legislative committees may simply work from the budget prepared by the budget board, and in adding funds for programs deemed deserving arrive at totals that are nearer the larger gubernatorial totals, which at least until recently, were larger.

While plausible, the first explanation probably overstates and the second probably understates the influence of the governor, and a third explanation seems more likely. The legislative committees may work from the budget prepared by the board, but they respond to pressures for additional expenditures from various interested parties, one of the more important of whom may be a governor acting as advocate for items important to his program. Other pressures on the committees are likely to be similar to those that were originally exerted on the governor for new programs or increased emphasis on existing programs. Thus, the additions to the board's base does bring the spending totals closer to the higher amounts recommended by the governor, and often a major portion of the increase goes to items advocated by the governor.

The influence of the governor in the budgetary process depends more on his informal powers and political relationships than on his formal budget powers. A governor who enjoys a favorable political situation and aggressively pushes innovative recommendations can have a major impact on the appropriations process; one who recommends a budget without significant programmatic change usually has little impact other than to establish a ceiling through his taxation policy. The legislature probably has a more significant role in budgeting in Texas than in most of the states, where use of a single executive budget gives the initiative to the governor. However, it is really a small group of legislators who wield most of the power—particularly the leadership and the appropriations conference conference committee. The typical legislator has little more control over the process than his counterparts in most state legislatures and the U.S. Congress.

EXECUTION OF THE BUDGET

Once the appropriations bill becomes law, the agencies revise their spending plans for the forthcoming fiscal year to bring them into accord with the amounts appropriated. With the beginning of the first year of the biennium (in our example, September 1, 1977), the third phase of the budgetary process, the spending of the money, is ready to begin. Many states have formal machinery, usually under the control of the governor, that provides for centralized planning and control over execution of the budget. Financial authorities are generally agreed that a system of budget execution is desirable. Among the particular controls that such authorities believe should be given the governor are the powers to require the submission of work programs for his approval, to establish allotments (controls over the rate and volume of spending), to approve transfers between categories of expenditures or even appropriations items, and to reduce appropriations.

In Texas there is little of a formal system of budget execution; at the onset of the fiscal year, the agencies are largely free to begin spending the funds provided—within the limitations set out in the appropriations act. The legislature does write some restrictions into the appropriations act in the form of riders. Riders have been used to establish gubernatorial controls, similar to those used by states having executive budget execution systems, by requiring approval of the governor prior to expenditure of specified items of appropriation. Rulings by the attorney general, however, have now held that such requirements are unconstitutional on the grounds that they violate the separation of powers clause of the constitution by delegating legislative authority to determine appropriations. A budget execution system apparently can be instituted only through constitutional amendment or revision.

Some control over spending is exercised by the comptroller of public accounts. Before an agency can actually expend funds it must receive authorization from the comptroller, who determines whether the proposed expenditures are within the agency's appropriation and do not violate the constitution or any laws. Such controls essentially determine legality and have little to do with financial planning or the wisdom or necessity of expenditures.

Another spending control of sorts emanates from the operations of the Board of Control, the state's central purchasing agency. The Board of Control exercises various controls over agency purchasing, both to reduce costs and to insure quality. Contracts for the sale of many items to state agencies are awarded to the "lowest and best" bidder, and the agencies must then buy such items only from that contractor.

THE AUDIT OF EXPENDITURES

It is generally agreed that sound financial administration requires an independent audit after the expenditure of funds by the operating agencies. This task is handled in Texas by the state auditor, who is appointed—with Senate approval—for a two-year term by the Legislative Audit Committee. The committee is composed of the lieutenant governor, speaker, and the chairmen of the Appropriations and Revenue and Taxation committees of the House and the Finance and State Affairs committees of the Senate. The auditor, who must have had at least five years of experience as a certified public accountant prior to his appointment, is directed to audit the financial records of all state agencies at least once every two years. This is to insure that the agencies use proper accounting procedures and to determine whether there was illegality or irregularity in expenditures. Reports embodying his findings and recommendations are sent to the governor and legislature. In short, the auditor is supposed to keep the agencies "honest," and the thought is that this can best be done by someone who is not a member of the executive branch.

THE PATTERN OF EXPENDITURES

The general trend in government expenditures—national, state, and local—in the United States in the twentieth century has been ever upward. While attention is often called to the great increase in national government spending, state and local spending has also increased tremendously.

A few figures will illustrate the point. In 1902 all governments in the United States collectively spent $1.7 billion.[15] Texas state government now spends more than that by itself in a year. The 1902 total figure was allocated among the three levels of governments as follows: national government, $572 million; state governments, $188 million; local governments, $959 million. Thus, over two-thirds of total government spending was done by state and local governments. By contrast, in 1976 total actual spending by all governments amounted to nearly $626 billion. This was allocated among the various governments, as follows: national government, $322 billion; state governments, $124 billion; local governments, $186 billion. Spending by the national government constituted 51 percent of government spending. But, if defense spending is eliminated from the analysis and only domestic spending is considered, a substantially different picture emerges. Subtract $100 billion for national defense from the national government's total spending, and $222 billion remains for domestic activities.[16] State and local governments still spend substantially more for domestic programs than does the national government. If spending can be taken as one measure of governmental power, all power has not yet "gone to Washington."

How can the huge increase in total government spending be explained? However ideologically satisfying, contentions that it is the result of the actions of power-hungry bureaucrats or politicians or of inefficiency in government administration lack real explanatory value, although they may apply to particular situations. Inflation undoubtedly accounts for part of the growth in dollar figures. Much of the increase in national spending stems from the costs of past wars (e.g., veterans programs and interest on debt incurred due to wars) and of current national defense programs. Defense-related expenditures accounted for over 40 percent of the national budget in 1974. National defense is largely outside the constitutional sphere of the state governments, and they spend almost nothing for this purpose.

In the domestic arena a number of broad, long-term socioeconomic and political developments have given rise to needs and demands for increased spending. Population growth has necessitated increased spending for traditional programs to provide services or protection for larger numbers of people. As the population has increased it has also become more urbanized and industrialized; urban populations have more need for governmentally provided services, such as police and fire protection, sewerage and water systems, and parks and recreational facilities. Along with population growth, urbanization, and industrialization have come rising standards of living, which result in greater demands for services and still higher costs.

The result is an urban-industrial society in which the independence and self-sufficiency have been replaced by interdependence as part of the human condition. As the economic hazards of life—old age, sickness, accident, unemployment—increase, government is called on to provide security, and consequently welfare programs originate and proliferate. The guarantee of human welfare becomes an accepted if not applauded responsibility of government.

The dominance of officeholders identified with the conservative faction of the Democratic party has not prevented the Texas state government from participating in the nationwide growth of governmental expenditures (Table 10.3). In three of the decades of this century expenditures tripled, and only in the depression decade of the 1930s did they fail to double. Much of the growth is attributable to increases in population and inflation. If per capita expenditures of constant dollars are considered, the growth was much more moderate—except in the first two decades of the century, when increases in the small dollar amounts represent very large percentage increases. Nevertheless, per capita spending of constant dollars in-

TABLE 10.3 • STATE EXPENDITURES IN TEXAS. ACTUAL AND PER CAPITA

Year	Actual expenditures (in millions)	Per capita expenditures (1967 dollars)
1900	$ 4.8	$ 3
1910	10.9	6
1920	33.5	35
1930	103.1	48
1940	165.7	64
1950	527.3	84
1960	1184.4	130
1970	2954.7	239
1976	6204.0	272

SOURCE: The population and expenditure data are from the *Texas Almanac, 1978–1979* (Dallas: A. H. Belo, 1977), p. 183, 641. Data on the value of the dollar are based on the wholesale price index in the *Statistical Abstract of the United States, 1977* (Washington, D.C.: Bureau of the Census, 1977), p. 472; and *Historical Statistics of the United States, 1789–1945* (Washington, D.C.: Bureau of the Census, 1949), pp. 233–234.

creased from $3 in 1900 to $239 in 1970. The decline between 1970 and 1974 was due to rapid inflation and undoubtedly was temporary.

Most Texas state spending goes, and has gone for some time, for three major purposes: education, highways, and welfare (Figure 10.2 and Table 10.4). The relative importance of the three in the overall totals has varied over time, with certain patterns discernible in the variation. Spending on highways amounted to over 40 percent of state spending in 1929 but declined to 10 percent in 1977. The 1977 percentage also represented a sharp decline from 1970, when over 21 percent of all spending was devoted to highways.

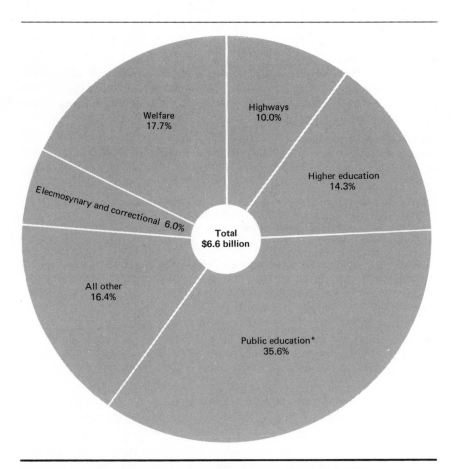

Figure 10.2 • Texas state expenditures by purpose, fiscal year 1977.

SOURCE: *1977 Annual Financial Report of the State of Texas* (Austin: Comptroller of Public *Accounts,* 1977), pp. 46–55.
*Includes all teacher retirement.

TABLE 10.4 • STATE EXPENDITURES IN TEXAS, BY PURPOSE (IN MILLIONS)

Purpose	1929	1950	1970	1977
Public education*	$25	$177	$ 961	$2354
Higher education	8	34	344	947
Highways	35	118	633	662
Welfare	2	132	554	1166
Eleemosynary and correctional	7	25	141	398
All other	7	42	322	1081
Total spending	85	527	2955	6607

SOURCE: Annual Reports of the Comptroller of Public Accounts.
*Includes all teacher retirement.

Welfare increased from less than 3 percent in 1929 to 25 percent in 1950, when most of the funds went to the politically attractive program of aid to the needy aged, but declined to 14 percent in 1967, when the percentage began an increase that reached 20 in 1972. The increase was primarily attributable to the program of medical assistance for welfare recipients, which followed the enactment by Congress of the Medicaid program. Not only was medical assistance costly, but its existence caused the costs of the categorical assistance programs to increase. Since the medical assistance program pays all covered medical services without regard to the size of the recipient's cash payment, many people who were potentially eligible for some assistance but who had not applied began to do so. Additionally, the welfare rights organizations have acted to ameliorate the stigma associated with welfare; more specifically, they have broadened eligibility standards through success-ful court actions, with a resultant growth in the number of recipients. In the 1970s the percentage again began a decline, primarily because of assumption by the national government of responsibility for the adult assistance programs, and in 1977, it was only 18.

The greatest growth in recent years has occurred in public education and the "all other" categories. The growth in the "all other" category, which increased from 8 to 16 percent between 1950 and 1977, apparently resulted from the general growth in expenditures for overhead, or general government costs, and changing attitudes that have resulted in the improvement of the salaries of state employees. The percentage of state expenditures for public education (essentially the program of aid to local school districts) increased from 33 to 36 percent because of changes in the system of state support which increased state aid and broadened the programs and services eligible for support.

Future patterns of expenditure are difficult to forecast, but it is highly probable that the portion of state expenditures devoted to highways will increase. In the early 1970s there were indications that officials of the Highway Department and their allies in the Good Roads Association favored a two-cent increase in the gasoline tax, but adament opposition by Gov. Dolph Briscoe led them not to pursue that increase. The increased costs of gasoline and conservation efforts had resulted in growth in revenue from the five-cent-per-gallon gasoline tax (the lowest in the nation) that was less than the rate of inflation. The 1977 session of the legislature diverted funds from general revenue to highways, but that may be a temporary measure; when revenue-raising legislation has to be enacted, an increase in the gasoline tax will be attractive. Funds now diverted from general revenue could return to that fund; highways would have funds from their "user" tax; and the public schools, which receive one-fourth of the gasoline tax, would receive more funds, perhaps thereby allowing the state to increase its portion of school costs and decrease pressures on local property taxes. Agricultural interests, traditionally conservative and oriented to local government, now favor state assumption of the full cost of the foundation school program, a reflection of the change in agriculture from a labor-intensive to a capital-intensive business.

The state government, of course, spends in support of a variety of other activities: regulation of business and industry, health, conservation, parks and recreation, support of the legislative and judicial branches. But however important they may be, they involve comparatively small expenditures of money. (Generally, service-providing activities are more expensive than regulatory activities, regardless of comparative importance.) In 1976 79 percent of the state's expenditure went for education, highways, and welfare.

TEXAS AMONG THE STATES

Comparative studies indicate that the levels of taxation and expenditure are determined more by a state's level of economic development (as measured by industrialization, urbanization, and income and educational levels) than by such political variables as party competition, voter participation, liberal-conservative political divisions. or legislative malapportionment.[17] (Other analyses indicate that the political variables do have a more important influence than economic variables on the allocation of burdens and benefits across income classes.)[18] While there is substantial variation among the states in spending for education and welfare, the wealthier, more economically developed states tend to spend more, the poorer states to spend less. To paraphrase, some have the money and some do not and it makes a difference. The budgetary process cannot be utilized to allocate resources that a state does not have, but particular states may, at least temporarily, move ahead or behind the norm for their level of development.

Governmental expenditures for domestic purposes will continue to increase in the foreseeable future. There has undoubtedly been a strong negative reaction throughout the country against the increases in taxes necessary to finance increased expenditures. However, the forces contributing to increased spending are still in operation and are helping to generate new or expanded needs and demands: demands for a cleaner environment, renewal of cities, new modes of urban transportation, income maintenance, equalized educational opportunity, and better treatment and rehabilitation for the inhabitants of state institutions. The reaction against higher taxes has been felt most strongly by local governments; increases in property taxes to support the elementary and secondary school systems and municipal services have been defeated with increasing regularity. State governments have also experienced adverse reactions to their efforts to increase taxes or find new sources of tax revenue.

There are indications that a tax plateau has been reached, at least temporarily, in many of the larger urban-industrial states and their cities, where the level of services and taxes are comparatively high. If this is the case, future expenditure growth will probably be financed from the national treasury, from which unearmarked revenue-sharing grants are now available. But urbanization occurred later in Texas than in most states, and state and local governments began to cope with problems well after many older urban areas. Consequently, a continued increase in spending and taxes is probable in Texas, for the level of governmental services is comparatively low.

Various indexes indicate that Texas is a low-taxation, low-expenditure, low-effort state. Per capita state-local expenditures rank forty-second among the 50 states and are much lower than the national average ($960 compared with a national average of $1191 in 1976). Per capita state-local taxes are lower than the national average; in 1976 Texas ranked thirty-eighth among the 50 states with a per capita tax of $581 compared to the national average of $731. And the percent of personal income taken for state-local taxes is lower than the national average; in 1976 the Texas tax burden ranked forty-third, with $105 per $1000 of personal income taken for taxes compared with the average of all states of $125.[19] Combined state and local figures are cited because differences in the distribution of responsibilities between state and local governments make those figures more comparable than figures for state governments only; but the latter comparisons are also low. The taxation-expenditure figures measure only dollar costs, not level of services. Reliable measures of services are difficult if not impossible to develop, but the quantity and quality of services are probably related to level of spending.

In the immediate future, pressures to increase the proportion of local school costs paid by the state to increase spending on highways, and perhaps to provide meaningful state grants for urban mass transit systems are likely to result in increased state expenditures. National and state developments indicate also that efforts are forthcoming to improve the level of care (and to place more emphasis on alternatives to care in large institutions) for inhabitants of schools for the retarded, mental hospitals, and adult and juvenile, correctional institutions. Preliminary forecasts for the 1980–1981 biennium indicate that the 1979 Texas legislature will not have to enact major revenue-raising legislation.

NOTES

[1]Clara Penniman, "The Politics of Taxation," in Herbert Jacob and Kenneth Vines, eds., *Politics in the American States,* 3rd ed. (Boston: Little, Brown, 1976), p. 433.

[2]Ibid., pp. 525–526.

[3]*Texas Observer,* May 2, 1963, pp. 10–11.

[4]A historical view is presented in Read Granberry and John T. Potter, "Some Texas Tax Trails," *Texas Quarterly* 7 (Winter 1964): 125–142.

[5]George A. Bishop, "Tax Burden by Income Class," *National Tax Journal* 14 (March 1961): 54.

[6]The report was prepared by the Fautus Company for the Illinois Manufacturer's Association and has been widely publicized in Texas by the Comptroller of Public Accounts. See *Texas Means Business!* (Austin: Comptroller of Public Accounts, 1977).

[7]Article VIII, Section 6.

[8]Article IV, Sections 9, 14.

[9]Article III, Section 49a.

[10]*Revenue Estimating for Texas State Government* (Austin: Texas Research League, 1968), pp. 9–26.

[11]This discussion draws on *Fiscal Size-up of Texas State Services* (Austin: Legislative Budget Office, 1978), pp. 9–11 and *1977 Annual Financial Report* (Austin: Comptroller of Public Accounts, 1977), pp. 69–77.

[12]Article III, Section 51a.

[13]Richard Fenno, *The Power of the Purse* (Boston: Little, Brown, 1966), pp. 667–668.

[14]For the specific wording of the riders, see House Bill 139, Article V, Sections 9 and 55, Acts of the Sixty-third Legislature of the State of Texas, Regular Session, 1973.

[15]*Historical Statistics of the United States, 1789–1957* (Washington, D.C.: Bureau of the Census, 1960), pp. 725–730.

[16]*Governmental Finances in 1975–76* (Washington, D.C.: Bureau of the Census, 1977), p. 20.

[17]See, especially, Thomas R. Dye, *Politics, Economics, and the Public* (Chicago: Rand McNally, 1966), chaps. 4–6.

[18]See, for example, Bernard Booms and James Halderson, "The Politics of Redistribution: A Reformulation," *American Political Science Review* 67 (September 1973): 924–933.

[19]*Governmental Finances in 1975–76,* op. cit., pp. 63, 68.

Index

80 81 82 9 8 7 6 5 4 3